D is for DIANA

W9-CQM-118

I would like to preface this book by stating that it is not a life story, and yet all the stories and facts are taken from my life as it has been so far.

On many occasions I have been approached to write an autobiography, and once or twice I have tried to do so, but my main reaction has always been that my life is by no means over, and that with luck there could be another forty years to come! By then of course I imagine I will have forgotten the early part, so I think I had better get something done now, not an autobiography, but a sort of A to Z of thoughts, opinions, experiences and anecdotes which the reader may find amusing, sad or shocking, but all written with complete honesty, and just a few names kept secret to protect the guilty!

I hope I will not have offended anyone in the writing of this book, it is not my intent, and I like to think the famous and infamous whom I have named, have all been gifted with a sense of humour which I have always maintained is essential in this world, and particularly the world of show business.

Perhaps some of you will be able to use my experiences as a guide to how not to behave, and therefore I will have the satisfaction of knowing that my mistakes have helped people to get along better in life, but whichever way you accept this book please remember it has been written to entertain and brighten up a dreary day, to cock a snook at hypocrisy which I abhor, and above all to put a stop to publishers and ambitious writers pestering me to do the complete story of my life — well at least until the year 2011, when I'm eighty!

FOR ADULTS ONLY

DIANA DORS

Associate Editor: Jack Hobbs

A STAR BOOK
published by
the Paperback Division of
W. H. ALLEN & Co. Ltd

To my Husband
for surviving somehow whilst I wrote
this book, and my Siamese
cat who watched me do it with
one eye closed

A Star Book
Published in 1978
by the Paperback Division of
W. H. Allen & Co. Ltd
A Howard and Wyndham Company
44 Hill Street, London W1X 8LB

Copyright © Diana Dors, 1978
Typesetting by Yale Press Limited, London SE25
Printed in Great Britain by
Richard Clay (The Chaucer Press) Limited,
Bungay, Suffolk

ISBN 0 352 30158 9

ACKNOWLEDGMENTS
We would like to acknowledge the following for the
use of their photographs: Michael Balcon; David White;
Sunday Mirror; J. Arthur Rank; Stanley Folb; Paul Popper
Ltd; *Daily Mail*; Bill Crespinol Jnr; ATV; Mark Gudgeon;
Michael Ward; Arthur E. Lemon; British Lion; Vista Photos Inc;
RKO Radio Pictures.
The publishers also wish to thank the photographers whom they were
unable to trace.

A is for APPLE

This of course is how sinning all started, and about the only thing I haven't, and can't be blamed for!

A is for AGA KHAN

I am speaking of the late Aga, Rita Hayworth's ex-father-in-law. Why couldn't I have managed to acquire a father-in-law with that kind of money?

I did have the pleasure of lunching wth him one day, however, at his luxurious villa with the indoor and outdoor swimming pools, just overlooking Cannes. We were all there for the Cannes Film Festival and he invited us to lunch with his wife the Begum. Susan Hayward, Ginger Rogers and Richard Todd were some of the stars in the party, and we sat down to a lunch served on solid gold plates with knives and forks to match. I found the old man very sweet, and happily we were not lost for conversation because he was fascinated by birds. I don't mean the human variety but the feathered ones, and particularly parrots. At the time I owned a marvellous cockatoo with a majestic lime green plume. The Aga listened for ages to my tales about the bird's habits and mischievous nature. One of the bird's favourite tricks late at night (which proved to be a boon when one had rather boring guests who would not leave) was to say in a very weary voice, 'Goodnight Poll,' and keep on repeating it until they finally took the hint realising it *was* getting late.

I think that lunch I had with the Aga was the last he gave for visiting celebrities as he was then in failing health, and died not long after. But it was an experience I will always remember, for in spite of the magnificence of the place there was an air of peace and informality seldom found in such impressive surroundings.

A is for AGE

You know you are growing old when the newspaper print becomes so small it is unreadable, when you fancy a handsome male or female at a party and find out you are old enough to be their parent or when you have been in the public eye as long as I have and a very elderly man comes up and tells you that you influenced his adolescent years at school and made him realise what women were all about. This actually happened to me recently, as did meeting my eldest son Mark, then aged seventeen, at Los Angeles Airport. Instead of finding a gorgeous little blue-eyed cherub, there stood a six foot charmer of Tarzan build with hair as long as mine, who looked down at me saying, 'Hi Mom,' with the words *I choked Linda Lovelace* scrawled across his T-shirted chest.

Luckily the only two good things about growing old are

that you know what you are prepared to put up with, and who you will tolerate after forty. This goes for husbands and lovers too; also everyone else is in the same boat, for all the young ones you meet, there are thousands who are older than yourself, and some who are the same age. I am happy to think Liz Taylor and I are in that group, and she is doing fine! Petula Clark and I are only twelve months apart. When I was fifteen and she was fourteen we were making films together. She was in gymslips, pigtails and socks, and I, as usual, was the 'tarty' one with all the make-up, high heels and busty sweaters. I used to feel so much older than her then, but age is a funny thing and as you go on ages merge and you catch up with one another.

I don't mind ageing; look at Mae West. I am going to look better than her at eighty-two (or so I tell myself). Things are not really so bad; age has nothing to do with life. The other day when I was feeling depressed by the memory of an eleven-year-old David Cassidy swimming in my Hollywood pool, a close girl friend confided to me she had had a romance with him — and she is the same age as me!

A is for AGENTS

I have had some two dozen of them in my time, and it would be hard a job to decide which was the worst. I think most actors like to complain about their agents and always think the grass is greener on the other side when it comes to their fellow actors' agents, but by and large they are not a bad crowd, and really a very necessary evil.

One agent of mine actually turned down the leading role for me (at a time when my career needed a good boost) in the successful film *Saturday Night and Sunday Morning*, on the grounds that it was not enough money. The part went to Rachel Roberts who rightly won an acting award for it, and it started her on the road to stardom. Another agent, who thankfully *I* was not under contract to, was approached by one of his clients once who timidly asked if she could be released from her contract with him, as they did not seem to be getting anywhere together. Expecting a volley of abuse and anger, she was mortified when he actually asked, 'Oh, are you with us?' Thank goodness I never had to deal with him, though I too have been lost in the shuffle with high-powered American agents, who have so many star clients on their books that unless you are in big demand, you do not stand a prayer.

A problem I have always suffered from is total amnesia where names and faces are concerned. I can remember lines of a play, people's birthdays, what I had for lunch on a Sunday ten years ago, and all sorts of totally unimportant information, particularly a bit of gossip, but names and faces can completely elude me. I have in recent years developed a trick whereby I pretend I know the person who approaches me and conduct a long conversation with them whilst searching my brain for their name. If this fails I finally ask when was the last time we met, bemoaning the fact that it has been too long, and when they inform me as to the time the name suddenly clicks into place.

Apparently this ploy was also used by an aristocratic gentleman, who one day was confronted by the late Princess Mary Royal somewhere in Bond Street. He could not for the life of him remember who she was. The conversation went something like this: 'Well it is lovely to see you after all this time. Er, when was it we last met?' 'Oh, don't you recall? It was at my brother's house,' she replied. 'Of course,' said the gentleman, lying through his teeth, still having no idea as to her identity. 'How is he . . . what's he doing now?' The Princess looked a little mystified but answered gaily, 'Oh he's still busy being King you know.'

Obviously this is dangerous ground to work on, but what can you do if you have this problem? When I was nineteen I did not know I had it until one evening, in a London club, I was standing by the bar with some friends, when I noticed a man at the other end of the bar who kept looking at me and making what I took to be come hither expressions. I repeatedly ignored him, turning my face abruptly from him each time he did it and trying to look cross. Finally he decided to leave, and had to walk right past me to get to the exit door. He approached me with a leer and I drew myself up to my full size saying in an indignant voice, 'Do I know you?' 'You should do darling,' he replied. 'I'm your agent.'

A is for ALAN

My third and positively last husband; a dark, handsome, brilliant actor, with a singing voice that tops Tom Jones', a gift for writing poetry in the style of Dylan Thomas, and as colourful a character as ever came out of Stoke-on-Trent! To this day his parents are mystified as to how they got him, and his looks are so pure Romany gypsy that he could be taken for any nationality! Such was the case when we once drove to Mexico. We had a slight altercation at the border. His hair was very long and as we found out, they were at the time extremely nervous about a certain sort of person entering the country due to hippies and the Charles Manson episode. Alan leapt out of the car and in an extremely British accent assured them that he was an English actor about to return here to play *King Lear*. 'Aha,' said the Mexican soldier commandant, 'You mean Shakespoke.' 'Exactly,' replied Alan and proceeded to blind the man with Shakespearian phrases in a dignified English manner. 'It would help if he took his earring out,' remarked a friend who was with us, dryly. Anyhow we got in and then, due to his dark, seemingly Mexican looks and the clothes he had purchased in Tijuana that day, we had difficulty trying to get *out* again, but we finally persuaded the border police that he was from Stoke-on-Trent, and not a Mexican wetback!

I first saw what was to be my future spouse in a television play called *Thief*, in which he gave such a marvellous performance, I was more impressed with his acting, than merely just fancying him! But some months later I was cast in a guest star role in a series in which he was playing the lead. Apparently the producers were highly excited that I had signed to do it, and one day just before rehearsals were due to start they told Alan that they had a fabulous star to play opposite him. 'You'll never believe it, but we've got Diana Dors,' they announced, expecting him to turn somersaults of glee at the prospect. 'Oh, Madam tits and lips,' said my charming future husband. He had never seen me in a film and belonged to the new young school of actors who being very dedicated to their work rather despised film stars, especially faded ones. Little did he know that his meeting with me, when I did not arrive dragging a mink behind me on the floor as he expected, and having learnt *all* my lines, would change his whole life. We fell in love literally on sight, like a corny magazine story, and were married seven weeks later after a whirlwind courtship.

Well here we are at the time of writing, nine years on, having suffered not only the ups and downs of marriage, but almost one tragedy a year. Broken backs and legs, prison sentences, meningitis and the loss of our last child (stillborn six weeks premature), amongst other things. But we have a beautiful son named Jason and our talents to get us through life's labours. We choose to consider they are God-given, and as God gave us to each other, for better or worse, that is how we will stay until *He* parts us.

A is for ARAB

As the Arabs seem to be the richest people in the world today, perhaps it would have been as well for me if my first husband, Dennis Hamilton, had accepted the offer made to him back in 1955 by an Arab Sheik. He had seen me in some sexy film or other and promptly dispatched a messenger with the offer of twenty-three camels in exchange for me. How he arrived at the figure of twenty-three I do not know. It is an odd number and I think it slightly mean of him not to have at least made it twenty-four, a round two dozen. Maybe one was sick, who knows? I also wonder what he would have done with me aside from the obvious, if I had actually been posted to

11

him. One thing is certain, I would have been a great deal richer than I am today.

A is for ARCHBISHOP

In this case the former Archbishop of Canterbury, who saw fit to denounce me from the pulpit as a wanton hussy, all because I had written my life story for the *News of the World* back in 1960. This was, of course, before Christine Keeler overthrew the Conservative government, before the Great Train robbers, the Beatles, and the whole Permissive Society. But in those days my 'ghost written' revelations in the *Widow's Bible*, as it is often called, rocked and shocked the Archbishop, along with Randolph Churchill who berated me on television, and also caused an uproar when I was chosen that year to be in the Royal Command Performance. I hasten to add that Buckingham Palace were not as shocked as the rest, for when the zealous journalists rang the press office at the Palace to see if they were going to ban me from appearing, they were told that the Royal Family saw no reason to do so — on the contrary they were quite looking forward to the show, whatever I was going to do! Obviously the Royals were way ahead of their time, and were not the fuddy-duddies the press had always tried to make them out to be.

Just recently in the more dignified *Sunday Times* Sir Oswald Mosley, who had seen me on the *Russell Harty* television show, publicly announced that I was the best thing that had happened to this country in years. In fact he put me on a par with only one other woman whom he said was of any importance and interest at all, namely Margaret Thatcher.

I'll bet there are not many women in this world who hold the distinction of being knocked down by an Archbishop and praised to the skies by a politician whose brilliant political career was marred by his Fascist leanings. It proves one thing at least, that all those jokes about the bishop and the actress are definitely not true!

A is for ARREST

I was arrested in 1953, fingerprinted, photographed, charged with housebreaking, bailed and finally wound up guilty of larceny. How did all this come about? The following facts will perhaps help to explain how such a silly situation mushroomed into something frighteningly enormous.

Having had a great success in a revue in London, really setting the town on fire with the notices I received, I had been offered a summer season in the blustering seaside town of Blackpool. So my first husband Dennis Hamilton and I installed ourselves in a flat for three months. The show was a big success, and during our stay we naturally met some very interesting characters who lived there permanently. They were nothing to do with show-business, one had a babywear shop, and two others had jewellery businesses; there was also another called The Gipsy, who apparently did nothing in particular, but he was always around for the parties and high jinks which used to take place either in our flat, or on the beach where we held midnight barbecues.

I mention all these people because they are a vital part of the story, particularly Frank Rogers, owner of the baby boutique. He was a strange individual and much to the annoyance of his friends, probably the meanest man in town. In spite of this he lured more girls to his flat than anyone in the group, which also irked his pals.

We must now jump a year to the summer of 1953, when I was in Manchester making a film with the late comedian Frank Randle. One weekend Dennis suggested we went to Blackpool for a couple of days, so off we went in our lovely Rolls Royce and checked in at a hotel on the front, which we knew all our friends always visited, especially The Gipsy. We then drove around to renew acquaintance with the two jewellers, tell them where we were staying, and organise a small party that evening. We telephoned Frank Rogers and told him to be at the hotel at eight and also, with a twinkle of mischief, Dennis added, 'Oh, by the way — Bring a bottle,' knowing full well there was no chance he would.

Everyone assembled at the hotel and the party began, but true to form there was no sign of Frank Rogers with a bottle under his arm, so Dennis decided we would drive to his flat and drag him back with the liquor. We all knew he had a well-stocked cocktail cabinet ready for his girls when they were brought there. One of the jewellers, Freddie Markall, came with us but there was no reply to our knocking. 'He's probably on his way home from the shop,' said Freddie. 'Let's wait in the car.' We did for about five minutes, until Freddie exclaimed, 'This is ridiculous! I used to share this flat with him and had a key. As it's not on me at the moment, we could climb through the window and wait inside in comfort.'

It was a ground floor flat, and as I was the smallest, I was pushed up through the kitchen window and proceeded to open the door for the others. Dennis took great delight in helping himself from the bulging cocktail cabinet, 'at last having a drink on Frank'! Eventually we began getting a little bored with the delay.

'I know what's happened,' said Dennis. 'The mean bastard has gone into hiding because I told him he had to bring a bottle.'

We agreed that he was probably right, and it was then that Dennis conceived the idea which was to lead to the real trouble. 'I'll teach him,' he exclaimed. 'We'll take these two half-bottles of gin, and whisky, ring him later and invite him again saying he need not bring anything. When he does come, we'll offer him his own booze and tell him afterwards he has been drinking his own stuff. That'll drive him mad.' So saying, he left a little note with a ridiculous drawing of Frank in a compromising position with one of his girlfriends, telling him we had been there, and asking him to come to the hotel and join us.

The party went on until the early hours, but no sign of Frank Rogers, and in fact the two bottles were still in the back of our car, when we all finally sank into bed. Suddenly the telephone rang, and Dennis heard Frank's angry voice shouting that his gin and whisky were missing, and demanded the bottles back straight away.

'Don't be so bloody silly,' said Dennis. 'You can have it tomorrow. Don't worry, no-one has drunk it. Come round at lunchtime and collect it, I'm certainly not getting up and bringing it back at this time of the morning.'

Rogers seemed somewhat appeased by this, and rang off. The following morning Dennis and I went flying at Blackpool aerodrome, and on arrival back at the hotel for lunch we found a nervous manager blabbering about the police having been there, searching our room. Thoroughly mystified as to what it was all about, we drove to the police station. As our car drew up outside, two detectives shouted, 'There they are,' and began running towards us as though they had sighted Al Capone and Dillinger.

We were hauled in for questioning, and to our astonishment were informed we were under arrest for breaking into Frank Rogers' flat, and stealing his property. Dennis was devastated, and at first laughed it off by trying to explain it was merely a practical joke, but they would have none of it and it was obvious they were out for blood. 'Come on,' said Dennis. 'If I am going to steal something from someone, I would hardly be likely to leave a note saying I was there. Anyway he can have his bottles back, they are in the car, in fact I had a date with him to come and collect them this morning.'

The police did appear to begin to understand the situation. By the time we had finished explaining, they too had to admit it was ridiculous, and that Frank Rogers was out of order in making a charge against us.

'Ask Freddie Markall why we got in through the window. He was there too; he's an old friend of Rogers',' said Dennis.

'Oh, Freddie Markall was in on it was he?' said the detective, and snapped at his minions to go and arrest Freddie without delay.

I can only imagine what happened next but it seems poor Freddie was in his shop when two policemen burst in, arrested him on the spot, and brought him back for questioning, leaving his horrified customer sitting there open-mouthed.

'We understand the position more fully now in view of what you have told us,' said the detective in charge. 'But a complaint has been made, and the wheels of the law have been set in motion, therefore you will have to be charged, fingerprinted and appear before the magistrates in the morning.'

We gasped. The effect it could have on my career would be terrifying, for what had simply been a practical joke would not look very funny in the newspapers. We pleaded with them to withdraw it, but they answered that the only one who could do so was the person who had made the charge, namely Frank Rogers. I saw Dennis clench his fists, and knew if we could get out of there, he would personally see that Rogers did just that. We were photographed, fingerprinted and placed in a cell, with the promise, after a lot of persuasion by Dennis, that we could be released on our own bail, and would not have to spend the night in the cells.

'What were you really looking for there?' asked the detective suspiciously. Then the penny dropped. Due to Frank Rogers various activities, the police thought we could help them unearth a much bigger crime, and were using our harmless joke as a way of setting a sprat to catch a mackerel. Eventually after what seemed an eternity, we were released with orders to appear the next morning at the Magistrates Court, and Dennis drove to Rogers' flat in a frenzy of anger. 'I'll kill him for this,' he threatened. Rogers opened the door and was pushed back into his flat by an angry Dennis, demanding to know what the hell he thought he was doing by bringing such a charge? Not only against us but against his old friend Freddie Markall? Flustered and ashamed, he stammered that he had been annoyed that we had taken his whisky and gin, and that was more or less it.

Dennis hauled him out, saying, 'Well, you are coming down to that police station now and withdrawing the charge before this gets into the press and ruins Diana's career.'

We drove him back and were met with the same opposition about the wheels of the law being put in motion and it having to be done in court the next morning.

'But that'll be too late,' cried Dennis. 'The newspapers will have printed it by then and we won't be able to cover the whole stupid affair up.' His pleas fell on deaf ears, and we were obliged to drive away miserably, with the thought of the next day hanging over us.

The following events were even worse. An anonymous caller telephoned my father in Swindon, and delighted in shocking him with the news that his daughter had been arrested for housebreaking and burglary. There was the added fact that Rogers' steady girlfriend, a sullen redhead, decided that if he was going to go into the box and withdraw the charge on our behalf, he should be paid for it. So we wrote out a cheque.

The next morning the court was buzzing with police and press, and the atmosphere when Rogers went into the witness box was tense. Even though he had been paid, he was such an odd-ball, it would have been quite possible for him to deny us suddenly and carry on with the charges. Thankfully he did not, but the chief prosecutor, Barnes, was not at all appeased by Rogers' attempted withdrawal of the charge by saying it was all a genuine mistake on his part, and asked for the whole case to be looked into further, and taken on to a higher court. This request was granted and so still on bail, we miserably left Blackpool for a week in order to obtain legal help, and wait for the wretched affair to begin all over again.

The following week we presented ourselves at the court and this time Barnes was ready for a fight. I noticed to my horror that he was in such command of the procedure that it seemed the magistrates would agree with every nod or shake of his head.

Finally the magistrates retired to consider their verdict. I have never known a more frightening ten minutes in my life as the thought of going to prison for six months, which was the minimum sentence, filled me with horror. As we all rose upon their return to hear the verdict, I know I was shaking, and when they pronounced us *guilty* I was nearly ready to faint.

Once more luck was on my side, as it has been so many times in my life. Our lawyer asked for the charge to be changed from house-breaking to larceny, which was a far less severe offence, and after agreeing that point, we were all three sentenced to pay a ten-pound fine. As it was my first offence, Dennis and Freddie both having had brushes with the law, I was given an unconditional discharge.

The publicity, oddly enough, did not damage my career. On the contrary it helped to make me a household name, and the public were extremely sympathetic, especially as I gagged my way through the occasion by going on stage at the beginning of my variety act and saying with relief for my opening line, 'Well, I finally got the handcuffs off and made it here,' which was guaranteed to bring the house down. But eventually, like everything, it all died a natural death, the only thing that remains to this day are my fingerprints and photographs at Blackpool police station, plus the fact that for the rest of my life I have a criminal record!

A is for AVA

There is only one Ava (Gardner), of course, the beautiful and talented. I have met her but once unfortunately. It was in 1955 at the Royal Command Film Performance. We were all lined up in alphabetical order in readiness to be introduced to the Queen and Prince Philip. I was standing between her and the late Steve Cochran who died years later as every man would probably like to go, on a yacht with six gorgeous girls! Ava was friendly and chatty, but quite adamant that she was *not* going to curtsey to the Queen as she was not a British subject. I suggested tactfully the old adage 'when in Rome', but she got it mixed up with Spain and raved on instead about her house there, inviting me to stay sometime, dance flamencos, and meet all her lovely bull-fighter boyfriends. I truly felt that when the moment came she *would* curtsey, as actors and actresses are a bit prone to creating potentially dramatic situations out of a desire for sheer flamboyance. But, true to her word, as the Queen shook her hand, Ava stood erect and, right or wrong, I had to admire her for having the courage of her convictions.

One delicious story about Ava, her sense of humour, and forthrightness of speech, concerned someone who was a great fan of the late Clark Gable, with whom she had made several films. 'What is he *really* like Miss Gardner?' asked the adoring fan. 'Well, it's like this,' said Ava, 'he's the kind of guy, if you say "Good morning, how are you?" — he'd be stuck for an answer.'

A is for AUTOGRAPHS

I have never understood the magic of obtaining some famous person's autograph on a bit of paper, or even in a proper autograph book, which I once owned as a child. The only signature I had in there of any value was that of the late comedian Tommy Handley (whoops, that dates me) and the only reason I had it was because my father had accompanied him on the piano at some show or other, and he acquired it for me! My idols were American film stars, but if I had ever met one it would never have occurred to me to ask for their written name on a page — it held no attraction.

Most autographs are written in the bustle of the moment anyway; outside a theatre where fans are mobbing the celebrity in question, and are scrawled in appalling haste with no meaning or message. I know, I have done it myself thousands of times and often wonder what people do with them once they get home. Do they sit and drool over the signature? I hope not, for the handwriting is always scrawled so badly it is hardly an advertisement for oneself.

Another point I have noticed over the years is that so many people ask one for one's autograph — but always add the rider, 'It's not for *me*,' and proceed to go into lengthy explanations, which one is not the least interested in, that it is for his brother's wife's sister's husband, or sometimes even more distant than that.

An old adage goes: 'The time to worry is when they do not ask any more,' and to an extent it is true I suppose. No-one minds obliging with their name providing it is requested in a polite manner! At times when you are shopping, running for a taxi or at other moments it is naturally a very boring and tiresome thing to have to stop and do, but then it is part of the price you pay if you set yourself up in the public eye.

Sean Connery is an old and very 'natural' friend of mine. He comes from Scotland and is completely honest — sometimes blunt or hurtful in the things he says, but at least you know where you stand with him. He is not a hypocrite. But like everyone else in the world of show business he is human and will only take just so much before he finally snaps. One such incident occurred when we all went to a big boxing match between Mohammad Ali and Henry Cooper. We had paid hefty prices for the seats — around fifty pounds each as I recall and they were all celebrities in our party. There was a lot of fuss and autograph signing when we sat down before the fight commenced. But eventually we settled back to enjoy ourselves; the lights went up; and the magnificent Ali made his entrance. The air of excitement was electric. Barely halfway through the first round a woman suddenly came rushing up to Sean and I and shoved a book under our noses to sign, completely obscuring our view! Had she offered it to me first I suppose I would have laboriously agreed, but unfortunately for her she aimed it at Sean. With typical Scots candour, and without too much restraint in his voice, he snapped, 'Get out of my bloody way woman. Do you think I've paid fifty quid a seat to sit here and look at *you*?' I wondered if she ever went to see a James Bond film again!

Another delightful story concerning a rather rude 'fan', if that is what she could be called, was related to me by fellow actor Ronald Frazer who was at one time making a film in Ireland with Robert Mitchum, also a celebrity like Sean who does not suffer fools gladly and speaks his mind regardless. They were, it seems, in a restaurant having lunch one day, when a very 'horsey' type of overbearing woman dressed in riding breeches, came up to Bob and in a loud voice that went with her haughty appearance, said rather sarcastically, 'You're some actor fellow aren't you?' Bob replied that he was of sorts and she appraised him with a look of disdain. 'I suppose I had better have your autograph hadn't I?' she demanded after a pause. There was an even longer pause as he unwound his large frame from the table and stood up, by now hovering over her. 'O.K. lady,' he drawled, 'If you'll just drop your drawers I'll sign it on your arse!'

B is for BANKRUPTCY

This is not a state anyone should get into if they can help it. I have many friends, not necessarily actors, who have had this unfortunate business forced upon them, and I too, through no fault of mine, but some mishandling by my first husband Dennis and his associates, have also been made bankrupt. I would merely go to the film studios in

B is for BED

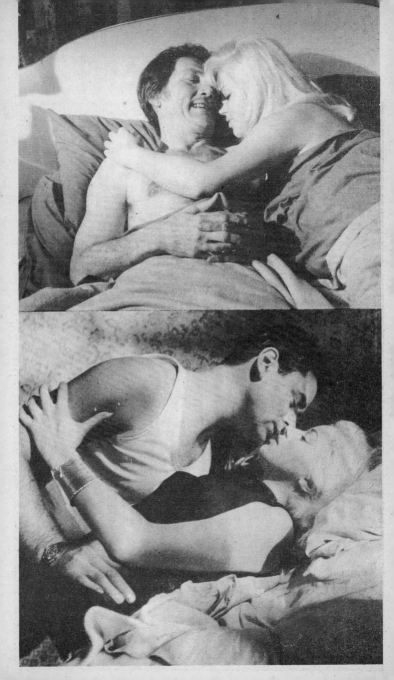

those days, do the work and earn the money, and when I was asked to sign some paper as I returned home at night, appertaining to some company somewhere, I would do so, thinking they knew best. Try explaining *that* to a judge! I hasten to add that it was the Inland Revenue who made me bankrupt! I did not owe money to tradesmen and the like. The court procedure and trial is not an easy experience to cope with but I pride myself that I conducted mine with great aplomb. It is particularly difficult if you are a public figure, for all the press are there waiting with pens dipped in poison. The judge and prosecutors grill you like the Gestapo and do not feel that they have done their job correctly until they have finally reduced you to a quivering jelly, or possibly tears if you are a woman. But the grand climax comes when they all get their emotional kicks as you stammer out that you have been a stupid fool, lived extravagantly beyond your means, and promise to be very good and never do it again.

An unfortunate incident happened to a well known pop star friend of mine to whom I had tried to give advice and sympathy on hearing of his impending bankruptcy. I rehearsed him in all the things he should do and say, told him not to be nervous or let them browbeat him as is their way, but when finally he got into the witness box his nerves got the better of him and he obviously forgot all he had been told. He had not eaten the day before and his stomach was in knots as the prosecutor hammered at him. With each fresh accusation he felt his intestines doing leaps and somersaults to such a degree that he could not help himself, and with the press virtually at his elbow, and hoping they would not hear, he was obliged to pass wind in order to relieve himself of the violent pains which were now racking his abdomen. The press luckily did not hear, as he had wished, but sadly his efforts had not been too successful, and he realised to his horror that he had actually done the entire job in his underpants! Thankfully it was the only bit of information which was silent and secret to everyone but him, on that dreadful day in court.

B is for BRIGITTE BARDOT

The French sex symbol, who like the rest of us, was hailed as the answer to Marilyn Monroe. Things were complicated as we all seemed to have double initials, such as B.B. in her case, D.D. in mine, M.M. as in Monroe herself, and then after Gina Lolobrigida and Sophia Loren, came Claudia Cardinale. This began to get so confusing that one columnist actually wrote, 'It is hard to figure this sex symbol scene out, what with Diana Dors hailed as England's answer to Marilyn Monroe, and Brigitte Bardot, France's answer to Claudia Cardinale? D.D., M.M., B.B. and C.C.! Goodness knows where it is all going to end!' I took his point. It was also not very nice being any country's answer to anyone, and no one likes comparisons. Even when I was expecting my first baby La Bardot was pregnant too, and the press seemed to think we had deliberately arranged it . . . My telephone rang on January 11th that year, and I heard an excited pressman on the line shouting, 'Well Bardot's done it, she's won the race.'

'What race?' I asked. 'She's pipped you and the Queen (who was also expecting) and she's had a son,' he announced triumphantly.

'I was not aware we were in a race,' I replied acidly, and put down the phone.

My only meeting with Bardot had been five years earlier at Pinewood studios where I was starring in a film called *Value for Money*. She had been brought over from France for the first time with all due publicity to do a film called *Doctor at Sea*. Her dressing-room was next door to mine, in what was then the stars' corridor as it was known, and other inmates were Peter Finch, Kay Kendall, John Gregson who was starring with me, and George Baker, then labouring under the title of 'England's answer to Gregory Peck.' I was not at all that impressed when we met.

The film Brigitte was making necessitated her singing a little song, which was not a difficult chore, but from the start she treated it as though it was an operatic event. A record player was installed in her dressing-room, and she put on a demo recording she had made, at every conceivable moment so that she could perfect the song. It would not have been so bad if she had played it softly, but she insisted on setting it at ear-splitting level, and for two days we all suffered in what was supposed to be the peace and quiet of our rooms, while it belted out on the record player. She ignored various polite requests from all of us to turn it down, or maybe even play it when she got back to her hotel at night, so after two days Dennis decided on the only course to take. He bribed someone to get another key to her room, waited for her to be called on to the film set and stealthily crept in to the Bardot boudoir. In his hand he held a large nail, and with great dexterity cut a groove in the disc, which to the naked eye must have looked like a crater. Everyone in the corridor knew what he had done, and we all eagerly waited for her return.

Eventually we heard her entering her room. As usual she immediately set the wretched machine going as loudly as possible, ignoring our pleas of the past two days, and the monotonous strains of the now horribly familiar lyrics and melody began churning round as before. 'There's a magic je ne sais quoi in the air tonight,' she squeaked in her tuneless French voice again, and then it happened . . . Dennis's artistry worked, and the disc stuck firmly on the words, 'There's a magic je ne, je ne, je ne,' we all breathed a sigh of relief, as we heard her rush to the record to see what was the matter, and thankfully, at long last turn the blasted thing off. That was the end of that, with Dennis definitely the hero of the day.

Well Brigitte, if you remember the occasion, I can now reveal the awful truth about the groove on your record, and how we all felt that day some twenty-two years ago over your singing, which we noted with relief you decided to abandon on your starry flight to the top.

B is for JACK BENNY

The marvellous American comedian who based a great deal of his act on pretending to be the meanest man in the world. In real life he was far from mean, and before his death gave so much, not only in money, but pleasure and happiness to millions.

I was once asked to appear on his television show in Hollywood, and a sample of the exquisite Benny humour, dry, and outwardly serious, began on the first morning we assembled to rehearse. As we began to read through the script, Jack suddenly paused, and looking up with a very straight expression said, 'Excuse me, but does anyone here know how tall a penguin is?' We were all mystified, not only with the question as nobody was an authority on penguins, but it had come completely out of the blue. Several people proffered suggestions, although they obviously had not the slightest idea what they were talking about, and gradually a serious discussion grew about the size and width of the birds. All the while Jack parried and answered questions, putting forth his own ideas as to how high the things stood, and finally it was decided by a maximum vote, that they could not possibly be taller than a foot and a half, if that. Jack sat back with a large grin all over his face, and sighed: 'Oh dear, then it must have been a nun I ran over in my car this morning.'

After the show had been completed I received a set of photographs of he and I, which I kept along with all the thousands of others I had acquired in my life, and one day years later, I had the idea of putting about a hundred up on the walls of a billiard room in my home. They were very interesting for people who played the game to look at whilst waiting for their turn, as literally everyone I had worked with was there, many stars and scenes from films and shows, over my thirty years in show-business. Naturally they were valuable, as like anything else, the older they got, the more interesting they became, and of course could never be replaced.

Once I decided in a mad moment to give Alan a great Dane puppy for his birthday and, after great research and

trouble, I bought a magnificent champion, with a pedigree to match, and named him Tiberius. Alan was delighted, but as Tiberius was not house trained, we bedded him down at night in the billiard room, carefully covering the carpet with newspaper, as like the dog it was very expensive!

Time went on and Tiberius had still not learned his social graces and proceeded to rip up the newspapers, and much to our dismay also the carpet underneath. The final straw came one morning when I heard Alan shout from below my bedroom.

'Whatever's the matter?' I called out as he reached the bottom of the stairs.

'Darling, the most terrible thing has happened,' he exclaimed dramatically.

'What is it?' I asked, almost too scared to want to know, and visualising the poor dog ill, or perhaps even dead . . .

'Tiberius has just eaten Jack Benny,' he cried.

B is for ERNEST BORGNINE

Although he looks so menacing, Ernie is one of the most gentle actors it has been my privilege to work with. We made a film with Raquel Welch in Spain and while Raquel was busy looking at herself in the mirror, (her favourite occupation — and I am not being bitchy), Ernie, the rest of the cast and I played cards and dined out in good restaurants, regaling each other with stories and experiences. Ernie was then married to a girl who had been, he told me, a stand-in for me when I first went to Hollywood. In fact Ernie had been married several times, once to the Mexican actress Katy Jurado, and once to Ethel Merman. His first wife was not an actress. He has since been married again, and I find it a continual source of mystery as to what goes wrong with Ernie's marriages. At the time he always seems so devoted. When Ernie's filming had finished in Spain he came round to say his goodbyes and it was then he told me of one of his pet grievances. 'It really bugs me,' he said, 'They get you to agree to do a movie and you sign the contract; they then fly you out to some foreign location where the director, producer and production manager all meet you on the tarmac as your plane lands, shake you by the hand and tell you what a thrill and honour it is to have you on the film, then they drive you in style in a big limousine to the hotel, and so you work your guts out away from your home and children until the big day comes and it's all over. Then suddenly something happens — they have had your life's blood, they've had your contracted work and best, but the producer and the director always seem to be missing on your last day! And the production guy says, "Hey sorry we got no car to take you to the airport, but they're all out on location, would you mind taking a taxi?" So there you are jogging along some road to the airport in a cab, wondering what you did or did not do that warranted no star treatment on the way back like you had when you first arrived.'

I knew only too well what he meant as it had happened to me and others too many times. It makes you feel like yesterday's laundry! To this day, if Alan, myself or any actor friends get the taxi routine worked on us whilst on location, we call it doing an 'Ernest Borgnine'. Recently I watched a re-run of one of his films *The Vikings* on TV and after seeing his last horrifying death scene, in which he leaps into a pit of wolves who tear him to pieces, I could not help turning to Alan and saying, 'I suppose when that was done, Ernie was to be seen jogging along a Norwegian road to Oslo in a taxi.' Thank goodness only actors know about the seamier side of show business otherwise it would certainly spoil the illusion for the general public.

B is for SCOTT BRADY

Scott is an actor who sadly, through no fault of his own, never made it as a really big star. He was as handsome as it is possible to be when he arrived in Hollywood, the younger brother of the late Lawrence Tierney, who had made such a great hit in movies with his first film *Dillinger* — the story of the notorious American gangster. Scott was a good professional actor who knew the ropes, so to speak, was always handy with stunt work, which saved the studios extra money, and was never late 'on set' (an unforgivable crime in films, in spite of his love of drinking and womanising). But with the luck of the show business draw he never got to the top and remained slogging away in what were then known as 'B' pictures. His one great chance came, he thought, when he was cast for the lead opposite Jane Russell in a film entitled *Gentlemen Marry Brunettes*, a follow up to Marilyn Monroe's successful *Gentlemen Prefer Blondes*. I worked with Scott many years later on a Hitchcock television series and found him a great character to act with, and to have fun with, during our leisure hours. He had a wonderful sense of humour and, in spite of his reputation as a bit of a hell-raiser and drinker, I found he had an extremely intelligent mind, and knew a great deal about Shakespeare and classical literature. He would regale me with stories which were always entertaining. One of them concerned the film I have just mentioned, or at least something that happened whilst he was in London doing it.

He arrived in England where the film was to be made and was given all the star treatment, including a luxurious suite in a top London hotel. All went well; Scott revelled in the whole venture; and for the first time in his career he played it like a star. One evening he and his stand-in were driving up Park Lane with nothing in particular to do, when he had the idea of picking up a couple of prostitutes and taking them back to the exclusive hotel, not for sex, but in order to give them a really good evening's 'pleasure and rest,' as he put it. As they entered the lobby, the hall porter who was kitted out in silken knee breeches, and wore a permanently disdainful expression on his face, looked horrified at the sight of what he obviously recognised straight away as two ladies of the night being brought into the palatial establishment.

Scott ordered him to send champagne and a banquet style supper up to his suite, and they proceeded to the lift despite the porter's obvious disgust at the situation. The night went well; Scott was in sparkling form; and after plying the girls with the food and drink, he quoted poetry, acted scenes from some of his films, told jokes and generally gave them an evening which they had never had before, and certainly did not expect. Finally, at around three a.m. he collapsed weary and tired with the whole project and politely informed them that they had better think about leaving, as he had an early call at the studio and would have to go to bed. The girls looked astounded, and one rather cheekily asked, 'Well, what about our money?' 'What do you mean money?' asked Scott incredulously. 'You've had a great evening haven't you? Champagne, the works and we've tried to keep you amused and give you a good time.' 'I'm glad you said that,' she replied. 'You've had our time you mean, and we want paying for it. It don't matter what you have or have not done to us, but you've had us up here taking up our time and stopping us from earning, so we want our money.' Scott could see trouble brewing, so he went into the bedroom and called down to the desk, the silk knee-breeched porter picked up the phone. 'Had enough sir?' he enquired sarcastically. 'Yes,' said Scott. 'Come up here now and get these dames out, they're causing trouble and refusing to leave.'

What followed next can only be described as pandemonium. The porter arrived hot-foot, eager to carry out Scott's wishes, and also delighted to prove that he had been right in his appraisal of the girls in the first place. They started screaming and lashing out at Scott, his stand-in and the porter, both verbally and physically, demanding their money and using extremely abusive language in the process. Somehow, in spite of his elegant costume, and aristocratic air, the porter managed to manhandle them, one under each arm, to the doorway of the suite. As each colourful adjective was hurled at Scott and his friend he managed to keep shushing them by telling them it was an exclusive hotel and he did not want the other residents awakened by their barrage of abuse.

As he dragged them down the corridor the one who had raised the issue about payment and time in the first place broke free from his grasp, and realising that she was not going to get her money, decided to deliver one last blast at her former host. 'Call yourself a star,' she shouted, arms akimbo. 'I've had dukes and earls! . . . *and* Donald Peers!'

B is for BROADMOOR

I think one of the weirdest evenings of my life was actually spent in this famous asylum (I hasten to add that I was invited, not sent there). A friend had acquired four tickets to see a play which some of the inmates were performing in aid of the Sunshine Home for Blind Babies. Not knowing quite what to expect, he and his wife, Alan, my husband, and I went along, and were ushered into a large room after being let in through various prison-style locked doors. Inside, a fairly large audience was waiting for the play to commence on a stage complete with curtains and lights. It began and continued extremely well. In fact it was so well acted, particularly by one man in the cast, that we could not make out whether the actors were inmates, staff, or outsiders. There was quite a fuss made of me when I was espied in the audience, and I was asked if I would go on stage between acts and make an appeal for the charity. We were then invited to remain behind after the performance and have a meal with the cast and production crew.

Tables and chairs were brought forth by the cast and stage hands, and with the uniformed warders in attendance, we were introduced to all and sundry, and sat down to coffee, cakes and sandwiches. I was seated next to the leading man and another who had produced the play. Their conversation was such that coupled with what I had just seen on the stage, it was hard for me to believe that they were actually inmates serving sentences in the dreaded place. A man with a beard sitting opposite asked me my opinion of the play and I said I had found it very amusing. He replied that his role that year was as prompter. In previous years he had acted but he did not like this year's subject. Stifling my longing to ask him what he was 'in for', I said as innocently as I could, 'How long have you been here?' 'Eight long weary years,' was his reply.

Meanwhile Alan, at the other end of the table, had just had an incredible conversation with one of the stage hands who had, after offering him a chair, sat down by his side and begun conversing gaily with characteristic Cockney humour. Alan, not being as retiring as I, asked him straight out what he was doing there, and he replied, 'Killed off a few warders, didn't I, when I was in the nick?' The leading man apologised to me that he had not seen any of my films as he had been too young to go to the sort of sexy films I was making in my heyday. Doing a quick mental deduction I realised that he must have been in there a hell of a lot longer than either the man opposite me or Alan's friend who had done in several warders. I managed to congratulate one man in the cast who spoke as though he had been educated at Oxford, and had given the best performance of all. I told him he had missed his vocation, and should have been a veteran comedy actor of the Wilfred Hyde-White calibre. He gazed at me sadly, thanked me, but said he had not enjoyed this production as much as the others in the twenty-four years he had resided there. 'It's a pity,' he said, 'you were not here two nights ago. The leading lady went mad in the women's wing yesterday, so her understudy had to go on tonight and she is not nearly so good.'

My mind was boggling. What could this man have done to have been there so long? Like them all, he seemed so sane and sensible. Again, I dared not ask, and suddenly, in the middle of the fun, one of the warders shouted, 'Right, everybody back to their cells.' They all hastily shook hands, bade us goodbye and filed off looking like sad lost sheep compared to the starry figures of an hour or so before. We were then taken across to the main club where the warders, wives, and doctors all hung out for their social evenings. I had noticed that not one of the doctors or people in charge had sat down and joined us for the meal with our somewhat bizarre table companions, and at the time I thought it rather mean of them considering they had acted so well and were conversing so politely.

Having been introduced all round to V.I.P.s and the like I then met the Governor of the place. I asked him what could possibly be wrong with these human beings, who seemed, on the face of it, just like he or I, and why were they there? 'My dear young lady,' he said tolerantly, 'do you realise that tonight you sat down to supper with more homicidal maniacs than anyone would meet in a lifetime?'

We left with a chill feeling of depression and also noted as we got into our car that there was a full moon. As we drove through the precinct a voice from some far away cell eerily called, 'Diana'. My friend's wife said, 'I don't believe what we've seen tonight, they all seemed so normal. What a shame to keep them locked up like that.' 'Yes,' I said, 'But do you realise that those faces we sat looking at over the coffee and sandwiches were probably the last faces certain poor victims saw on this earth?' We drove home in silence.

B is for BUTLER

I have been butled in my time and it was lovely. Of all the servants I have ever employed he was the best. His cooking was superb, he cleaned my house until it shone, and when pressmen called unexpectedly at the door he stiffly announced that not only was I unavailable, but 'her Ladyship has her dignity you know.' I don't quite understand what he meant by this, but as he had worked for so many titled folk I suppose he meant well. My breakfast was always brought up on a tray with freshly picked flowers from the garden in a vase on the corner of it, and whilst guests were sampling his culinary delights after he had served dinner so elegantly, with the plates warmed to utter temperature perfection, he would rush into the drawing room where we had been before, emptying ashtrays and plumping up cushions. What was wrong? There is always a snag to everything and everyone. He was queer which I didn't mind, but he hated living in the country. I had a farm at the time and he felt he was missing out on the bright lights and the fun of city life. He also had a fetish about Gracie Fields, not that that mattered, but his room was covered with photographs of her, and one felt that if she had reared up at any time all the breakfasts and flowers along with the rest of it, would be abandoned as he rushed headlong towards her, leaving me in the lurch. As it was he did disappear early one morning, and there was a curt note left on the kitchen table saying his yearning for the bright lights had got the better of him.

One especially memorable incident, however, occurred before he left. A male friend of mine who considered himself a Casanova with the ladies, and who drove a pink Cadillac, was always trying to get me to 'lay on birds', saying 'Tell 'em about the Cadillac, it's a good bit of flash.'

One night he asked me to see what I could do on his behalf, and for a laugh I decided to dress up the butler. We put an auburn wig on him, false eyelashes, falsies, a lurex trouser suit with high-heeled shoes, and sat him down in the drawing room under a soft red lamp telling him to pose and not speak more than he could. My friend arrived dressed to kill, reeking of aftershave. I told him I had got a bird named Margaret who was a knockout, but that he would have to really go to town as she was very shy. The whole evening was a riot. The butler only uttered squeaky 'yes's' and 'no's' and caused the aforementioned Casanova the most frustrating evening he had ever had. There was nothing he could do to get started with 'her'. Finally she left with a quick excuse that she *had* to go, even refusing his offer of a ride home in the Cadillac, and to this day he thinks he failed to 'pull a bird' in front of many witnesses and cannot understand why!

C is for CAPRICORN

This is my downfall zodiac sign in the love department. It

is strange that I have had four serious affairs with Capricorns not by intent, but accidentally. The first Capricorn in my life was a married one and from him I learned my lesson about the evils of 'dallying' with men who are locked in matrimony. It ended in tears, but the next Capricornian came along only a year later and I lived with him for nearly two years. He was not married — in fact we were both under twenty-one, the age of majority in those days; and as neither of our parents liked our chosen partner we would say that we were engaged and would probably marry when the time came. Thank God we didn't! The third was many years later in Hollywood when an extremely handsome, sullen looking actor (all Capricorns seem to have a rather brooding, moody quality which I obviously go for) appeared on the horizon and lasted a few months, again ending in tears! Finally, just before I met my present husband I was unfortunate enough to meet another, thankfully the last. I look back on that episode which went on for a few years, as a sort of final completion of sentence regarding my association with Capricorns.

C is for CARS

I have always loved big, fast, expensive cars. It is not merely the luxury of owning and riding in them, but that I only feel safe with a big engine in front of me, for if I am unlucky enough to have a head on collision then at least I have got some protection. My main style of car over the years has usually been a Cadillac, though I have toyed with the odd Rolls Royce and several American makes as well. My most famous Cadillac was one I took to the Cannes Film Festival. It was a powder blue convertible and it matched the gown I wore to my own film premiere. Of course it cost a great deal of money, but then I was earning it at the time so I figured why not? I will never forget one day as I was driving in it along a rather narrow country lane another car swerved round the corner and we

nearly had a nasty accident. The driver, on seeing who I was, leaned out of his car window and snarled, 'You silly cow, I had to *work* to get this.' 'What the hell do you think I had to do to get this?' I shouted back. It's a funny thing but a lot of people do not think showbusiness folk work at all but merely pursue a life of glamour and pleasure, forgetting we rise at five in the morning to get to the studios for an early call, and put in a gruelling twelve hour day. I once had a nurse for my youngest son Jason who each time I went through the door on my way to work would call out 'Have a nice day,' as if I were off to some social function.

One car I did own was not a Cadillac however, it was a specially built Delahaye which had been designed for a rich property dealer. It was such a fantastic looking affair, it had been on display at the Paris Motor Show amongst other things, with a crystal steering wheel and all solid gold fittings. Whenever I parked it outside a restaurant or shop, crowds would gather in the street just gazing at it; for it looked as though it had landed off Mars. That too was powder blue — it used to be my colour.

Nowadays I really do not mind what I drive around in, providing it is large and it goes. Up until recently I did lay claim to a white Rolls Royce which was very beautiful, but contrary to what they say about Rolls Royces never going wrong this one never seemed to go *right*, and I spent a fortune on it. My final gasp was one day whilst driving up the motorway on an important engagement in the north of England. Suddenly there was a loud bang; she spluttered and gradually stopped. There I was, stuck on the motorway with all the cars zooming past me, not knowing what to do, and desperate, for I did not wish to arrive late. I decided to thumb a lift and must have made quite a funny picture standing there with the wind blowing my platinum locks and my thumb in a signalling position. I was wearing a T-shirt I had bought in Hollywood, as it happened, with my name emblazoned in sequin letters across the bust and a big picture of Paul Newman on the back . . . I wondered which way to turn in order to get the fastest pull up from a passing driver. I am sorry to have to say this Paul, as I am a great fan of yours, but *I* won!

C is for CHARM SCHOOL

This unlikely sounding place was, believe it or not, an attempt on the part of the J. Arthur Rank Organisation to create a sort of acting academy for their young contract players, who were inexperienced or untrained in the job of acting. When I was given a ten-year contract at the age of fifteen, I was sent there, much to my chagrin, as I was *not* untrained, and indeed had just completed a two-year course at L.A.M.D.A., where I had also received and been awarded my diploma, plus the Alexander Korda trophy for the girl most likely to . . . succeed in films of course!

There were many young boys and girls at the Charm School, but I was the youngest, and I often wonder what happened to them all, for only a few like Christopher Lee, D.J. Pete Murray, and Barbara Murray, (no relation) were ever heard of again. As one may imagine, it was not an establishment to admit with pride that one was attending, such as R.A.D.A. for instance. I loathed it, but it was compulsory if you were under contract — to keep you out of mischief as they put it.

Another compulsory affair was the weekly cocktail party held by the head of the Rank contracts department for producers to mingle with young starlets and possibly arrange film parts for them in their pictures. The real reason was, as everyone knew, that a good bit of lechery could be indulged in under the guise of business, and many a young actress was tricked into some hot situation by the promise of a starring role. My tender age, plus the fact that to have sex with a girl under sixteen is, and was, against the law, saved my bacon for everyone was afraid to make any improper suggestions to me, but eventually came the time when the worst almost happened.

A chief executive, who shall be nameless, could obviously contain himself no longer as far as I was concerned, saying that he wished to see me one Saturday

evening at his flat. I was thrilled with the news, as I thought that at last he was going to tell me what I had hoped all along — I was to be their next big star project — and to reveal all the wonderful scripts they had lined up for me. I telephoned my parents in Swindon, to say that I would not be home that weekend as usual, for this was going to be the meeting to end all, and the Rank Organisation were finally going to make me a star!

On the Saturday evening I duly arrived at his flat, concealing my excitement as well as I could. He opened the door himself, and showed me into the drawingroom, whereupon we sat down and he made conversation of sorts for about ten minutes. *When* is he going to get to the point? I thought impatiently. Eventually he drawled, 'I've asked you here tonight to discuss something which is worrying me. I know you are only fifteen, a child really, but your weight is becoming a problem. Of course it is only "puppy" fat, and it will go, but I think you had better start dieting.' I gazed at him, crestfallen. Was this the whole reason for the summons to his presence? Was I not to be made a star after all and what was I going to tell my parents who were also excited about the big news, whatever it was going to be?

Things had only just started to move from his end however, which I at that moment was blissfully unaware of. As I mulled over my 'puppy fat' rather miserably, he stood up and said abruptly, 'I would like to see for myself just how fat you are. It is impossible to tell with that suit you are wearing. Take all your clothes off and I will be back to inspect you in a minute.' With this he strode out of the room. I stood there in a panic. What should I do? If I refused, he might cancel my contract and get very angry, but the whole idea of stripping off alone there in his flat was almost too dreadful to think about. I realised the latter was the only alternative I had, and I nervously began to unzip my skirt, when to my delight, not to mention relief, I heard the front door bell ring. I had been literally saved by the bell! He rushed through to answer it, and in came his secretary, with whom I found out later he was having an affair. She was anxious no doubt to see what he was up to with me, as she had arranged the appointment on his instructions. He offered her a drink, and after a great deal of flustered conversation, told me I need wait no longer now as we had finished our talk, and to see myself out. I needed no second bidding, and have never been so happy to escape from anywhere in my life. My next problem though was what to tell my parents? I telephoned and said the meeting was nothing very interesting after all, and that I had to go on a diet. My father who was always ready to believe the worst where I was concerned, decided, and told me to my face when I next went home, that I *must* have been misbehaving myself, and not concentrating on my work properly at the Charm School.

I was too young and embarrassed to tell him the real truth, that the respectable man who controlled our destinies and careers, merely wanted to make it with me. Anyway I knew that even if I had tried to do so, he would never have believed such a thing was possible, thinking I was simply covering up my faults. *That* is what happens if you have an ex-army officer for a father! As for the Charm

School, it died a natural death like most of our contracts did when the Rank Organisation made everyone redundant in 1950, and the executive went too, along with his secretary, his cocktail parties, and the problems over the starlets he had to handle . . . in more ways than one!

C is for COMMUNIST

A dirty word in America after the McCarthy witch-hunt of the early Fifties, when many famous Hollywood names were kicked out of the celluloid city, with their careers in ashes, as confessions were revealed of their once belonging in a mad moment to the Communist party in the Thirties. Communism is still a dirty word in America, though things have eased up a great deal since then, and some of those actors and writers have actually been allowed back to work in Hollywood.

This was not the case when I arrived there in 1956 however. Imagine my surprise when one morning in the *Hollywood Reporter*, the late Mike Connolly, a columnist well known to have Fascist leanings, accused *me* in print of being a Communist!

Before I left for Hollywood I had arranged with a leading film magazine in England to write a Hollywood column every week, but as I was not a writer and would be busy making films, a 'ghost' writer would do the work for me. He made a very good job of it for a month or two, until in one edition he wrote a piece about actress Dawn Adams not being allowed to work in Hollywood any more, because she had once made a film with Charles Chaplin, a known Communist who had been booted out along with all the rest.

At the time of my ghosted column, Chaplin was certainly not popular, and neither was Dawn, which the column stated, quite fairly, was all wrong as she had no Communist leanings, but was merely doing a job of work as any actress might have done. Even though I had not written it, it was done under my name, and I could not, and still cannot see anything wrong with one actress giving another a little help publicity wise, and commenting on a very unfair situation.

Mike Connolly did not see it like that however, and, proceeded to shriek at me day after day in his column, with paragraphs such as: *Diana Dors thinks it is unfair of us not to let Dawn Adams work here on account of that commie Chaplin. Up the Hammer and Sickle girl, and gather those Yankee dollars while ye may,* and so on. The head of R.K.O. studios summoned me to his office, and was horrified by the accusations, asking me if I *was* a Communist and why did I not check before I let a ghost writer print things under my name? He was also afraid the publicity would effect the film I was making, and lose the studios a lot of money, which was understandable, and having heard *my* side of the story, announced that I must telephone Connolly right away and put matters right.

But there was no appeasing him! 'You hypocrite,' he screamed down the wire. 'I was nice to you when you got here, gave you great publicity, and all the time you were writing this kind of filth against me and my country.'

I tried to explain I was not a Communist, or even a Liberal, but to no avail, and my pleas about the fact I did not know what the ghost writer was doing for me back home, were merely hissed at by the raging columnist.

For the rest of my stay in Hollywood, he 'had a go' at me whenever possible. Some months went by after my return to England, and Christmas came around, I was sending cards to people I had met in America, and thought it would be in the spirit of Christmas to send him one, and try to bury the hatchet. A few weeks later, he sent it back with the message: *How dare you wish me a Happy Xmas, you English hypocrite!* Well you cannot please everybody!

C is for SIR NOEL COWARD

The late and brilliant playwright whose acid wit, on stage

and off, was famous; and who, I am happy to say, I had the priviledge of knowing. So many stories are accredited to him; such as the day when David Niven was sadly lamenting the fact that all his friends seemed to be dying. 'It's terrible Noel,' he said. 'Everyone I know is either dead or dying, it makes me feel ghastly.' 'My dear boy,' replied Coward, 'I count myself very lucky if mine last until lunch!'

On another occasion, he was standing on the balcony of a friend's house at Brighton overlooking the sea when a small boy, who was also staying there, came out to join him. As they looked down on the pavement below, they saw two dogs in the act of making canine love. The little boy excitedly pointed at them and said to Coward, 'Look Uncle Noel, what are those two dogs doing?' The master paused for a moment and then explained to the child as carefully as he could. 'Well you see, my child, the dog in front is blind, and the one at the back is being very kind and pushing it all the way to St. Dunstans.'

C is for CUFFLINKS

A certain Oscar-winning Hollywood actress was famous for being extremely generous to her lovers. If they were heavy romances she would shower them with the most costly gifts, but if they were merely 'one night stands' she would always present them with a set of cufflinks. This last act was so well known that if anyone was seen wearing her gift it was quite apparent that they had been to bed with her. A British film columnist went to interview her on one occasion and arrived back sporting a pair very proudly, not realising that everyone knew what he had been up to, and that they were not simply a present from her because she thought he was a good writer!

Long before that, in the late thirties, for she was at it even then, a new young actor arrived in Hollywood from England, and was summoned for dinner at her home. He presented himself at the appropriate time on her doorstep and rang the bell. To his amazement the hostess herself opened the door looking breathtakingly beautiful. Her hair was groomed to perfection, make-up flawless and she wore a white gown with frills — in fact the whole effect looked like a scene from one of her movies. 'How sweet of you to come,' she cooed and ushered him in to the most magnificent house he had even seen. 'I have mixed the martinis,' she said. 'They should be chilled and just the right temperature.' At this she poured him out a stiff one and one for herself. They clinked glasses and he admired the house and furnishings remarking that as the place was so immaculately kept she must employ a staff of dozens. 'Oh no,' she replied, 'I would not trust anyone with my valuable things, and besides I prefer to clean it *all* myself.' More martinis followed and he was then invited to the kitchen from whence delicious smells were wafting. As she donned a lace apron over her frilly gown, he realised she was also cooking the dinner herself and he could not help feeling that she looked even more as though she were playing a scene from one of her films. 'I do all my own cooking too,' she added, but there was no need for her to do so as he could see for himself that she was a sort of living phenomenon.

Dinner was served out by the swimming pool on a table elegantly laid with solid silver and cut glass crystal goblets for the perfectly chilled wine. They dined, drank and eventually rose to dance around the pool to the sounds of the filtered music coming out on to the terrace from the living room.

By now the scene had changed somewhat, for a great deal of drink had been consumed, and the lady was not looking quite as immaculate as she had done at the beginning of the evening. Her hair was beginning to fall down around her eyes and the make-up was slightly smudged, but they danced on and drank on and finally in a rather inebriated tone she asked if he would care to see the bedroom. 'Naturally,' he answered and together they staggered into the all white boudoir. The strain of the dancing and drinking was beginning to tell on the young actor's energy and gratefully he sank into an ornate gold chair, whilst the lady really began getting down to business, kissing and clawing at him like a demented animal.

Eventually, her passion aroused to fever pitch, she decided to 'do her thing' sexually and climbed up on to the chair, lifting up her now crumpled white dress to relieve her bladder over the actor's head. 'Hang on there,' said our hero, and he rushed into the bathroom, grabbed a shower cap and returned to the chair saying politely as only an Englishman could say it, 'Now do pray continue.'

D is for DEVIL

I am a little superstitious, and I do not believe in tempting fate, for too many times in my life have I done this, and usually to my cost. The Devil does not frighten me as much as he might have done before I became a Roman Catholic. But I did have a nasty experience a few years ago when doing a television play entitled *Thriller.* I was asked to portray a wicked, evil nurse, who it turned out in the end was the devil himself present on this earth in the shape of a woman. It was an eerie play, and my inward fears about appearing in it seemed to be confirmed on the first morning as I drove to the studios for the read-through of the script. As I journeyed there a thunderstorm started, which caused such terrible flooding that I was forced to take off my shoes when I arrived at the studio and wade through deep water to the reception desk. Quite a unique experience! The read-through went all right, but as I closed the script and rose to my feet, the crucifix I was wearing snapped off the end of its chain for no apparent reason — and fell to the floor!

I tried to forget the incidents and shrugging them off as possible coincidences I sailed on. Exactly two weeks after the play had been filmed, I was suddenly taken ill, and rushed to hospital in a coma with meningitis. I lay at death's door for twenty-four hours. The doctors were quite mystified as to how I had contracted it, as it is a contagious disease and no-one else within a hundred miles of me had caught it. Such are my powers of resilience that I not only recovered, but came through intact. Miraculous, for if one *does* get over this illness, which is rare, then it usually leaves its victim with brain damage, blindness or paralysis.

To end on a note of advice, particularly for my female readers, there is a saying which can be helpful when dealing with men, and works like a charm — 'indifference beats the devil' . . . think about it!

D is for the TWO MR DORS

No man likes to be referred to by his wife's name. For one thing it wounds the male ego, and for another it is extremely rude, but sadly in show-business the press always make good use of the fact when a husband is not on an equal footing with his wife, especially if she is the one who is more successful.

When Brigitte Bardot married her second husband, actor Jacques Charrier, the honeymoon lasted until he was forcibly made to join the French army under their conscription laws. Aside from the situation being intolerable for the poor fellow, with all his army companions teasing him and asking questions regarding Brigitte's sex life, he was continually referred to as 'Mr Bardot', until he finally suffered a nervous breakdown.

Nothing like this has ever happened to any of my husbands, but they were obviously made of sterner stuff than Monsieur Charrier! Dennis Hamilton actually *revelled* in being called 'Mr Dors', but then his situation was different. He was not a temperamental actor, and looked upon me as a big business project, using all the tricks and gimmicks to build me into what he described as 'a female Errol Flynn' (a title I did not particularly like at the time) but I had to admit that in the end he was right, and I became a household name long before I had done anything of importance. Whenever the press wrote 'Mr Dors' regarding something Dennis had done, he would be delighted, for he looked upon it as one more occasion when *my* name was blazened in print.

This was of course a healthy state of affairs, probably the *only* healthy part of our marriage, for the rest was very fraught, amusing at times, but eventually I rebelled and escaped from his domineering and possessive grasp. My second husband, Dickie Dawson, was totally unlike Dennis in every way and detested being called the dreaded 'Mr Dors'. He was then a comedian aspiring to be an actor, and his personal and professional ego could not stand it. Things were not too bad at first, but when we finally went to Hollywood to live, one of Dickie's great ambitions, the situation got the better of him, and for years as we struggled to keep the marriage afloat, he fought against even being seen at parties with me, for fear of being labelled merely the negative 'Mr Dors'.

It is odd how opposites attract, and looking back one wonders why certain people meet and fall in love. The beginning of a romance is always roses, but at the end when anger, bitterness and whatever else transpires between two people has subsided, there is an empty gap with nothing left even to talk about, and it seems hard to remember the breathless, exciting start of it all . . . Actually looking back over my life and the loves I have had, they present a pretty depressing picture, and I have often thought that if they were all lined up for inspection as to what they had contributed and given, either emotionally or financially, the net result would be pretty dismal.

Well, as the song goes 'It's all in the Game, the wonderful Game of Love', but the sad part when a marriage fails are the children involved. Luckily Dennis and I had none, for the simple reason he would not allow it, thinking they would get in the way of my making money. Dickie and I had two sons, Mark and Gary, and it has always been the tragedy of my life that through the marriage rift, I have seen so little of them, missing most of their childhood. Happily, things are different, we are all adult and able to talk things over, but try explaining marriage problems to tiny tots!

Dickie, unlike Dennis, was an entertainer, saving all his humour and personality for the stage. Dennis was a charmer, handsome, amusing, devilish and angelic all at the same time. He could charm the birds from the trees if necessary, driving me, and any friends who were around at the time, along in a gale force wind which took one's breath away! When *he* jumped everybody jumped and some people often tried to copy him. I once saw him knock a man downstairs in a rage after an argument, and watched fascinated as the victim stood up and thanked him for doing the right thing.

His practical jokes were endless, his dominance stifling, and he conducted his life as though he were riding along on a whirlwind, with not a moment to lose. Dennis's tragic death at thirty-three after burning himself out with too many women, and an excess of everything, left everyone numbed and to this day those who knew him cannot believe he is really gone. He was an ordinary boy from an ordinary background who, when he left home, could not speak grammatically, and had no special talent for anything, yet when he died, such was the mark he had made in society that newspapers headlined their front pages with the news, and television shows were interrupted to announce the tragedy. It was almost as if royalty had passed on, and yet aside from manipulating me, what had he actually ever done?

This was the sort of man who comes along only every now and then. No doubt my reader will find all through this book I seem continually to refer to him, but it is only because he played such a strong part in the early shaping of my life and career, and though I never really loved him, he fascinated and held me for many years before I made my final getaway.

Dickie was a totally different matter. He made me laugh, which is the chink in my armour which I dare now to reveal, for I am married to my third husband Alan and am in no danger of being married again, wooed, courted or otherwise. Dickie and I worked together in a stage show first of all. Working and playing, combined with laughter, led to romance and eventual marriage. He was not an extrovert like Dennis, did not have his wicked sense of humour, but he was kind, sensible in so many ways where Dennis had been wild, and conserved his energy for professional purposes.

Sadly the jokes and impersonations with which he used to amuse me during our romance all disappeared after the wedding, suddenly I found a different man to whom I would not even dare speak before noon, and certainly no more Jerry Lewis and Robert Mitchum impersonations before breakfast! His professional frustration, and the strains and stresses of living in Hollywood, plus being married to someone like *me*, caused him a great deal of misery, and sadly, despite our two beautiful children, the marriage cracked at the seams and fell apart.

Happily Dickie is now highly successful in American television, and I am delighted for him. He is a secure, well-adjusted and much nicer person than he was during our early struggles, and success has made him a confident, more contented person.

No longer is he called 'Mr Dors'. Such is his popularity now that on one occasion when I returned to Hollywood to visit my sons, we went to a premiere, and the fans pushed *me* to one side in order to get *his* autograph.

I often wonder when I see other actresses' husbands described as 'Mr So and So', whether *they* argue and fight about it at home? Even husbands who are not in show-business must suffer, for no man likes to think he is on a lower par than his wife. But come to think of it, Prince Philip seems to get along quite well, and try as I may, I cannot imagine him snarling at the Queen over the breakfast table when he reads some ego-shattering headline about his role in life.

D is for KIRK DOUGLAS

My first meeting with this handsome Hollywood superstar was at the home of actor James Mason and his then wife Pamela, later the greatest woman friend I have ever had.

But this was 1956, and my first trip to the celluloid city. In those days, Sundays at the Masons were a big social event. Any number of famous folk would be there, arriving at all times of the day and sampling the wonderful hospitality provided. One of the main functions was the tennis. James would organise the proceedings almost as if he were still portraying Rommel, the German Field Marshal he played in a film some years before. Unless you put your foot down firmly as Pam did for instance, you were designated to play tennis at any hour and be partnered off with some of the best players in Hollywood. It was my bad luck that on my first Sunday there I was literally thrown on to the court, with who else but Kirk, and to make matters worse we were playing against James himself, who fancied his chances very strongly at the game, and Ginger Rogers, a player of professional standards. Now I *had* played tennis before, but I was pretty hopeless at it, however I always looked good in the latest tennis gear, as I did that day at the Masons but I knew they were all going to be in for a shock when I commenced the game, as my chief fault was and is a complete inability to run for the ball.

The game began, and the other three threw themselves into the affray with all the fervour of Wimbledon champions, but it became increasingly obvious to them and the spectators that I was doing Kirk no good at all as his partner, and he became rather annoyed.

'Run for the ball, Diana', he shouted desperately, totally unaware that this was my big hang-up regarding the wretched game.

'Why didn't you run for the ball', he kept snarling, gritting those famous teeth (the way he does on screen) and ferociously sucking in great gulps of air.

The ordeal finally came to a halt, with Ginger and James scoring a fantastic triumph, and Kirk looking sullen as he stalked off the court. He had every reason to be cross, but I suspected he was probably not a very good loser at the best of times, so enthusiastic was he about playing tennis.

Much to my relief I was not asked to play again that day, or for that matter ever again. This was probably how my friendship with Pamela got started, as she never played, and we used to sit gossiping, our favourite past-time!

Kirk, of course, did not share her opinion, but he must have forgiven me, for years later, when I was living in Hollywood with my second husband and two children, Pam threw a birthday party in my honour, and one of the surprise guests she had invited was Kirk. He came alone and oozed charm the entire evening, so I figured he must have completely forgotten our abortive tennis partnership.

'Please do me a favour, Diana?' he asked during the party. 'Don't become good friends with my wife. They all do, and it ruins my relationships with women.'

I did not know quite how to take this, and hoped he did not mean what I thought he meant, but shrugged the subject off as merely the evening's *joie de vivre* and the effect of Pam's champagne!

At around eleven o'clock he excused himself by saying that he had to return home. I suspect his wife was probably due to telephone but he did not say this of course, preferring to go out in true Kirk Douglas style, as he does at the end of all his marvellous movies.

'Do me another favour,' he said, gallantly kissing my hand and edging towards the door. 'When midnight strikes, I shall be lying in my bed all alone and thinking of you. Please think about me too!'

Sadly the party got rather hectic after his departure and, like Cinderella, I forgot the time until it was too late. To this day I wonder what Kirk Douglas was thinking about all alone in his king-size bed at midnight.

D is for DRACULA

Dracula, far from being the fictitious character so chillingly portrayed by Vincent Price and Christopher Lee, was once a real person, hundreds of years ago, somewhere in Europe. Count Vlad Dracula's activities were so frightful and barbaric, that they beat anything written or acted in this day and age. Amongst his other ideas of fun (and I imagine blood-sucking was possibly one of them) he murdered his own wife, and frequently delighted in impaling people alive, hanging them up over his dinner table with relish. One evening a guest complained that he could not enjoy his food due to the stench of the overhanging decor. Dracula pulled out his sword, speared the unfortunate fellow, and hung him up with the others!

D is for DRINK

Thank heaven I have never succumbed to this poison, though by rights, with all the tragedies and experiences I have had in my life, I should have become an alcoholic long ago.

I have analysed myself on this subject, for naturally in my youth I drank to keep up with the crowd because I thought it was the sophisticated thing to do! Luckily for me, when I had had too many I became as sick as a dog, and the resulting illness and hangover made me vow each time it happened, which was not often as I am not a masochist, that I would stop trying to keep up with the others. I am perfectly capable of getting high on *people*, which is very fortunate for me.

I also discovered at a very early age that I did not like smoking. At fourteen and armed with a cigarette case, puffing away happily — it seemed the smart thing to do — I encountered, on the five a.m. workman's train (I had an early call at the film studios) carriage loads of dirty old workmen sucking away at their non-filtered cigarettes. The sight of them made me feel so ill that suddenly smoking was no longer the grown-up, sophisticated thing I had watched my mother's friends doing when I was a child.

Thus I was saved from the perils of smoking and drinking. I have watched so many famous people ruin their lives and careers by drinking themselves to death. To me it is a tragedy. When talent is such a rare and God-given thing, it is tragic to dissipate and abuse it.

Of course there are always exceptions. Some people can drink non-stop without too much bad effect. And funny stories relating to drunks, especially actors such as Robert Newton whom I will deal with when I get to the letter 'N', are plentiful. I once knew a man who lived in Blackburn, he was a bit of a villain, but very nice and owned a little drinking club there. He would start first thing in the morning with a whole bottle of Vodka, and continue through the day, his quota being about four or five bottles of the stuff. I never once saw him drunk and he was as strong as an ox, but his kind are all too few. The great Winston Churchill who lived to over ninety, was well known for his love of brandy, and brilliant as he was, my guess is that towards the end of his life, he was pickled and preserved like a walnut.

The majority of men and women (and is there anything worse than an intoxicated woman?) who drink heavily fall by the wayside, and to use the words of my mother-in-law whom I will be dealing with later in this book, drink is nothing short of lunatic's lotion which in the end kills the liver and the brain cells.

I do not necessarily believe in ghosts or the supernatural, although equally I do not disbelieve it, yet I have seen many cases of people who, when under the influence of alcohol, behave as if possessed by evil influences, and in some cases the Devil himself. For I firmly believe that if such forces *do* exist then it is when a person is drunk that they are most vulnerable to evil.

Ending this rather grim subject on a funny note I will relate a story about the Oscar-winning star Lee Marvin, who was renowned for his drinking habits. Lee was in England many years ago making a marvellous film called *The Dirty Dozen*. Late one afternoon he had to deliver a very big dramatic speech from the top of a roof on the set. Everything had been rehearsed and was all ready to be filmed, when the clock beat the camera crew and, true to union rules, shooting stopped to be continued the following morning. During that night Lee went on a bender, and the next morning he arrived at the studios. The scene was already lit, the extras in their correct places, and everything ready to go. Lee marched on the film set rather like a robot and, stiff as a board, solemnly climbed up to his rooftop position. The Director called 'Action!' and the cameras whirred. Lee delivered his speech as well, if not better, than he had done the evening before. Indeed it was so well-performed that as the director shouted 'Cut!' he turned to the crew and Lee with delight saying, 'Fantastic, just what I wanted! No need to do it again. It's a *one* take!' As he beamed around with pleasure, Lee stared through glazed eyes, and in a loud voice exclaimed, '*That* is why I get paid a million dollars a picture.' At which point, his rigid body fell backwards flat on the floor, and he was ceremoniously carried off the set feet first, taking two days to recover.

E is for EGO

Vanity and conceit in a woman is bad enough, but then in the case of some ladies they can be forgiven, for what else have they got to think about? But the ego which never ceases to amaze me is that of the male!! Man's conceit over his prowess for pursuing, and catching women has been going on since time began.

Very early on in any girl's life she is subjected to being chased by a man, perhaps he takes her out to dinner, if he has any finesse, or maybe it's just a trip to the cinema with a packet of sweets thrown in. But at the end of the evening not only does he expect, but demands, kissing, canoodling, or often a great deal more! Many a good evening out has been spoilt for a girl by the thought of the struggle which must inevitably ensue on the way home in the taxi, or at her front door, and all because the male ego considers he is utterly irresistible! His amazement, and downright angry reaction to her refusal of his beautiful body knows no bounds, and it has always seemed to me so wrongly taken for granted on the man's part! Happily I am not the only one who thinks this way, and it was finally brought home to me by a very experienced woman friend of mine who said, 'Always remember if you say no and mean it, never feel guilty about the rejected suitor. If they've got the cheek to demand it in the first place, then you certainly have the cheek to refuse!'

My final word on the male ego must be summed up by the fact that ex-film star, Ronald Regan, who ran for presidency in America, and was also governor of California at the time, decided to commemorate his wedding anniversary celebrations by having an enormous portrait of himself made in sugar above the cake. Needless to say his wife did not feature!

E is for EMBARRASSMENT

I have often been asked what has been my most embarrassing moment, and the trouble is if I am asked on television or at a public function, there is no way I can really relate the incident because . . . it is simply too embarrassing! However this is an adult ABC so I will recall it now with no holds barred!

The worst moment of all concerned my youngest, Jason, aged six at the time. As children do, he had picked up a few swear words and whilst I do not mind swearing I try to deter him as he might use them in school or amongst adults who *would* take offence. One of the unfortunate expressions he had acquired was 'arse holes'. Now, we do not often take Jason to Church as we do not believe in forcing religion down his throat and would prefer him to make his mind up when he is older. And anyway the Catholic service can be boring for a child if he is too young to understand what is going on. But one Sunday he decided of his own volition to come. Alan and I sing in the choir, which is perched up on a balcony and consists of a few of the local congregation, some playing flutes, one on the organ, and a couple of young priests with guitars. The service proceeded as usual and finally came the sermon which was preached by an Italian priest whose English is good, but naturally not perfect. 'The trouble with a-people today,' he began with his delightful accent, 'is that a-they are praying for the wrong things, they are a-praying for a new a-washing machine, a coloured television set, a nice a-new car, nobody is a-praying for the right things, everybody should be a-praying for our souls!'

I need hardly explain at this point that the phonetic sound of his last two words, even to the adult congregation let alone to a small boy, sounded like the dreaded words we had forbidden Jason to say. With lungs second only to Dame Nellie Melba, he shouted down from the balcony with finger pointed like Caligula at the unfortunate priest, 'He swore, he said arse holes!' I grabbed him in a panic. 'Shut up!' I hissed, 'He didn't swear.' 'He did, he said arse holes!' piped my youngest. And once again the words ricocheted around the holy building . . . How can you explain the difference to a child of six at a moment like that, or that the Father is Italian and has an accent, especially with half the people craning their heads around to see where this terrible volley of abuse is coming from?

The second of my most embarrassing moments came at the hands, or rather another part of the anatomy, of my eldest son Mark, then only eighteen months old.

I had journeyed with him to Barcelona from our home in Hollywood, to make a somewhat dubious film for an Indian film producer. I say dubious, because the gentleman concerned had made a number of highly successful sex movies in Finland, and was now setting his sights on something straighter and, he hoped, bigger even financially than his Finnish efforts. The film was to be entitled *Appointment in Majorca* or some such nonsense, and the salary he nobly offered me was around $75,000. He had also generously thrown in heavy expenses, and the promise of a villa complete with servants during my stay there, so off I went taking Mark and his nurse.

I have never liked the idea of trundling children around when I work but on this occasion it was a necessity. It turned out that things would have been much better for all concerned if I had let them remain behind in Hollywood.

As our plane approached Barcelona the nurse, who had

eaten lobster for lunch against previous medical advice, was forced to rush to the toilet, leaving me with a screaming Mark, and made her descent to Spain sitting on the loo.

We were then met by the producer, and whisked away to a hotel where we would be staying until the 'luxurious villa' was ready. I could not help thinking how much like Peter Sellers he looked and spoke (when Peter is doing a funny portrayal of an Indian), and hoped that his promises and plans for me would not turn out to be as comical as a Peter Sellers type movie. Having deposited us in the hotel he rushed off, and to my dismay I found the place totally inadequate for our needs, in fact rather sleezy! Amy, the nurse, was by now groaning with pain on a bed somewhere in the room she had been allocated, and although exhausted from the flight, I took Mark off on a taxi-tour of Barcelona to try and locate a decent hotel. After endless searching I found a super one, with a penthouse suite overlooking the city, and finally after much shifting and shunting of baggage, I transported the wailing nurse and Mark there, and we settled down for the night.

The next day my manager and his wife arrived from England to make sure everything was in order. (These were the days before he started managing Elizabeth Taylor and Richard Burton, and devoted most of his time and energy to me!) It was decided that we would lunch in the skyline restaurant of the hotel. We had to take Mark with us, since the nurse was still in bed moaning.

It was quite obvious this was very much the *in* place to lunch in Barcelona. The customers were all elegantly dressed, there was an orchestra playing at one end of the room, and we were dutifully bowed to a table at the far end. Heads turned as we walked in; the waiters all fussed around us; and I noted that we had obviously been given the best table which was surrounded by glass windows giving a grand panoramic view of the city. If I had known what was going to happen I would have settled for a small corner table near the door!

I quickly ordered some sort of baby fare and asked them to bring it immediately, so that we could peruse the menu at a relaxed pace and savour the scrumptious items which were on it. The next events were to say the least frightful. Having consumed his 'mush' Mark who, though I say it myself, was one of the most beautiful cherubic blond children, climbed down from his seat and stood by the window gazing at the view. The waiters had just brought our first course, mouth-watering plates of melon, when my manager's wife looked at me and said, "What a gorgeous child Mark is. Those blue eyes! And look at that *smile* he's giving me.' I stared down at him with parental pride, and had to admit she was right as not only was he lovely but the smile he was bestowing upon her was almost celestial! I sat there for a moment preening, when suddenly to my horror I became aware of the reason for the look of jubilation on his face, he had just relieved himself in his nappy, and worse still, the nappy had obviously been a bit loose, for beneath him on the polished floor was the result. I gasped frantically, and indicated to her what he had done. My embarrassment knew no bounds, and I could feel the blood rushing to my head. My manager limply proffered me his scented silk handkerchief to wipe the offending mess up, but it was ridiculous, I could not bear to look down. Worse still were the waiters hovering around us, blissfully unaware of the disaster area at my feet. I could only think of escaping fast and so saying I grabbed Mark by the hand, and began the *long* walk out, I could not carry him as he was in such a mess, and it was difficult for the poor little fellow to walk quickly as his pants were bulging. The entire restaurant went silent as we made our way to the door, I could hear the odd whispers: 'That is the British film star,' and never have I felt less like one. We made an odd pair Mark and I — Diana Dors the glamorous sex symbol, and her blonde-haired toddler son covered in muck and walking forcibly bow-legged out of that smart restaurant.

Eventually after what had seemed an eternity we reached the door and I never dared enter the room again. There was to be a final twist to the tale, for as we passed the orchestra making our slow plodding progress, they decided to do 'the little English bambino' the honour of striking up the best British tune they could think of, and so we endured the strains of 'Colonel Bogey' which had been Alec Guinness's triumphant musical marching piece from the film *Bridge Over the River Kwai*, with Mark not managing to present quite the same dignified gait as Guinness as he waddled along!

Nothing worse could have happened to me after that, although the film, as I had suspected from the start, ran into troubled waters. I never got the villa, and after two weeks' gruelling filming, received not a penny from the producer. The company and crew received no money for their labours either, and worse still the hotel had not been paid for our stay there. I had to fly back to England to attend to some business with my manager, so he sent one of his staff out there to cope with the thunder clouds. It was at this point that Mark and the nurse, now fully recovered, were held hostage in the hotel until the bill was actually paid. This state of affairs lasted a whole weekend until reluctantly, as there was not much an eighteen-month-old baby and his nurse could do about the financial position, the management allowed them to leave, but they kept the unfortunate agent who had been sent to deal with the affair under lock and key! Whether they released Mark and his minder because they were merely incurring more credit, or whether it had something to do with that ghastly incident in the restaurant and their not wanting a recurrence of it, we will never know!

The third and last embarrassing situation which I was placed in by one of my children, came via my middle son Gary, and was thankfully the mildest one of all. Nevertheless it was an embarrassing affair, which could have ricocheted into something much bigger.

In 1966 when Gary was about four and I was working every hour that God sent, I used to fly back to my home in Hollywood at every opportunity to see my two sons, and stay a few weeks, until tearfully I would be on my travels again. Gary was then my youngest, and really I had never seen as much of him as I would have liked. It was a sad thing, but happily it did not affect our relationship, and he loved me almost as much as I loved him.

On one of my trips there I asked him if he would care to sleep in my bed one night for fun, and like any small child who loves a change around, he eagerly accepted.

The next morning, as it happened, I had invited an English friend of mine who was working in Hollywood as an agent, over to have breakfast by the pool. Terry arrived and we sat in the sunshine drinking coffee and chatting when suddenly I noticed Gary who was swimming around, looking rather lost and 'out of it'. He was alone, as Mark was at school, and feeling rather guilty at having devoted myself entirely to my friend, I happily pointed at him and exclaimed, 'Who slept in my bed last night?' hoping this would bring him into the conversation. Little did I know what was coming! After a few moments' thought, Gary stared back hard at Terry and pointing his finger in much the same way I had done to him, said 'He did'.

Now had it not been an old chum, I would have been very embarrassed, but as it was a platonic friend, we both laughed out loud. Gary meanwhile became very excited with himself realising his joke had gone so well, and bounced up and down in the water, shouting, 'He slept with you', again and again until we had to beg him to stop as the joke was beginning to wear a bit thin.

'That's the sort of remark which could get anyone hanged,' said Terry. 'you know what people think . . ? Children never lie, and why should he say I slept in your bed if there was not at least some vestige of truth in it?'

I agreed entirely, and we sat there musing the fact that many unfortunate folk had been tried and convicted by the, so-called, innocent words of children.

'Imagine me telling my wife about this', remarked Terry, (he had just married comedian Phil Silvers' ex-wife and inherited four daughters). 'Well, that's something you do *not* do,' I warned. 'For though *we* know it's not the truth, she might just take it the wrong way.'

Unfortunately Terry did not heed my advice, he was so sure that his bride would be tickled by the story. He related it to her when he got home that evening, laughingly going over the details, and the moment when Gary had pointed the accusing finger at him. His wife did not laugh though, in fact she hardly even smiled. Later that night after what had been a rather stony silence she finally turned to him and in a cold questioning tone which only a wife knows how to conjure up, smiling like a razor, she asked nonchalantly, 'Tell me, dear. *Have* you ever had an affair with Diana Dors?'

'No, no of course not! Don't be so silly,' stammered Terry, now feeling guilty.

'That's odd,' she said icily. 'Children never lie. I wonder *why* he said it?'

E is for ANITA EKBERG

The one-time fabulous Swedish sex-symbol with a body that was only surpassed by the beautiful bone structure of her face. We first met at a cocktail party given in her honour by a film producer friend of mine. The press were all set to have a field day with the war between the Swedish and British 'answers' to Marilyn Monroe! The evening went very calmly however. Not a picture was taken of us snarling at each other, and we chatted away quite pleasantly. In fact things were so dull that the pressmen started getting edgy for want of something newsworthy.

I had taken a close friend of mine, actress Jean Marsh, who later found fame as the demure Rose in *Upstairs, Downstairs*, and who was then possessed of a pretty kooky sense of humour! One of the pressmen sidled up to Jean knowing she had come with me, and kept pestering her for some spicy bit of information about me. At first she declined to co-operate. But, being unable to get rid of him, she suddenly blinked her great big eyes and said, 'Yes

I do know something which would shake your newspaper rigid.' 'What is it?' urged the man almost foaming at the mouth. 'I can't tell you now,' replied the wicked Jean, 'But I promise I will at the end of the party.' 'You swear you won't tell anyone else. Keep it for me as an exclusive and I'll see you right,' he said giving her a horrible wink. 'Promise?' she whispered. The evening dragged on and finally as guests started to disperse, unable to contain himself any longer, he grabbed her and pulled her into a corner. 'Come on, what is it?' he sizzled. 'Well' said Jean furtively looking around. 'She's got some spaghetti up her knickers!' . . . I did not see his expression, as she told me the story later, but I can imagine his dismay!

Anyway this subject is E for Ekberg (more of Jean Marsh later), and a highly entertaining thing happened just after she had married the British film star Anthony Steel. She had completed a film with my old chum Victor Mature called *Zarak*. A gigantic poster of Anita was placed in Leicester Square advertising the film, and of course her magnificent body was stretched across it from one side to the other. Sadly, the site of the poster was one no longer to be used for publicity, in fact a big building project was in progress there. No-one to this day knows who pasted a strip of paper right over the most intimate part of the Ekberg anatomy, with the words: *This place reserved for steel erections!* written on it.

F is for FANS

Fans are marvellous, they love you when you are up and hate you when you are down. Or even worse, forget about you altogether! They sometimes get you completely mixed up with someone else, as in the case of Doris Day and myself. I have often been referred to as Doris, but only because they are probably nervous and the Doris part becomes confused with Dors. Besides we are both blonde! Whatever they are we cannot do without them, and a typically sad story concerns an elderly actor, now passed on, named Ernest Thesiger. He did a good deal of character work in his time and one of his prize possessions was a pearl necklace given him by the late Queen Mary, with whom he used to sit and do tapestry, which he always wore under his winged collars. Ernest had got to look rather old towards the end of his years and had one of those faces that look 'well lived in'. The story goes that one day he was strolling down Regent Street in London when an excited fan rushed up to him and said, 'Excuse me but *weren't* you Ernest Thesiger?'

Now this has not happened to me as yet but I did have one bewildering experience at London Airport, when a man kept staring and walking up and down behind me. Eventually he plucked up courage to come and speak. In a strange voice he said, 'Are you Diana Dors?' I assured him that I was, and his face became stranger than his voice as he replied, 'Good heavens, I never would have believed it.' To this day I am still wondering what he meant. Did I look so good, or was he so surprised to see me in the flesh? Or was it that he expected someone much better, and thought I was obviously a terrible let-down in real life.

Fan worship can be sychophantic and it is also fickle — either people love you or they hate the sight of you. It also has its nastier moments. Oddly enough my fan mail has always been mainly from women. I've also had my share of crank letters, threats and so on, but one day just after the birth of my son Mark, I received a letter which disturbed me more than any had done before. Usually I throw crank letters away, particularly when they are extremely obnoxious and the writer hasn't the guts to include his name and address.

This letter came, anonymously of course, from someone who demanded that I put two thousand pounds in a paper parcel outside the gates of my house — on a certain day at a certain time, and that if I did not, the writer would kill my baby. I mulled it over, should I throw it away as just another 'nutter' or should I call the police? I called them — something inside me told me to do so and as it turned out it was as well I did. The detectives told me to do as the letter stated but place a parcel containing old newspapers outside my front gates at the appropriate time, and they would wait within to see if anyone came.

I did as they had told me, and on the appointed day we concealed ourselves just inside the driveway. I will never forget the sinister sight of a hand creeping around the gatepost to grab the parcel, 'Get him,' shouted one of the police, as they rushed out of the house and down the lane in hot pursuit of the offender. Apparently he gave them quite a chase for they had to run nearly a mile before catching up with him. When they brought him back, he turned out to be a youth of sixteen in jeans, who swore he had picked up the parcel for a man in a green sportscar, who had given him a pound to do so. The police took him off and within a short time he made a confession that he *had* written the letter because he wanted the money to buy *himself* a sportscar . . .

He was subsequently brought to court and looked very different in his smart suit and tie, unlike the ruffian in jeans of the week before. His parents were there and I felt sorry for them; he was a naval cadet and his age saved him from going to prison, but the Navy said they would take him into their charge and deal with it. I do not class him as a fan naturally, but then this is what must be expected if one is a public figure, and at all times keep it in mind that fans can be funny folk!

F is for W. C. FIELDS

The incredible W.C. who since his death, has probably been impersonated by almost every comedian in show-business.

Naturally I did not meet him, as he was before my time, but his reputation as a child and animal hater, together with all the other stories surrounding his life and career, have delighted me on many occasions.

Amongst many stories about W. C. Fields, there is one which typified his attitude to the studio bosses, coupled with the fact that he was worth so much money at the height of his career. He would get on a train, go across country alighting at obscure towns, and open bank deposit accounts, to hide his vast fortune. To this day no-one knows where all the accounts were, and indeed still are, hidden. His behaviour when at his zenith is shown in an incident which happened whilst in the middle of filming. Apparently W. C. had found an alluring female friend, and decided to give work a miss for a while, so he took her, together with his valet, to some mountain retreat. Several days went by, and Jack Warner, the studio head, was going beserk, since the delay caused by the star's absence was making the already expensive film costs soar higher.

Desperately he telephoned the mountain chalet, pleading with the valet to persuade his master to return and finish the film, but the pleas fell on deaf ears, since W. C. would not even speak to him. Finally, frustrated with rage, he telephoned and issued the valet with an ultimatum: 'You tell that son of a bitch that if he is not back in my studio tomorrow morning to continue his movie, I will personally see to it that he never works in another studio or theatre anywhere in the world for the rest of his life . . . Now, go and tell him what Jack Warner has just said, and I'll hold on.'

The valet, did as he was bid, and timidly opened the bedroom door saying, 'Mr Fields, it's Mr Warner on the phone. He says if you don't go back and finish the film, he will ruin you, not only in Hollywood but all over the world.'

There was a long pause as W.C. absorbed the threat.

'Well, what shall I tell him, sir? He's waiting on the telephone for your decision,' enquired the valet nervously . . .

'Give him an evasive answer,' drawled Fields in his inimitable way. 'Tell him to go and fuck himself!'

F is for PETER FINCH

The late hell-raising actor-rebel, who made history by winning an Oscar after his death. Finchy was a great character and I knew him well. We laughed together on many an occasion, and he cried on my shoulder one night when a love affair with a dusky English songstress had gone wrong. Whatever he did, and wherever he went there was always fun and excitement, he rebelled against officialdom, especially the star system which we were all expected to adhere to in the old days with the J. Arthur Rank Organisation. On one memorable photograph call at Pinewood Studios, as we were all lined up to be photographed he insisted on shouting, 'Shit!' each time the cameraman tried to take a picture of us all looking as though we were happy to be Rank stars. And as I remember it, he deliberately shocked the producers and 'powers that be' that day, by refusing to go and visit the Gents toilet, thus putting out the log fire in the bar in his own way!

Despite all the wild man publicity, and the press ballyhoo about his private life, he was a splendid actor, and he will be missed greatly.

A film which was one of his best was *The Man With the Green Carnation*, the story of Oscar Wilde, and each time I see it I cry.

His performance was so sensitive and moving. No doubt I will cry again when next I look at it, for now he has gone, and the world is an emptier place.

F is for FIREWORKS

In days gone by, I have held firework parties and watched whilst monstrous chances were taken by over-excited people throwing them at one another, usually after they have had too much to drink! When actor Jon Pertwee lived near my home in Maidenhead, we would sometimes go round to his little cottage knowing he was there with a girlfriend, and let fireworks off under his window to frighten him. Now I recall it, we all took a sadistic delight in torturing poor Jon for some reason. One evening he arrived at my house, which was built over an Olympic-size swimming pool, empty at the time, and as he and his girlfriend were settling down to wait for us (we had hidden, pretending to be out), someone let off some fireworks in the empty pool. The noise sounded like nothing less than a bomb attack which sent the girl flying over the room falling headling over a large tiger skin, while Jon, thinking it was my ex-husband Dennis, seeking vengeance, yelled frantically, 'No, no Dennis! Don't shoot! It's only *me*, your old friend Pertwee!'

This sort of thing was merely a bit of fun, but the terror of fireworks in my life began at a party held one November night in 1961 at the riverside home of a showbusiness friend. He was Tommy Steele's manager, and I had been invited there with many other people all of whom were asked to bring a pound's worth of fireworks to be let off after the barbecue. All went well, stars of stage and screen mingled with advertising executives, businessmen and the like. Then someone thought they would be clever and threw a jumping jack into the main living-room to give us all a scare. At no time would this have been funny, for the house, a brand new wooden ranch-style affair, was covered in white wall-to-wall carpet, and, had I been the host, I would have reacted very angrily.

The white carpet was the least of the trouble however, for stacked in a chair near the French window through which the jumping jack had been thrown, were all the other fireworks and rockets waiting to be let off. The firecracker hit the chair, jumped around setting light to the rockets, and within twenty seconds, the whole house was a blazing inferno. I had backed into the kitchen alcove to get away from the exploding rockets, which was the worst place possible, full of electrical gadgets soon to blow sky high. But in a panic no-one stops to work things out too carefully. Guests screamed, and a pregnant woman kicked a glass window to try and get out, whilst three men,

I might add, all stood back helplessly and let her do it. Flames were spreading everywhere, and one girl who was actually on fire jumped into the river to put herself out. Seeing no escape from my retreat, I spied a small window at the top of the kitchen and climbed up to it. I was pregnant at the time, expecting my second son Gary, and without any thought as to the extent of the drop below which must have been some twelve feet, I jumped! A friend who came out the same way just behind me told me afterwards that the flames were then so close, they singed her hair. After I landed I staggered up the path, dress torn, legs cut and bleeding, looking like something out of a Hammer horror film. By now the hysteria had reached its zenith. There were further fears for all the cars lined up on the drive, for one spark could have set the petrol alight and all hell would have broken loose. Mercifully this did not happen, and some of the cars near the house were moved, but the dreadful toll of injured rushed to the nearby hospital was only exceeded in tragedy by the death of three people. One man died of a heart attack on the garden path. Two others, a handsome male model, and a businessman's wife were lost in the inferno and never found again.

To this day I still have a scar on my leg to remind me of that terrible night, but thankfully Gary, my expected baby, was unharmed and weighed a hefty and healthy ten pounds, two ounces at birth. The late actor Sid James received injuries through breaking a window to help people escape, which left him with a permanently paralysed finger, and the host lost his house and all its contents which were not insured.

F is for ERROL FLYNN

Undoubtedly the most handsome, colourful character ever to hit Hollywood! His book told of his early life which was even more interesting than when he became an actor. The

stories of his romances, experiences and jokes are endless along with his love of living until the end came through too much vodka and whatever else he poisoned his beautiful system with.

I only met him once, briefly, at a film garden party here in England, and he courteously had his picture taken with me. His good looks were beginning to fade a little even then in 1951, but his charm and *savoir faire* were delightful and I could see that under the polite veneer lurked a mischievous twinkle.

I would never have liked to have had a love affair with Flynn, but I am sorry that I did not know him well like others did, namely his old sparring partner David Niven, for I feel I would have got on tremendously well with him as a friend. I know my first husband Dennis would have done so too, for they were so alike with their wonderful sense of humour and outlook on life.

Towards the latter end of his career when things were not going so well and he was no longer the great movie star he had once been, Flynn came to England to do a television series, which turned out to lose money all round. By then he was, I think, subjecting himself to all kinds of cheap work in order to keep up with the cost of his beloved sea-going boat. This he adored even more than his third wife Patrice Wymore, who had been a long suffering spouse right from the start. Even at their wedding reception a summons for a paternity suit was served on him. Hardly a romantic and peaceful beginning to a marriage!

No doubt the strain of working in the rubbish he was forced to do caused Flynn to reach for his beloved vodka bottle more often than ever, and at the end of a day in the studio when one is exhausted, anything, regardless of vodka, is likely to happen.

The television series was being shot at Bray studios, a quiet and pleasant place where I spent my happiest times living in a house in a tranquil backwater. But at the time of the 'Errol Flynn saga' as it came to be known, I had not arrived. Perhaps if Dennis and I had been living there then Flynn would have had somewhere to go and relax at the end of the day. As it turned out he was forced to take refuge in the only hotel Bray boasted, a delightful old world establishment right in the middle of the tiny village. As it was not very big, his bedroom was on the first floor just above the entrance door. On one memorable summer evening, as Flynn wended his way from studio to hotel his car was held up by a farmer driving a herd of pigs along the narrow country lane. This caused some confusion but it finished with Flynn getting out of the car, offering the bewildered farmer a sum of money, and buying the pigs on the spot! What he thought he was going to do with them only he knew, but I have a sneaking suspicion that he wanted to annoy the hotel proprietress, a rather snooty lady who laid claim to being a friend of Prince Philip, and looked disdainfully down her nose at everyone. Having assembled his pigs Flynn took them back, snorting and grunting, to the hotel and left them to run around in the forecourt whilst he went up to his room, completely ignoring them from then on.

All hell broke loose in the village; owners of cottages dotted around telephoned complaints and some actually came in person to the proprietress to air their opinions.

Flynn was summoned to appear to explain himself but refused to descend the stairs. He appeared at the window of his room shouting obscenities; this mingled appropriately with the noise of the unfortunate animals below which by then were running about in all directions.

As I was not there I do not know how the tale ended, but I have a pretty good idea, and I do know that he was not asked — but *commanded* to leave without further ado. As for the pigs — who knows what became of them? But with Flynn's sense of humour he probably took them all back to Hollywood for screen tests . . . such was his opinion of the film city!

F is for FOOD

My favourite subject and pastime. Being a Scorpio I adore indulging myself in all manner of spicy dishes, and yet thoroughly savour plain and what I call 'peasant food', like sausage and mash, fish and chips etc.

If I were not a female, and people had not become accustomed to seeing me once upon a time with a dream figure, things would have been easier, but I have to try and do something to quell my love of food and stay in shape, even if it is plumper now than before. A fact about which people never stop reminding me. Now if I were someone like actor Robert Morley what a joy life would be. He bought me breakfast once in a super restaurant in Park Lane, when we were doing some television commercial together. He has also bought me lunch in an exclusive show-business establishment, when we were doing a publicity interview and on each occasion we gorged our way through marvellous courses of goodies, with Robert telling me enthusiastically to 'tuck in.' Naturally I needed no second bidding. I now know that he would have a disastrous effect on my waistline, if I spent too long in his company. It's fine for Robert as he revels in his size and it does not interfere with his career. I have seen him on TV in America, chattering on about the delights of treacle puddings, much to the curiosity of the American people, who do not know what the hell treacle puddings are . . . and that's one of the reasons I could never feel happy there!

A sad little story about dieting comes to mind, and makes me realise even more that I am not the only person in this world without will-power. I recall my old friend and boss, Hollywood producer Herman Cohen whom I worked for once in a film starring the late Joan Crawford. Herman loved to eat, but found his figure becoming heavy and unattractive, so he decided to try and diet. His secretary, who was also overweight, knew him well enough to know he had not got a cat in hell's chance of staying on it, cheerfully suggested they should attempt a diet together. The first to weaken would have to pay the other a substantial sum of money. A pact was made, and they promised solemnly to confess if either cheated whilst not in the other's company. The ordeal began, and things went along smoothly for quite a while, with both behaving impeccably, but whilst the secretary started to lose a little weight, Herman seemed to stay the same. One day I asked him what he thought was wrong, and with a naughty twinkle he whispered the horrible truth to me. After a couple of days had elapsed, Herman's hunger pangs got the better of him. Not wishing to back down that early, or lose the financial bet, he had provided himself with a stack of candy bars which he kept secreted in his office desk drawer under lock and key. Whenever he felt hungry, he would merely announce rather officiously to his secretary, that he was going to be involved in heavy business matters, and on no account was he to be disturbed for any reason, whereupon he would creep 'Tom and Jerry' fashion into his office, lock the door and sit there all morning munching away happily. I am not aware of the final result of the deal, or who broke down and paid who, but I do know that Herman decided one day to put himself into a small scene in the picture, in the same way that Alfred Hitchcock is always seen in his films. Herman darling, I saw the movie, and all I can say is, Hitchcock is a very large gentleman too!

F is for FRAME-UP

F is for FRENCHMEN

I am going to state right away that I do not like Frenchmen! The great French lover myth is just an enigma to me, a legend created by the antics of gentlemen at the French court years ago, who along with the coquettish women, leapt from bedchamber to bedchamber indulging in glorious debauchery, until, with the coming of the French Revolution, they all had their heads lopped off, poor souls.

Frenchmen have never appealed to me, indeed I find them rather feminine. Give me an Englishman every time, or better still an 'Italian-American'. I stress this title because ordinary straight-forward Italians on their home ground, have deteriorated badly down through the centuries, whereas the ones whose ancestors emigrated to the States are much more like Italian men used to be. In short if given the choice between being swept away in the arms of a drooling Frenchman, or pinned to a wall by some jealous Sicilian threatening me with love or death, I would opt for the Latin lover every time!

Many years ago I made a film with an American actor named Eddie Constantine who had once been a chorus boy in his native New York, but journeyed to France in search of fame and fortune, and found *both* in an enormous way. He became their biggest star for a while, playing rough gangsters who slapped women around, instead of doing a 'Charles Boyer', which was what they were used to! His treatment of the female sex proved extremely fruitful, and Eddie was the Number One star there for a long time. Eventually he decided to set his sights on English territory and arrived here to make a film all about brothels, entitled *Passport to Shame*. Of course I was a natural piece of casting for this type of movie in those days, and we hammered out a fairly good little epic, which was so successful at the box office in America that the wily producer sent it round again under a different title, *Room 43*, thus making himself a small fortune!

The critics were not very kind however, and lambasted

it well. I did not mind very much, as I was quite used to receiving bad notices for the films I appeared in then, but Eddie's reactions were entirely the opposite. Having staked his whole career and reputation on it, he was hoping to make it really big in the States, and no doubt possibly return there with all guns blazing, like the conquering hero, to be respected and adored by his own countrymen.

The New York critics were even more scathing than the British in their reports, but the one which really hurt said, 'After seeing the performance of Mr Eddie Constantine in this latest offering, and knowing him to be a very successful star in his newly acquired country, France, we can only assume that "fifty million Frenchmen" must be wrong.'

G is for GEORGE

Of all the people I have known in my life, this was without doubt the wildest, most colourful character I ever met.

My old friend Kim Waterfield first introduced me to George in 1950, just after he had come out of prison for the *first* time for stealing two umbrellas and a bicycle from Harrods. He had been helped in this silly escapade by a member of the aristocracy, whilst both were slightly 'in their cups'. The aristocrat had 'got away with it', leaving poor George to face the music and receive twelve months, which was quite a harsh sentence for a first offence. Had the magistrates known who they were dealing with, they would probably have locked him up for good and thrown the key away there and then, which would have at least prevented the world from suffering the havoc which he was to cause after he came out.

By a strange coincidence George was then married to an understudy of mine, a Canadian girl named Barbara, and we were appearing in a play in the West End, so naturally I saw a good deal of him at that time. My first insight into his odd behaviour and pathological lying came when, having seen him arrive by bus, I asked him what sort of a journey it had been. 'I did not travel on a bus,' said George grandly as if the indignity of using such a public vehicle was unthinkable. 'I wished to get here quickly, so I travelled on the tube.' Not knowing his character then as I do now, I argued that he could not possibly have done this as I had seen him getting off a bus. But the more I argued the more adamant he became about his tube ride. It was at *that* moment I found out George could not help lying over the tiniest thing however unimportant. He was the sort of person who, if he said it was a beautiful sunny day outside, you knew immediately without even looking through the window, that it was pouring with rain.

As the years rolled by, my association with him was a sort of 'on and off' friendship, usually because he was either in jail again, or rushing round the world at breakneck speed, drinking, womanising and generally conning people into believing that he was the 'Duke' of this, or the 'Earl' of that. On one occasion he drew up in his car at a local garage demanding petrol on an obviously extended credit account, was saluted by the garage man, and respectfully addressed as 'Lord Carlton'. At another time he devised a plan whereby he and a friend dressed themselves as Army officers and went on a spree throughout the country, living at hotels and 'bouncing' cheques, until they were finally caught in Manchester, and he was once again sent down for a period of time. (During George's enforced stays in prison, the English population could happily relax and enjoy a peaceful rest until he was released.) His marriage to Barbara was dissolved eventually, and one day when I asked him foolishly what had become of her, he shook his head sadly replying that she had returned to Canada and committed suicide. I was naturally shocked by this, but as the years went by he married again. Imagine my surprise, even knowing him as well as I did, when I received a letter from Barbara in Canada, stating that she was very worried as to his where-abouts. It appeared he had been there visiting her, but made a somewhat hasty departure, hotly pursued by the Royal Canadian Mounted Police. What he had done to warrant this attention I still have no idea, but I was furious with him for lying to me on such a serious subject as his ex-wife's death, and was determined to have it out with him the next time we met. I actually looked forward to challenging him, delighting in the prospect of watching him squirm under my interrogation, and openly stating that I could not wait to see what excuse he would use *this* time to get out of the situation. I had to control myself for a long time before I had the pleasure of doing this, since George had got himself into trouble again, this time with the Dutch police and was confined in a Rotterdam jail for a lengthy period. However he eventually managed, through his acting ability (having once been an actor amongst other things) to obtain a parole, by telling the authorities there that he was dying from cancer and needed urgent treatment in England. The Dutch in all good faith had flown him back home, provided him with a wheel-chair as he went through his Oscar-winning performance and sent him directly to a first class hospital where he was kept in luxury for a while and then released yet again upon the unsuspecting British public.

Having captured him in my house and heard his adventures and revelations, I gleefully confronted him with the news that I had received a letter from the 'dead' Barbara during his absence, and *what* did he have to say about it?

'Why did you tell me she was dead?' I demanded . . . George sat back, paused for a fleeting moment, and just as I thought I had ensnared him, replied incredulously, 'Well, I thought she *was.*'

His talent for getting round any situation was amazing, he looked very much like an English Lord, and therefore it was no problem for him to occupy a large suite at the Ritz Hotel on many occasions under some bogus title, treating us all to dinner there often, with the staff bowing and scraping in every direction. How he paid the bill I never knew.

George sometimes arrived bag and baggage for a surprise overnight stay at my home, clutching a bottle of champagne, and would then proceed to drive me mad, until I could stand it no longer and literally threw him out. Regardless of this he would always bounce back with the same ebullience as his bounced cheques, ready and eager to carry on where he had left off, drinking and chasing women! He also developed a talent for cooking, and having opened a restaurant somewhere, would then reign like a beloved king over the local inhabitants, usually getting me to open the place for him with a blaze of press publicity. I would stand back and listen to the complimentary remarks made by all and sundry regarding his warm landlordly behaviour, smiling quietly to myself, for I knew that it would end in tears, and the same people who were paying such homage, would soon be searching frantically for him to pay their bills etc.

During George's colourful career as a restauranteur, one of his points of disembarkation was Malta. While residing there, he almost had the whole island under control, dining at the Palace, and coming out on to the balcony to wave to the crowds on public holidays!

In many ways he reminded me of Toad of Toad Hall. He was an incorrigible rogue, but a lovable one and thereby hung his charm and ability to sail through life. He managed to hoodwink my first husband (a virtually impossible task), but Dennis was very like George when it came to charm and personality. He also nearly ruined a film appointment which my present husband Alan had at the Ritz with film director David Lean one day, by sticking his nose in as usual where it was not wanted, and behaving like Toad in a noisy and embarrassing manner, for he considered the Ritz to be his own personal domain.

Alan had been a bit dubious about him ever since their first encounter. George took him on one side for an intimate talk about me (his old and loved friend), finally announcing to my future husband, 'I think she will be faithful *this* time,' which gave my reputation a bad jolt from Alan's point of view and hardly cemented the relationship between us very happily!

I could write a complete book about George, but I will wind the subject of him up by relating a typical story which happened some years ago. I was booked to appear on a television show in Birmingham, and George, who had made his usual surprise arrival at my home, announced that he would like to accompany me there. He assured me he knew the management of a big hotel in the city very well, and could get me the penthouse suite for nothing, but I took this last piece of information with the usual pinch of salt, and foolishly let him browbeat his way into coming with me. He also extended an invitation to a girlfriend of pop star P.J. Proby (who was away touring Australia at that time), and to my astonishment she accepted. George had meanwhile left his second wife and four children at home in Derbyshire, and so it was with great surprise that the morning after our arrival, I was awakened by him, rather breathlessly, on the telephone from his room to mine, 'You'll never guess what happened in the middle of the night,' he began. 'My bloody wife arrived in the lobby, God knows how she found out I was here! I was woken up by the hall porter just as Sarah and I were getting along fine, and he told me.'

'Good heavens, George. Whatever did you do?' I gasped.

'Do? What do you mean, what did I do? I simply told him off for daring to disturb me at such a late hour and said she must wait downstairs in the hotel until I was ready to receive her this morning,' came his indignant reply. He might have been visiting royalty, or a Field Marshal who had been interrupted by some important event from the front the way he was describing the situation, and his irritation knew no bounds.

'You mean she is downstairs *now*,' I said suddenly grasping the full meaning of the situation.

'Yes, that's the problem,' he answered. 'She is actually on her way up, and I've got to get rid of Sarah.' With that, he hung up abruptly. I leapt out of bed and rushed into his room. Dragging the poor girl from her bed, I managed somehow to propel her into the service elevator, with the sound of the customers' elevator coming up the other shaft, literally with George's wife inside.

To this day I do not know how the two did not collide, they passed each other en route, but luckily George's wife never saw Sarah. How will he talk his way out of this one I wondered? There was a long scene in the bedroom, after an interminable time, his wife came out with tears rolling down her face, and grasped me with both hands. For one horrible moment I feared she may have believed that *I* was having an illicit affair with her husband — perish the thought! I loved him, but not in that way. My fears were eased as she said sorrowfully, 'George has made a completely clean breast of everything to me.'

Holding my breath as to what this statement could possibly mean, and not imagining it was possible for him to compile a dossier of his sex life in such a short time, I asked furtively what he had told her?

George had done it again! Playing on her sympathy he revealed, with hand on heart, that the doctors in London had told him he only had a short while to live, due to gallstone trouble, and would she forgive his behaviour as he had been so worried and wanted to try and keep the truth from her.

Like everyone else before her, the poor woman believed every word and probably still thinks, for they separated later, that his hours were numbered that day in Birmingham. Tragically George's convenient lie *was* to come true many years later, when he died suddenly, just at the height of a new business venture he had embarked upon in Bombay. True to form George could only die as spectacularly as he had lived, and was mourned by many of his new unsuspecting followers over there . . . but for once in his life he did the decent thing by dying! If he had not, England would surely have been at war with India!

G is for GLASGOW

I have nothing against Glasgow, but my memory of the old Hippodrome where I was first sent to work in variety, will be etched on my memory for all time. Firstly, in my own defence, I must state that I was not the only one who quivered at the sound of the place. Established acts would refuse to play there, the veteran comedian Max Miller plainly stated he was afraid to go further than Newcastle-upon-Tyne, and singer Des O'Connor once staged a dummy faint in the middle of his show and allowed himself to be carried off, because his comedy act was going so badly before the dour and rowdy Scots audience.

I was out of work when an agent, who shall be nameless, suggested with cash registers lighting up in his eyes, that I should try my hand at variety. It was 1953 and music halls were just going through their final death throes before television killed them off altogether. He told me a lot of money could still be made for both of us, and all I had to do was to rehearse a twenty-minute act, go out cashing in on my film name, and collect the percentage of the takings at the end of each week. Filled with doubt, as I was really an actress and not a variety artiste, I did as he suggested, and when all was ready he proudly announced he had booked me into the Hippodrome at Glasgow.

Dennis Hamilton, the agent and I journeyed north on an overnight train, and arrived tired and nervous at Glasgow station. Our taxi turned into a street some three blocks from the Hippodrome, and we saw an enormous queue of people lined up four deep. The queue went around the corner into the next street, turned the corner again, and to my agent's now hysterical delight, stretched right up to the box office of the theatre.

'My God!' he exclaimed. 'It's for you. I thought you might be a draw but I never imagined anything as fabulous as this.' He jumped up and down in his seat, and I could see he was already counting the money he was going to make out of me that week. We leapt out of the cab and entered the stage door, feeling elated at the prospect of the business ahead.

'Good morning,' I said to the stage-door keeper brightly. 'What a wonderful queue out there. We should do great business this week with that amount of customers.'

'Och,' he replied in a thick Scottish brogue. 'That's not

for you, it's for the Sunday concert next week. It's a great bill full of *Scottish* artistes.'

I was crushed to say the least, but undaunted he continued, 'I'll show ye to your room, it's the star one ye know, we've had all the biggest ones here: Danny Kaye; Judy Garland; Frankie Laine . . .' and on and on his voice droned, reeling off stars of such magnitude that it suddenly hit me what I was doing for the first time. Here was I, my first week in a medium I knew nothing about, topping the bill where they had had scores of international stars, I might just as well have been opening at the London Palladium!

From that moment on my knees went to jelly. I had not the experience I have today, I was in a foreign field, and trying to cash in on a screen name at what was to prove to be the toughest theatre in the world.

'Have you got your lighting plot?' asked the stage manager.

I did not even understand what he was talking about. I muttered something about leaving it to him, and he looked mystified but left it at that. The opening night was horrific. Before I went on in the star spot, a comedian said to me, 'Whoever booked you here must be mad. It's like throwing a baby in a pond and saying "now swim".'

The manager had already warned me about the Friday night audience being so unruly that he could not hold himself responsible. I could see they were eating fish and chips in the circle on a Monday, so heaven knows what was going to happen on the Friday, or for that matter any other night, in the gallery. To add to my terror Monte Rey, an English singer who had chosen the Italian sounding name to suit his Italian songs and mode of dress, was in the middle of his act and prefaced a number by saying that although he had an Italian name he was English too. I assumed he was trying to endear himself to the audience but his scheme backfired miserably, for no sooner were the words out of his mouth, when a raucous voice from the gallery shouted out, 'You bloody liar. I was shooting at bastards like you during the war.' It killed Monte's act stone dead, and caused him to get off stage quicker than he had planned.

I made my entrance to a great fanfare of music, and then regaled them with all the expensive material I had gathered for my act, assuming it would knock them cold . . . it did just that, only not in the way I had expected.

Every joke, every line of each song which was even vaguely amusing, received nothing but total silence, and only the smallest trickle of applause at the close of each number. I came off stage a complete wreck. 'My God,' I gasped. 'I died a thousand deaths out there.'

'Nonsense,' said the manager, standing in the wings. 'You went very well. At least they kept quiet and didn't throw things. I was expecting worse than that with you.'

The rest of the week followed with icy coldness. I was contracted to do two shows a night, and each show saw me trying a different act, changing words, jokes, songs, *anything* to try and melt the stony Scots, but to no avail.

Finally on the Saturday, thankfully the last night, the manager came to the dressing room with my weekly salary. To my utter amazement, I received the sum of £300, more than I had ever earned in my life for a week's work, and truly unwarranted for I had been very bad.

The last nail in the coffin of the Glasgow Hippodrome came years later when I was reclining beside my swimming pool in Hollywood, sunbathing and feeling miles away from England. The telephone rang, and upon answering I heard a Scots voice echoing down the crackly line. It was a Scottish newspaper man telling me they were finally pulling down the old Hippodrome and did I have any sentimental memories or thoughts about the place? . . . I do not remember my exact words, but I know I suggested as politely as possible, what in my opinion they could do with it!

G is for JACKIE GLEASON

The American comedian who gave such a wonderful performance in *The Hustler* as Minnesota Fats with Paul Newman, for which he was nominated for an Oscar. Of all the branches of entertainment business I think comedy is the hardest, and if comedians have the capacity to make people laugh they can certainly make them cry; it is much more difficult.

To leave Jackie and his fellow comedians for a moment however, I have three sons and although the eldest, Mark, is the image of me to look at, it is rather an embarrassing fact that the other two, Gary and Jason, look incredibly like two actors I have met once and only briefly. Jason particularly with his enormous blue eyes, could easily be the offspring of actor Malcolm MacDowell, especially when he pulls some of his wistful expressions — but I was only introduced to Malcolm at a restaurant in London one evening, so there was hardly a chance of consummating the association on that occasion. Gary, when he was two years old, looked unbelievably like Albert Finney who had just scored such a success with the film of *Tom Jones.* Wherever I took him in Hollywood elderly matrons would point fingers at him and gushingly squeal, 'Oh Gee, it's Albert Finney!' I had never even met Albert at that point and did not do so until years later when introduced by my husband Alan who had filmed *Charlie Bubbles* with him. But back to Jackie Gleason and the birth of Gary at the Cedars of Lebanon Hospital in 1962. When you leave a hospital in Hollywood, especially after having a baby, a great fuss is made and you are wheeled right to your waiting car. Naturally, as I left with baby Gary wrapped in a blue shawl, television newsmen and press gathered around taking our pictures. 'Who do you think he looks like?' they asked, and as Gary was an enormous baby — he weighed 10lbs 2oz at birth and had a very round face surrounded by a mop of black hair — I gaily quipped, 'Jackie Gleason!' This was of course duly screened that night on television and the next day a telegram arrived at my Beverly Hills home addressed to Richard Dawson, my husband at that time. It read 'There are more reasons than one why that child looks like me. My regards to Miss Fluck. Signed Jackie Gleason.' We roared with laughter, but I was curious as to how he knew my maiden name. The answer was revealed later when I discovered he was filming at the time with a British actress and friend of mine, Glynis Johns, whom I had not seen since 1955 when we filmed *The Weak and the Wicked* together. She was at the bottom of it all — but to this day, I have still never met Mr Gleason.

G is for GODFATHER

The Godfather, since the advent of the best selling book and highly successful film, has suddenly given this rather serious and responsible position a dreaded sound, whereas the word 'godmother' merely implies, at its worst, the wicked fairy godmother in the children's story *The Sleeping Beauty*. This does not deter anyone however from selecting several responsible people, either relatives or friends, to preside over their adored infant at its christening.

At my last son Jason's christening a rather bizarre thing took place. It has a sinister ring to it like *The Godfather*, but it must also be looked on with humour.

One of the friends I had chosen to be a godfather was an old and dear chum of mine, and a very well-known musical genius into the bargain. I figured it would be good for Jason to be able to say proudly that this man was his godparent, but as it turned out I wished afterwards I had not made the choice.

I arranged a beautiful reception to take place at my house after the baptism. But before we left for the church, I asked all the guests to assemble there first and organised chauffeur-driven cars to transport them back and forth.

My two elder sons had flown over from Hollywood for the occasion, and were looking forward to the event with great excitement as they had never been to a christening before. When the time to set off drew near, I began marshalling everyone to the cars, leaving one large car free to take my sons, Alan and I. It was just as well I did, for suddenly I realised that the proposed godfather was missing. We dashed all over the house, and to my amazement I found the door of my bathroom locked. 'Who's in there?' I called, and a throttled voice answered that it was he. 'Come on, hurry up. We are leaving,' I said anxiously. Finally he opened the door and emerged looking ghastly, with white talcum powder all over the front of his suit. I presumed he had been trying to cover the dark rings under his eyes with the stuff.

Having got him suitably presentable, I grabbed his hand and led him to our waiting car. On the journey to the church he began to act very strangely, shouting the fact that he was an aetheist and did not believe in God. This was much to the fascination of my two sons, but certainly not to mine, as I was beginning to wonder whatever had possessed me to ask him in the first place.

The ceremony went off without a hitch, although there were a few moments when I suddenly realised how dumb I had been. I consider myself pretty wise about the ways of the world, but obviously I was completely taken in that day. The stuff I had innocently thought was talcum powder was actually cocaine which he was well hooked on, and *there* was I brushing dope off the godfather's suit before my baby's christening! I was genuinely shocked and surprised, and though it sounds like a funny scene now years later, it was not at all amusing at the time.

There were naturally a great many show-business people at the reception and I think the whole affair was summed up by my mother-in-law, who always in her typical north-country way sums up everything. 'Ooh, duck,' she said to me when everyone had gone home. 'I've never seen such a shower of people in my life. The show business folk looked as though they had all escaped from Billy Smart's Circus.'

G is for GOLD

There is to my mind nothing as sexy as gold, particularly when it is displayed on a suntanned skin.

A very amusing film producer friend of mine once said, 'The trouble with Diana is that when she has a lover she insists on hanging him in gold from every angle.' He was right, I could never resist the urge to buy watches, bracelets, rings, and large coin necklaces for my beaus to wear nonchalantly dangling on their chests, all carefully inscribed with loving and cutely coded messages, to remind them of me when I was not around!

I always seemed to make my purchases at Harrods in those days, and the salesman who used to serve me came to know my tastes very well as, with the advent of each new lover, I would rush to order some lovely new gold trinket as a display of my affection. He always treated me with a bit of 'tongue in cheek' humour, especially when it came to the inscriptions, and I must confess I did feel slightly embarrassed when dictating a new message of love to have engraved on the jewellery. The last time I saw him the joke was really on me.

Having just met and married my second husband, Richard Dawson, I immediately set off on my pilgrimage to Harrods to buy him a gold cigarette case which I knew he wanted badly. The salesman greeted me with a quizzical look, as if to say, 'Who is the lucky fellow this time?', but I ignored his expression and happily set about selecting the most expensive items I could find. Having made my choice, I asked for the case to be suitably inscribed, but before I could spell out the wording, he stopped me, and advised me not to do so as it reduced the value of the article. (I had been having inscriptions written for years, never dreaming that the wretched things devalued the gold in any way.)

Seeing my downcast face at not being able to write my usual message of undying love, he gave a big smile and said cheerfully, 'I shouldn't worry about it too much, if you do not have this one engraved it will save you quite a lot of money.'

'Why?' I asked incredulously, as I had never considered the cost of the inscription in the past.

'Well,' he explained, and this time his tongue was well into his cheek. 'With all due respect Madam, if there is no name on it you can make it do for the next one!'

G is for GRANDMOTHER

We all usually start out with two of these. The grandmother I had on my father's side, Catherine Carter, I was not much interested in. She was the youngest but one of twenty-five children of a Gloucestershire farmer! However, as he had had two wives, this made the total number more understandable. Even so it was obvious that with or without television, some pretty heavy sex was going on after the milking had been done! Catherine became a model in Gloucester when she grew up, as she was the proud possessor of an eighteen-inch waist. There she met and married a man named Albert Fluck — hence my being born with what was possibly the *worst* name any one could inherit at birth. I hasten to add in its defence that it was of German origin, and I have seen it written on posters over there with the umlaut accent over the 'u' — i.e. Flück, which has a totally different sound.

My maternal grandmother was a completely different 'cup of tea.' Georgina Dors was also a farmer's daughter, but from Somerset. Her father, John Dors, died eventually in his late nineties and was such a character that his death was announced in th papers as the passing of 'the grand old man of the Mendips'! The Dors were from the start a sexy lot. When I was only ten, my grandmother's brother, Great Uncle Arthur Dors, tried to make it with me in the stables. I did not really understand what he was up to and never dared tell my parents. However I got away from his cider-soaked clutches (he was permanently paralytically drunk on the stuff) and remained happily *virgo intacta!*

Georgina Dors was one of a family of eight and I reckon started the Permissive Society way back in the 1890s. She married at sixteen and had four children, one of them being my mother. By the time she was twenty her husband Elijah Payne obviously did not notice that his young wife in spite of her pregnancies, was casting an amorous eye at his brother James who was casting the same at her. In short the romance grew so hot they decided to leave home at dead of night taking my mother and her brothers with them, and set out for Wales. Why they chose Wales no-one will ever know. My mother hated the place so much during her childhood that she was often heard to say in later years that she wished Grandma had left her in Somerset.

My grandfather on learning of the disappearance of the couple gave chase on his horse, but failed to catch them and he never saw her again. The family were outraged and from then on Georgina's name was never mentioned, not even in a whisper. Life was hard for the lovers in Wales. They went from village to village because each time she became pregnant they had to move for fear anyone would find out the awful truth that they were 'living in sin.' As a result of this union my grandmother had five sons and one daughter — all illegitimate, a terrible word until quite recently!

My mother hated her Uncle James and life was far from idyllic in those days. They were extremely poor and Georgina took in washing to make ends meet. So much for love and romance — was it worth it? At the beginning of World War One my mother's oldest 'legitimate' brother went off to fight leaving behind his young village fiancé. James Payne lost no time, and deciding he had had enough of the former Miss Dors, ran away with her! Grandma never saw him again and lived out the rest of her days alone in a little pink cottage in Llanthrythidd after all her children had grown up and left, but she still had not learned her lesson. She adored men with brown eyes (as I do), and just before her death, though I was a tiny child, I can remember an old flame with dark brown eyes named Tom sitting beside her fire.

G is for JOHN GREGSON

The late actor friend with whom I had the pleasure of working in several films, as well as knowing him for many years. Since writing this book so many famous people, besides being friends of mine, have passed on. It does not seem possible that they are not still around, however if one has good memories then it compensates a great deal for the sadness and loss. John had a wonderfully dry sense of humour, which was just as well, when one night I gave a party and he came along quite unexpectedly to join in the fun. There were many beautiful girls there but the one who took John's eye was standing rather aloofly in the middle of the room. I think someone had brought her in their group as I did not really know who she was. John asked me for an introduction but as I had not the slightest idea of her name, I could not help him. 'Oh just go on over and chat her up,' I said. Off he went, only to return rather sadly, but still with the Gregson humour overcoming the situation. It appears when he made his bid for her attention the girl, much to his surprise, for he was a pretty well known actor, had given him a rather cold reception and enquired haughtily, 'What do *you* do?' This threw John considerably, and he announced quietly that if that was the way things were and the only girl he fancied in the room did not even know of his existence, then the game was definitely up, so he might as well go home.

Actually John was not the only star at the party who experienced a somewhat depressing encounter. Comedian, Eric Sykes, informed me that much to his chagrin upon arrival, a pretty girl had rushed up to him because as he thought and hoped, she fancied him! Sadly for Eric, the girl had merely been concerned about his welfare, for he felt about ninety-three when she asked politely, 'Mr Sykes would you like me to fetch you a chair?'

H is for HALLOWEEN

I have always thought it a great pity that we do not really celebrate this witches' night here in England. In America the children have enormous fun dressing-up as goblins and ghosts, going around knocking at people's front doors, and saying 'Trick or Treat'. This actually means that if the occupant does not give them sweets (which they always do) a horrifying trick will be played on them. In a vain attempt one year to introduce this sort of Halloween frolicking over here, and always ready in those days for an excuse to have a party, I arranged a magnificently catered affair at my home, complete with pumpkins and candles decorating the rooms to give it all a ghostly atmosphere. The guest list read like a *Who's Who* in show-business. I also hired a funny effeminate little fellow, who had been recommended to me by some fairy dancer I knew, to come dressed up as a witch and serve mulled wine from a cauldron out on the terrace. Halloween night arrived, and with it a ring at the front door. Upon answering I found the aforementioned fellow standing there saying 'Good evening, I'm the witch!' He was shown out to the terrace, and placed in front of the cauldron and I must say looked very authentic as he had brought along his own witch's costume, complete with flowing grey wig. All this would have been most effective if when the fun began there had not been the most terrible howling gale, and both witch and cauldron were blown around all evening in a very uncomfortable fashion. I will say in his favour that the poor little chap stayed his ground and remained for hours, only being seen when someone opened the glass door and grabbed a cup of wine from his hand as he was blown past.

Whether it had anything to do with Halloween or not, the most extraordinary things kept happening that night, and also many of the guests, like Tom Jones, Bobby Moore, Ty Hardin and so on, were all quarrelling bitterly with their respective spouses, which added extra charge to the atmosphere. The late American singer, Bobby Darin, gatecrashed the party with actor Richard Harris, both totally inebriated, and proceeded to lock themselves in my bedroom with a young lady. Strange noises were heard emanating from within, and when they finally vacated the room, ordered rather sharply to do so by me, left the unfortunate girl in the most unfeminine position, head downwards in the bushes outside the front door. I imagine she must have been pretty intoxicated herself, as for one thing she could never have hung there in that 'batlike' position for so long, but there she was, and no-one knew here name, or whom she had arrived with.

As the clouds raced across the moon, and the traditional witches were supposed to be flying around on their broomsticks, here was a party filled with husbands and wives arguing and fighting, a male witch dressed in all his clobber practically being blown away by the wind storm and frozen stiff into the bargain, boxer Billy Walker running around complaining there was not enough spare 'crumpet' and an unknown girl upside down in the bushes, showing all she had got, unclaimed by any one. At length when everyone had peered at her face and rear-end from all angles trying to decipher an identity, and after many of the battling couples had finally gone home, black singer Kenny Lynch did the gallant thing and hauled her down from the perch giving both her and the now numb witch a lift back to London.

To this day I do not know her identity, and neither I think does Kenny, who is well-known as a practical joker, together with his great friend, actor Harry Fowler. Perhaps it was the atmosphere of that party which inspired them to hoax the entire Kings Road in Chelsea one day. During the peak shopping hour they drove the full length of it in a convertible car, with Kenny standing up and holding a banner which blazed the headline 'Keep Britain White!'

H is for HANGMAN

The story of my happily brief acquaintance with Albert Pierrepoint, sometime head hangman in this country, began in Manchester in 1953 where I was making a film with the late comedian Frank Randle. One day he informed me that Pierrepoint, an old friend of his, would be coming to visit the set. 'Whatever you do,' he warned, 'say nothing to him about his occupation. He is very reticent about it and never wants to discuss the subject.'

I promised faithfully to keep my 'trap shut' (if you will pardon the pun!). Curbing my desire to see what this sinister figure looked like, I awaited his arrival at the studios with interest. To my amazement, Frank Randle appeared with a tubby little man wearing an ordinary suit, pork pie hat, loud hand-painted tie and sporting a large cigar stump in his mouth. He looked more like a bookmaker than a hangman, but then with hindsight I realised he would hardly be likely to walk about wearing a black hood over his head. I was introduced to Mr Pierrepoint, who behaved in a loud, rather brash manner, and true to my word, let him do all the talking, without once referring to his occupation.

After filming had finished that day, he invited Frank, Dennis and I back to the pub he owned just outside Manchester. I do not know what sort of a pub I imagined in my mind, but it certainly was a surprise when we got there. Naturally, on the Oldham Road I did not expect to see a prettly little place with roses around the door, but what I did see was a sign swinging backwards and forwards in the wind and rain, heralding a grim looking building named *Help the Poor Struggler*.

This was the first of many minor shocks I was to experience, for when we got inside I saw it was more of a beer house than a pub, and there were 'sick joke' notices pinned up everywhere like *No Hanging Round the Bar* and so forth. Once inside his own domain, Albert Pierrepoint became his real self. The customers treated him like loyal subjects, and his brash humour now knew no bounds.

We were ceremoniously ushered into the back parlour, and introduced to his wife, a pleasant, mild little woman who, when eventually I asked her what it felt like to be the wife of the hangman, replied, 'Oh well, someone's got to do it haven't they?' as if resigned to her fate and strange status in life. Albert played host with a vengeance, liberally pouring out beers for the men, all the time cracking corny jokes, and sometimes bursting into song. Suddenly, as if the curtain had lifted on stage, he began talking non-stop about his job, reeling off names of people he had 'topped' as he put it and giving intimate details of how they went. Spurred on with excitement, he produced a large book of press cuttings about himself, and I realised as he flicked over the pages, revealing his various publicity headlines, that he had an ego bigger than any film star.

Once we realised he *wanted* to talk about himself, we peppered him with questions. He showed us an incredible book which contained the names of all the people he had hanged, their ages, weights, length of the drop, and the crimes they had committed. 'I have been offered £35,000 for that book,' announced Albert proudly. 'Then why don't you sell it, get away from all this and go and live in the South of France?' I answered, all too late realising my remark had offended him by suggesting that his beer-house was not a particularly nice place.

'If I did that,' he said huffily, 'I would have to retire, and I'm not ready to retire yet.'

I could see that the man loved his work, so I changed the subject as quickly as possible, although within me there lurked a nasty feeling about Albert's real reasons for his profession.

More pictures and press cuttings followed, this time connected with the Nuremberg Trials, and it was evident that Albert had had his nose well put out of joint by the Americans who had apparently packed him off home to England, thinking they could hang the Nazi war criminals better themselves. Apparently the man who had been hired for the job, one Sergeant John Woods, had made such a hash of it that they were shamefacedly forced to recall Albert to finish off the work professionally. *Hangman Flies Back* screeched one newspaper headline which he proudly showed me, together with some pictures of Nazi corpses, with their necks stretched like chickens.

'They hadn't got a clue how to do it,' announced Albert

grandly. 'The rope they used you could have towed the *Queen Mary* with, I use a very fine one.' He mimed the size and style of his apparatus with great pride.

Drawn like a snake to the charmer, I pursued my questions, horrified by his revelations. When I asked him if people panicked as the moment came for them to die, he grew rather irritated at my naivety, stating quite seriously, 'I go to the prison the day before, shake them by the hand and say, "Now you know who I am, do as I say and you'll be quite all right".' He paused as if waiting for me to digest this scene, and then added, 'Yes, I've had some lovely letters from mothers, thanking me for taking care of their sons.'

Helplessly I turned to his wife hoping that somewhere in this dingy back parlour, a ray of light would appear, and said flippantly, 'How does it feel to go out and buy the groceries on Christie?' He was a notorious murderer awaiting sentence at the time, and indeed Albert had already shown us the Home Office letter requesting his presence at Pentonville prison to carry out Christie's hanging, but she merely shrugged and smiled half-heartedly. I asked the question because I'd heard that the fee for a hanging was extremely small, only about fifteen pounds a time in those days, so Albert could not possibly have been in the business for money.

Happily that was the last time I ever saw him.

H is for RICHARD HARRIS

The actor, hell-raiser and drinker who features on the back cover of this book, nestling in the confessional at St Peter's, Rome, is one of the wildest, yet greatest, people in show-business today. Not only is he a damn good actor, but he gives the profession a bit of excitement which is all too sadly lacking nowadays, in the same style as when show-business first began with rogues, vagabonds and strolling players. No doubt there are a few producers still reeling from the effects of having employed Richard, despite his enormous box-office appeal, for if, when on location, he suddenly decides to take off for pastures new, then nothing and no one can stop him.

Like the late Robert Newton there are many stories about him, but for the moment I had better deal with the one which caused the confessional photograph on the back cover to be taken.

As Alan had never visited Rome (it has always been my favourite city, surpassing Paris by miles in my opinion) we decided to go there for a sort of second honeymoon. Excitedly I told him all about the wonderful sights, the fountains, statues, and above all the beautiful church of Saint Peter's in the heart of the Vatican. We were also on the brink of becoming Catholics so he looked forward to seeing this particular place very much.

Having settled down after the first day, I rushed him at once to Saint Peter's, eager to show him the works of Michelangelo, and all the other magnificent paintings and sculptures there. We entered the building and the atmosphere which always prevails seeped through us and thrilled our spirits, but just as we were quietly admiring the work of an artist, a loud voice rang out behind me, making me rock on my heels. 'Diana Dors, what the hell are you doing here?' On looking round I saw Richard standing with a photographer and a reporter from an English newspaper. To this day I do not know why he was there. He is a Catholic of course, and was making statements about getting in to see the Pope, regarding the Northern Irish problem. At the time I did not pay much attention and talked happily to him as we had not seen each other for quite a while. Richard's natural ebullience got the better of him however and the more we talked the more excited he became at seeing an old friend so far away from home. He was alone (by this, I mean with no girlfriend) and anxious to arrange a good night out on the town as he was leaving the next day. The reporter, always on the look-out for something good to send back to his paper, suddenly had the idea of photographing us in the confessional and duly sent the pictures to England. But his paper considered they might be a little offensive to Catholics, so they were never printed — until now.

That night we all met up at Richard's hotel, and noted that his previous problem of having no girlfriend had been rectified, for in his suite were several Italian beauties waiting to be escorted around Rome. Where he had gathered them from I do not know, but finally we all left with one in particular hanging on his arm. It was the sort of Roman night one dreams about, we dined by candle light in a thousand-year-old cellar, and the party became very lively as the hours rolled by. Richard and Alan, both fortified by the potent Italian wine, sparked electrically, singing and joking, until four a.m. when we all reluctantly decided it was time to leave. Outside in the little cobblestone street, dawn was beginning to break, but undaunted by the hour, Alan and Richard continued their merry-making somewhat noisily, culminating in Alan singing an operatic aria with all the strength and sound of the Concorde landing and Richard giving full vocal support. As their voices rang round the little street square, a window opened and an angry Italian lady roused from her slumbers proceeded to rain down an avalanche of abuse at the singing duo. On seeing their apparent indifference to her plight, she disappeared and then re-appeared with a large bucket of something and threw it at them. Unluckily Richard's girlfriend was standing in a position where she received full blast of the contents, but the two main culprits were quite untouched. I often wondered afterwards whether she thought it was really worth a night with Richard Harris, to be soaked by someone's slops!

H is for RUSSELL HARTY

I have done so many television chat shows with this adorable interviewer that on the last one I said, 'tongue in cheek', I thought people might begin to start talking about us. 'Let 'em,' he replied, and it turned out in an odd way my words were not quite so silly.

One day after Alan and I had had a fight — and when

we do, which happily is not often, we really fight *well*, my little son Jason came to me and said, 'I think you had better get a divorce Mummy.' 'Do you darling?' I answered miserably. There was a long pause whilst he mulled over the situation. 'I know,' he suddenly stated briefly, 'you could marry Russell Harty — he likes you!'

H is for HOLLYWOOD

I have continually referred to this tinsel town, celluloid city, land of broken dreams, or whatever else it may be called, that now I have arrived at letter 'H', I had better deal with it as generally as possible and relate my experience of the place.

When I was a child, and then a young teenage actress, my one ambition was to go to Hollywood. To me it was the Mecca, the ultimate, and the only life I wished for. All through my childhood those endless magical nights spent at the cinema with my mother, the fantasy and excitement connected with film stars themselves, filled me with longing and a burning determination to some day become one of them. I wrote in a school essay, at a very early age, that I was *going* to be a film star and live in a big house with a cream coloured telephone and a swimming pool. Goodness knows why the cream telephone came into it, but that was my goal. The fact that all the other children wrote what they would like to be, as opposed to my statement about what I was *going* to be, confirms my amazing determination even then!

Just a few years ago I found it necessary to fly to Hollywood to settle a rather sad domestic situation with my sons, and as I flew towards the film capital I could not help thinking that here was I going to visit my sons who resided there permanently and regarded it as perfectly ordinary. At their age, wearing a black disc over the left side of my spectacles in order to correct a lazy eye, I was little mousey-haired Diana who lived in a small suburban town, dreaming her dreams of one day living in Hollywood.

But to begin at the beginning; my first arrival there was hailed with almost as much publicity as the coming of the second Messiah! I had negotiated through my husband and manager Dennis to make a film entitled *I Married a Woman* for RKO Studios, and was being paid a fortune into the bargain. The ballyhoo arranged by studio publicity men began as our ship sailed into New York and photographers and reporters scrambled all over the decks to get at me. Eight studio public relations executives were assigned to look after me, and, as up until then Dennis had been doing a remarkable job all on his own, I was rather overwhelmed. Well what girl wouldn't be with eight men at her disposal!

The blazing fanfare followed us to California, with a grand reception organised in the Crystal Room of the Beverly Hills Hotel, where reporters and the like mingled with many stars all anxious to welcome me to their town (*and* get a picture of themselves in the trade papers by shaking my hand!). I learned very early on that 'nothing is done for nothing' in Hollywood, and though I was totally bowled over by the reception, the sunshine, the scenery and all the glamorous trappings, not to mention the heady wine of success, there was even then a strange feeling of artificiality about it all, as if things were not quite real. The too smooth chatter of the Americans, the banks, post offices and ordinary buildings there all looked as if someone was going to 'strike' them as they do a film set when the scene is finished.

Of course the two feared and dreaded women columnists who literally ran the film business with their ability to make or break stars and studios, Louella Parsons and Hedda Hopper, were present at that first reception, and I was taken to them to pay homage and let them give me the 'once over' like an item in a shop window. Louella cooed and gushed in her rather sickening way, but Hedda was much more abrupt and snappy, and for the first time in his life Dennis, who could charm anybody, was completely taken aback, when after paying her a compliment hopefully thinking it would ingratiate us, she turned on him and snarled 'Okay Hamilton, don't overdo it!'

This was to be the beginning of a totally foreign and new way of life for both of us. And after three weeks or so had gone by, the novelty of being there had started to wear off as it does with everyone, no matter how successful. We began feeling homesick for England, its seasons, showers of rain, or a little country pub instead of the glossy bars and perpetual merciless sunshine beating down amongst the lush palm trees.

There was an enormous sign erected high in the Hollywood hills, and the story went that a fairly rich man, who had been spiritually broken by the business methods, and ruthless pedlars of flesh there, had paid for it to be built. I noticed the sign on my first drive from the airport, and it looked odd to me just perched up in the middle of nowhere — chalk white letters spelling out 'Hollywood' — stark and glaring in the sunlight. Apparently my ominous feeling about it was not entirely wrong, for when it had finally been erected, the man who had commissioned the extraordinary thing climbed to the top and threw himself off in one last and final gesture displaying his dislike of the place.

There was no danger of anything like this happening to me, I thought, when the tale was related. But by the time Hollywood with all its pressures, ruthlessness, way of life and business, had finished with me, I came home to England weighing nearly two stone less than before I left, and with my mind in shreds, not to mention my marriage!

In that town I learned so many things new to me in the world of films. The lack of privacy. The dislike of the British (in those days). The waiters, chamber maids, barmen, many of whom were on the payrolls of ever-powerful columnists, ready to report what celebrities had for breakfast, and who with! The competition was so fierce too. A jungle compared with the steady pace of England, and the clichéd route through bedroom-door to stardom or disaster, which I thought had all been over long since, was just as prevalent as it ever had been.

If I paint a dismal picture then I am sorry. It was naturally not so bad, all the time. Who could not like the climate, the glamour, the marvellous professionalism at the film studios, plus the star treatment (providing you were at the top) which made the British way of filming seem like *Tom and Jerry* time? If you have ever had to chip the ice off your car windscreen at five a.m. in England, then who could complain about being driven by a uniformed chauffeur through the luxurious, sunlit avenues of Hollywood — and on reaching the studio, have many people employed to service every need and whim. Why, one girl was there to simply make-up my *ears*, as it was classified as body make-up!

The honeymoon lasted for a month or two, and then began to wane. An artiste, after all, only remained popular until some newer and bigger one overtook and redirected the limelight. I was reminded of the experience of dear Peter Finch who also experienced the full star treatment on arrival. And suddenly when the excitement inevitably grew cold some months later, he discovered hosts at parties would no longer dwell in his company for long, but excused themselves to rush and welcome some new personality who had arrived. Eventually Peter's invitations to be present at all became non-existent.

There was the ghastly and now world famous incident when I was pushed into my own swimming-pool by over-zealous pressmen and photographers at a party I gave for all the show business people who had welcomed me there. It resulted in Dennis, who had been dunked too, along with Bob Hope's agent, nearly killing the man responsible. It was then that the bad publicity started.

From being able to do nothing wrong, *now* I could do nothing right! I was accused of being a Communist; told in large headlines to, 'Go home and take Mr Dors with you'; branded by the Women's Catholic Guild as immoral; and generally pilloried at every twist and turn. To cap it all, the first film I had made turned out to be bad, and in Hollywood you are only as good as your last film! By this time I had signed a three year contract with RKO and was in the middle of making my second film *The Unholy Wife* with Rod Steiger. This was to be the final nail in my coffin, for I made the mistake of falling in love with him. He was married but verging on divorce, so *that* was bad enough, but I was married too and for publicity purposes living happily ever after was a 'must'. In actual fact a marriage in Hollywood needed to be made of granite and steel to endure the temptations, marital frustrations, and temperamental egos.

Around the time I committed my 'crime', I had earned something like a quarter of a million dollars in five months, but such was Dennis's bad business dealing over there, he had signed so many pieces of me away to

managers and companies, that I was left owing ten per cent
to somebody after my weekly salary had been paid! This
however was not the reason our marriage began to go
wrong. Who knows where or how it happens? But when
Rod Steiger entered my life, everything took an
unbelievable turn. I was completely besotted with the
man, I adored acting with him too, for he rekindled some
of my early ambitious enthusiasm, which had been dulled
over the years by bad films, money-making schemes, and
the usual all-round disenchantment which hits many
people in show business.

I have never been able to hide my feelings, and Dennis
soon found out what was going on. His guarded watch
over my every thought and move was claustrophobic, and
the result was frightful. He came to the studios and
threatened Steiger with a gun. The film bosses had me on
the carpet and forbade me to continue my affair for fear of

the Women's Catholic Guild. They also threatened to pull what is known as the 'morals' clause in my contract if I defied them. And the columnists had a field day! Dennis flew back to England and it hit the press there too. Then, in a vain bid to patch things up between us, he flew back and tried to save the day on the publicity surface.

The director of the film we were doing was the late John Farrow, father of Mia. He and his wife, actress Maureen O'Sullivan, were great friends of Louella Parsons. One day he confronted me on the set, ashen faced, and reported that Louella was hopping mad because I had lied to her about my love affair with Steiger, and unless I went and apologised, she would ruin me the way she had ruined Rex Harrison, by publicly denouncing him on the radio years before, because of an affair he had had with an actress who later committed suicide. I could not understand why my romance was of such interest to everyone, including her. 'They are all trying to destroy my love for Steiger,' I cried. 'I am doing no-one any harm! What does it matter? Why is it all so important?' 'You are a married woman, *and* you are English,' he warned. 'Maureen and I will pacify her as much as we can, but you and Dennis must go to see her and apologise personally.'

The next evening was one of the most sickening events in my life. Dennis, who was anxious to protect his business and financial interest, namely me, drove us to Louella's house. We were ushered into a drawing room which rivalled that of any film star (but then film folk in those days showered she and Hedda with presents — cadillacs, minks, jewellery and the like, just to keep them sweet). Such was their power, and thank God all that is finished now!

I have never liked to crawl, and as we waited for her to make her entrance I felt inwardly nauseous. Finally she walked in and I began my carefully prepared speech, 'But why did you lie to me?' she drawled. 'I *asked* you if you were having an affair with Steiger, and you denied it.' 'I'm sorry Louella,' I heard myself grovel, 'you see I was misguided and trying to save face, I also hoped that perhaps things would be all right with Dennis and I.' This last statement was a deliberate piece of lying, but I had been drilled as to what to say, and delivered my lines with all the aplomb of Bette Davis. Eventually after a lecture from the old crone, with her religious shrine lit up in pastel shaded lights glowing in on us from the garden, she wagged her finger at me like a school teacher, and pronounced her forgiveness of my terrible behaviour, making me swear it would never happen again . . . or if it did to please let her be the *first* to know before Hedda Hopper! And with *that* she bade us a sugary farewell, expressing her wish that our marriage would now have a happy-ever-after, Hollywood-style ending.

The eventual, inevitable break-up between Dennis and I, plus the bad publicity, finished me in Hollywood for a long time to come. The love affair ended in tears too, which did not help my spirits, already pretty low due to my flagging career. I flew home to England one cold November day and after two days of talks with Dennis, flanked by the press camped day and night outside our home, reporting bulletins every hour to the newspapers regarding our discussions and decisions, we finally decided to try and make another 'go' of it now that we were away from the heady Hollywood atmosphere which had trapped and killed us.

Our marriage lasted some six months longer, but then broke up completely, and whatever else can be said, for or against the place, I could not blame *that* on Hollywood!

H is for BOB HOPE

The reason I went to Hollywood in the first place was actually due to Bob. For many years he had, amongst many other pilgrimages to American servicemen all over the world, made Iceland his mark at Christmas time. When he went he would always take along a glamorous female star to help boost the boys' morale. He invited me on one occasion, but I was filming and could not go. So the next time he came to these shores, he requested that I appear on a big television show he was doing here for American viewing. At the time I was at the height of my career, in the Fifties, and Bob being a shrewd judge of box office appeal and glamour, had a specially scripted sketch written for us plus a lot of comedy material which we did in a 'stand-up' routine. I recall the first meeting with him in his suite at the Dorchester Hotel, there were no less than seventeen script-writers sitting there, all on his payroll, and ready to supply him with gags and jokes for every occasion.

The show was eventually seen in the States, and this was the very first time anyone there came to know of my existence. Monroe was at her zenith, and with Bob's help, and nationwide show publicity, everyone suddenly became aware of a British blonde, whom they thought naturally had merely aped Marilyn and was hoping for stardom by jumping on her wagon.

Bob had an agent who had worked for him during his entire career. He was an incredible old character named Louis Shurr, or Doc. Aside from looking rather like a garden gnome, he had an eye for the ladies. Doc wore a rubber girdle to keep his stomach in, was driven everywhere by a coloured chauffeur named Hopkins, who looked much more dignified than his boss, and had a gimmick which all Hollywood knew and chuckled about! It is a recognised thing for a man to give a girl a mink coat if he can afford it, or if the mood takes him, but Doc Shurr was different. He was a bachelor and knew hundreds of pretty girls, and whenever he would escort some starlet to a film premiere he would provide them with a fabulous mink coat, which he owned, just to wear for the evening, rather on the lines of Cinderella having to give her ball-gown back at midnight.

When I was pushed into my swimming-pool at the party mentioned earlier, Doc Shurr was unlucky enough to be standing next to me just at that moment and went under too. Later, Bob Hope quipped in one of the trade magazines, 'Doc Shurr has ordered his new formal party outfit for the season, white tie, goggles and snorkel!' The picture of me climbing out of the water was circulated all round the world, and Doc Shurr's head was just below me, looking like John the Baptist after Salome had finished with him.

Doc had negotiated my contract with RKO and arranged for me to go to Hollywood, so he and Bob felt quite responsible for me, as if I was their property, which was extremely nice. At one point before my star began to wane, there was a strong possibility that Bob and I were going to re-make some of the old Jean Harlow films — comedies like *Blonde Bombshell*. Sadly, plans fell by the wayside.

About this time I received, and stupidly turned down, the lead in a film entitled *The Girl Can't Help It*, thereby giving Jayne Mansfield her first crack at film stardom which she seized with both hands!

I did do another television spectacular with Bob however, and it was great. My old and undisputed favourite James Cagney was guesting on it too, and I am proud to say I have met and worked with him.

Bob's studio Paramount was just across the road from mine at RKO and he and Dennis used to send jokes and messages back to each other all the time. I also visited his fantastic home in Bel Air, with its enormous trophy room full of awards and honours collected by Bob over the years. He *was* actually born in England, though he seems to be such a typical American. One day I said to him: 'What would have happened I wonder if your parents had not left Eltham and gone to live in the States?' 'Quite simple,' he quipped 'I would have been the English Tommy Trinder.'

H is for HOTSEAT

This is a terrible game devised, I am ashamed to say, by myself with fellow actor Andrew Ray, son of comedian Ted, one rainy Sunday afternoon, when a group of friends were at my house with nothing better to do. . .

The idea was quite basic really and involved simply telling the complete truth. One person must sit in the middle of the room — the 'hotseat' — and all the others are allowed to question him about any personal or provocative subject they choose. The victim *must* tell the truth and if he is discovered to be lying, or the vote goes against him, then a ghastly forfeit has to be paid.

Such was the case when one evening, a certain agent was playing the game and insisted that his sexual prowess reached incredible heights. He was given the chance to change his story or admit he had not told the truth, but steadfastly refused. So he was carried out to the goldfish pond in bitter cold weather and dumped in, whilst the pond's inhabitants swam around his posterior with great curiosity!

Now this wicked game is all very amusing if you are on your own, minus wife, husband or lover, for, whatever question is asked, it can be answered with complete freedom and sometimes to the delight of the questioners, who are all dying to hear the intimate details of your life. But woe betide the victim if he or she plays when accompanied by any of the aforementioned people. For as sure as the sun rises in the east there will be fireworks! I have seen marriages break up on account of 'hotseat'.

At some of my parties where people like Bruce Forsyth, Stanley Baker, Ronnie Carroll, Sean Connery, Eric Sykes and a host of well-known names would gather after a day's golf at Wentworth, hysterically funny stories would be related, and some very embarrassing questions answered in complete honesty. American star Ty Hardin, late of the television series *Bronco*, was once challenged by his fourth wife as to whether he had ever had an affair with her sister (which she obviously suspected and which had been gnawing away in her craw for a long time). Ty launched into a long description of how when she was away in Rome, and it was a very cold night, he merely invited his sister-in-law into his bed to keep warm. 'But at no time,' he declared in his Texan drawl, 'at no time did I ever penetrate her!'

For some reason, known only to him, Sean Connery

H is for HUSBANDS

Top: Dennis Hamilton
Centre: Dickie Dawson
Left: Alan Lake

would always take charge of the game like a ringmaster, shouting instructions and abuse (with a thick Scots accent) at all concerned! Players had to adhere to the rules or tell the truth, for he was adamant that no-one should be a hypocrite or ever dare hide facts. Sean was more interested in extracting the truth than getting anyone to pay a penalty, which seemed peculiar, as forfeits were the most amusing part of it all.

One night, Ed 'Kooky' Byrne, another American star whom I had met in Hollywood, arrived fresh from his television series *77 Sunset Strip* (in which his gimmick had been to pull out a comb in any emergency and drag it through his hair) with a police motor cycle escort! I hasten to add that he did this since he didn't know the way out of London to my home, so he did the obvious thing and asked a policeman!! The cop brought him to my place like a homing pigeon, and I never knew whether that was something I should be pleased about or not!

During the ensuing game of 'hotseat', with Sean presiding like Judge Jeffries over the proceedings, Ed was put in the chair. He was being interrogated by all and sundry, when Irish singer Ronnie Carroll, who had always rather admired Ed, saw fit to ask him an odd question. 'Tell me,' he enquired with his Belfast brogue, 'have you ever had an affair with a man?' The answer he received was frank, and rather funny, or at least so I thought, but it ruined Ronnie's evening . . . 'SURE, HASN'T EVERYBODY?' quipped Kooky!

H is for HYPOCRISY

Second to cruelty to children, this is one of the things I hate most, due no doubt to my being brought up amongst middle class hypocrisy. Class distinction in England is a way of life which will never change. There will always be aristocracy, upper and lower middle classes and the working class. I had no choice as to where I was born but loathed the middle class from an early age. I wished I had been born either into the aristocracy or the lowest working class. This is how I have conducted my life — this is the way I am made.

It was the narrow-mindedness of the hypocrites practising the 'respectable' mode of living which pulled me away from the church as a child; for not only was I too young to understand the service, I was repelled by the presence of pious and sanctimonious looking women who were really only interested in who was wearing what, and who had a new fur coat.

My father was somewhat Victorian and my mother worried about 'what the neighbours would think'. I grew up with the words ringing in my ears 'We are respected in this town, and your father has always walked with his head held high.' Now I am older I can appreciate their feelings, but I certainly did not do so then. My constant curiosity was aimed at who THEY were, as it was always sentences which began THEY will talk, or THEY will think, which were foremost in our mode of living. Finally it reached me: THEY were the hypocrites of this world, not merely the inhabitants of my home town, but a vast multitude of so-called do-gooders and pontificating, sanctimonious, 'respectable' people. Sadly a great deal of this behaviour goes on under the guise of Christianity and before I became a Catholic convert I used to point a finger at so-called Christians who confessed and then went off and sinned again.

However since joining the Catholic Church I have realised that a good deal of my former criticism was based on nothing but ignorance.

The persecution I received from the Women's Catholic Guild of America still rankles with me despite my new found faith, and whilst many Catholics are good, there are still too many brainwashed ones for my liking.

Not too long ago I was asked to 'kick off' at a football match to promote funds for a Catholic Church.

It was a very hot day and I wore a cool, low cut dress.

A week later I was rebuked by the organiser, an avid churchgoer, as the photographs were useless he said, owing to the low cut of the dress — my bust being too prominent for a *church* paper.

Unable to suppress my anger at this piece of hypocrisy I snapped: 'AREN'T YOU SUPPOSED TO HAVE TITS IF YOU ARE A CHRISTIAN?'

I is for IGNORANCE

A terrifying state of mind, sadly all too prevalent in this world.

The great Greek philosopher Socrates once said, and I quote . . . 'Ignorance is something against which even the Gods are powerless!'

I is for IMAGE

To build up a public image is naturally a very clever thing to do, the only drawback being that whilst on the one hand you are making yourself into a household name, on the other you are 'typing' yourself. Once 'typed' it is extremely difficult ever to do something else! Such was my case when I tried to drop the sex-symbol glamour image and become recognised as an actress.

The public, having accepted you as one thing, understandably continue to believe for the rest of their lives that you are what they have been told you are, and my image, no matter how hard I try to change it, will be *Dors* — the glamorous sex-symbol of yesteryear, driving big American cars, throwing extravagant parties and sitting in nightclubs sipping pink champagne with somebody else's husband! No-one can imagine I live a normal life, or that I do not even smoke or drink, and why should they? For they have all been weaned on my flamboyant publicity. This easily explains one particular nurse's attitude whom I had engaged to look after Jason when he was a baby. After waiting excitedly in the hall on her first morning at my home, she confided to the charwoman that she could not wait to see me come down the stairs in one of my fabulous rhinestone evening gowns, obviously thinking I dressed that way even at 9 a.m.

A typical example of my image working against me happened years ago at the B.B.C. when I was sitting in a side room, awaiting a programme that I was about to do, called *Desert Island Discs*. A studio assistant put his head around the door and asked me if I was all right. I assured him I was and then he said perfectly naturally, 'Would you like a gin?' I politely declined but secretly felt amused that he would immediately associate me with *gin*, a drink I cannot ever bear the smell of! Had it been Dame Anna Neagle that day he would have offered her a cup of tea!

On many occasions I too have been guilty of drawing the wrong conclusions about actors merely by reading publicity blurbs, or perhaps seeing their performances on screen and coupling them in life with the roles they play. Therefore it was quite understandable to me, whilst making a personal appearance somewhere and being ushered through a large crowd, to hear one woman say to her friend, 'I've never liked her till now, but she's quite *nice* really isn't she?' 'Aint it surprising,' replied the other, and they toasted me with their shopping baskets as if setting the seal of approval on a whole new appreciation of Diana Dors.

Sadly images often work against a celebrity, as in the case of the late Irish playwright Brendan Behan, whose capacity for drink earned him the reputation of being a heavy boozer. I met Brendan one evening at the height of his success after plays such as *The Quare Fellow* and *The Hostage*, and on seeing people plying him with Irish whiskey, which he knew was dangerous for him to drink, I asked him why he allowed them to do it. He answered wearily with the air of someone who had become resigned to his fate, 'My image is killing me,' he said. It did.

I is for IRELAND

'The trouble with Northern Ireland,' said comedian Frank Carson, 'is that it's full of Catholics and Protestants but not enough Christians.' A sad and yet true statement, not the kind of description anyone should be making about such a beautiful country — let us hope and pray that one day peace will come to this trouble-torn land again. I hold no political beliefs regarding the situation at all — for political is what it is, and it angers me when I see and hear things being done in the name of religion. I am sure everyone involved has his point, whoever gets into the argument, though when I see young children on televison throwing stones and fighting too, I wonder! Now I do not agree with actors voicing their political beliefs in public, for one thing they lose a lot of fans and for another, as in the case of Vanessa Redgrave, it is extremely boring. So you will never find *me* marching with her just before an opening night of a play in London, which she once did, keeping the other actors on tenterhooks as to whether there was going to be a play at all, and salaries to go with it! Miss Redgrave is entitled to her views, and what she does is her own business, but I wish she and her kind would not keep on trying to inflict them on other actors. To digress from Ireland for a moment, there was one memorable occasion when Vanessa was trying desperately hard to interest my husband Alan in some revolutionary movement, and he mischievously told her that whilst *he* was not interested, another actor, Charles Gray, was right up her street and shared her feelings on politics, knowing full well that Charles was the *last* person to approach. La Redgrave rushed to claim a new follower to her camp and belaboured him for nearly five minutes with party politics and the like until Charles could stand no more. He had not wanted to seem impolite when she first grabbed him, but finally yawned right in her face and said, 'My dear Vanessa, I am agog with boredom!'

When I changed my religion and became a Roman Catholic, I did it very quietly as I considered it to be a very private affair and did not want the press making it look like a cheap publicity stunt. It did of course leak out to some newspapers, and I received a letter from an outraged woman who actually blamed *me* for the terrible Tower of London bombings where many little children were killed. So even if I had marched with Vanessa or gone out on a date with the Rev. Ian Paisley, I could not win — there is an old saying, 'You cannot please everybody'.

Once I *did* please everybody in Ireland back in 1957 and long before all the trouble started, although I suppose it was brewing even then. I was asked to make a personal appearance at a big furniture store in Belfast and away I went, not realising for a minute that I was as popular as I turned out to be. I arrived with due pomp and ceremony in a big limousine at the store amidst crowds of waiting fans and was ushered inside. I did my job and went all over the place having the usual photographs taken, and on reaching the top of the building I was asked if I would go out onto the rooftop balcony and wave to the crowds below. I do not know what had happened whilst I was inside, but as I walked out on to the roof and looked down, thousands upon thousands of people had gathered in the street and were pinned shoulder to shoulder with police cordons everywhere. They were stretched right across the road, and literally swaying from side to side. It was a frightening experience as I have never liked crowds and I became claustrophobic. 'How am I going to get away?' I asked nervously, as my limousine had completely disappeared. This presented the organisers with a big problem — they could see there was no possibility and I had to be at the airport to catch a plane back to England within the hour.

Someone had a brainwave, and without further ado a television removal van was brought around to the back of the store and I was bundled into it and told to lie down on the floor. Once round the corner, the van would go 'hell for leather' and try to escape from the masses. Thank God it worked, but there was one awful moment when some people sighted it and made a rush towards us, no doubt suspecting what was going on. We made our getaway from those jam-packed streets of Belfast, and I have never been so glad to see the beautiful green fields of the Emerald Isle displayed before me on my way to the airport.

I is for IRISHMEN

By and large they are a funny breed. I have had one or two love affairs with Irishmen, but the two who stand out most in my mind were most certainly not connected with my personal life!

It has been my dubious pleasure to appear in cabaret at a rather rough public house in Shepherds Bush, London, on several occasions, for an Irishman named Butty Segrew.

Butty is an extraordinary character, who once worked for a circus as a strongman, and one of his specialities was lifting motor cycles up with his teeth, a thing I believe he still does when the fit takes him! His circus career started him along the road of showmanship, and when he acquired a pub, aside from making it a very successful business, he was always ready to think of the odd publicity stunt to promote the place and give it a bit more colour. I never understood why he needed to go to such lengths to make press space, as his pub, whenever I saw it, was always bursting at the seams regardless of Butty's publicity escapades and cabaret shows.

On one occasion he had installed a boxing ring in the middle of the pub, and asked ex-fighter Jack Doyle to introduce me. This sounds all very well on the face of it, but firstly Jack, who as is well known loves his pint, began an introduction for me and became so obsessed with his performance that he could not be induced to get off the 'stage' and let me get on with my act. In the end Butty had to physically yank him off, though with his prowess for picking up motor cycles this was a simple task. I finally managed to climb up the ladder and stand there for twenty minutes, with my painist tucked away in a corner where I could neither see nor hear him, and attempted to entertain the shouting mass of humanity. To be fair to Butty, when he sensed the audience were becoming too rowdy, he would always rush to the front and make wild signs with his watch, saying I might as well cut the whole thing there and then, which was both a great relief and made no difference to the generous fee he paid.

My first encounter with Butty however, before we hit the starry heights of Shepherds Bush, began about ten years ago when he owned a scruffy little pub in Kilburn, London, again bulging nightly with drinking Irishmen. He had really surpassed himself with an idea for news headlines. It appears that one evening in a mad moment, another Irishman called Mick (but then they are nearly all named that!) had announced he would be prepared to be buried alive for sixty days in a coffin near Butty's pub. Butty's side of the deal was to pay him a nominal fee of one hundred pounds, and get fantastic publicity for his pub into the bargain.

The arrangement was signed and sealed, and true to his word down went Mick amidst much fanfare and photography, in a super lined coffin with things needed for his stay, plus a hole in the top so that he could receive air and messages from Butty and whoever else wanted to converse with him.

This affair created world headlines, much to Butty's delight, and soon the Americans were at it too. One misguided fellow was buried in Ohio and announced that he would stay there longer than Mick, so it made a contest out of the event, to such a degree that the television companies decided it was such a unique situation, they arranged a transatlantic hook-up between the two men one night. Viewers were able to listen to the pair of them swearing at each other and declaring their intentions about how long they were going to remain underground in their respective coffins.

One American woman tried to get into the act at this point, but having bade her husband and children adieu, and hopped into her coffin, she eventually panicked and was rushed up for air, vowing she would never attempt such a thing again.

In the end and running true to form, Butty's man won, the American having been hauled out semi-conscious a few days earlier, and at this moment in the story, I came in. Butty, drunk with power, decided he wanted a film star to dig Mick up. So I was asked to go along and help with the job.

The streets outside Butty's place were lined with cheering Irish, all eager to welcome Mick from his self-imposed grave, and then get on with the serious business of drinking and celebrating. I was placed in a room above the pub to await Mick's arrival. Soon enough the bizarre cortège appeared amidst such noise and shouting from the crowds. There, perched on top of a lorry, was the coffin, with every now and then Mick's hand and arm popping through the hole in the top to wave to the fans he could hear yet not see.

It was then explained to me that they were going to lower him through the window of the room I was in, which had been conveniently taken out for the occasion, and once safely inside Butty's emporium, I was to open the lid of the box and let him out.

This I did amidst press and photographers all flashing away with their cameras, to reveal a white-faced Mick, very dirty and, to put it mildly, smelling to high heaven! It was not his fault, obviously he could not wash whilst lying there for three months, and indeed really did nothing much except pray, which was what he informed the press later he had done during his long ordeal. 'Come on, come on, Miss Dors give him a kiss,' cried the excited newspapermen . . . but this was where I drew the line. Not even for the fee Butty was paying me could I bring myself to do that!

I is for ISTANBUL

'Istanbul was Constantinople' went a certain song written about this romantic, mysterious city in Turkey, with its large domes covering exotic styled mosques. I always assumed all kinds of exciting happenings going on under-neath them, so it came as rather a disappointment that nothing was really occurring there at all, aside from a bit of wailing and worshipping!

I have no doubt that my illusions about the mysterious East were brought about by films like *Topkapi*, and Turkish belly dancers who can be seen swivelling their hips almost anywhere in London, but certainly not in Turkey! Little did I know as I arrived there exhausted after a long flight which had brought me from North Carolina in the U.S.A., where I had been appearing in cabaret, that I would come close to being branded a jewel thief myself, in true 'Topkapi' style.

The reason for my hysterical reception by the Turkish public and press way back in 1965, was that I had a contract to do a week's cabaret in Istanbul, at a doubtful sounding joint called the 'Klob X'! I quickly checked in at the Hilton Hotel as it was the only bit of civilised territory I could find, and after that saw very little of the city, other than on my journey nightly to the club, as it was the only place I felt genuinely safe in. The atmosphere was one I did not like at all, and as I gazed at the dirt and poverty in the streets from my taxi window, I shuddered and was glad I had only a week to perform there. Around the middle of the engagement, I received a telephone call from an incredible English character I had once met in Derbyshire, Bunty Scott-Moncrieff, who was amongst other things a dealer in old Rolls Royces. He was quite famous in his field and lived in a magnificent baronial mansion, with hardly any furniture and peacocks who strutted around the lawns, eating nothing but chocolate cake, or so he once told me! Bunty was there in Istanbul for a holiday, and like everything else he did, was revelling in it with gusto! I was very happy to hear from him, but then with all due respect to Bunty, I would have been relieved to hear from *anyone* providing they were English, so miserable and alone was I in that faraway place.

'Now where have you been since you arrived?' he inquired enthusiastically, 'Nowhere except the "Klob X" where I am working,' I answered. 'Really Bunty I'm a bit frightened to go out on the streets.' 'Well we will have to change all that,' he exclaimed, 'Now get yourself ready and we will go this very day and visit the famous covered bazaar.' Deaf to my pleas and attempted excuses, he arrived carrying a rather grand walking stick, which I learned later was a sword stick. To anyone who is not familiar with these objects, there is a lethal sword inside the stem of the stick, and in cases of emergency, one merely pulls the handle and whips out the blade.

Bunty had obviously never been out walking with a blonde film star before. In an ordinary street it is difficult enough, with people staring and rushing up for autographs, but in Turkey, it is very definitely NOT the thing to do. Blondes are unheard of there for one thing and for that matter, women are seldom seen walking around anywhere. Added to this, I was famous, as my photographs were dotted around on hoardings advertising the 'Klob X', and I was wearing shocking pink, skin tight slacks, an extremely unwise decision on my part; but then I never seem to be wearing the right thing at the right time.

To put it mildly, as we walked towards the bazaar, with Bunty striding along holding his sword stick on high like the British flag, we amassed at least two hundred male Turks, who it seemed had nothing else to do but follow us, getting closer and closer as seconds went by, until I began to feel like a female Pied Piper of Hamelin! At least *he* was not being groped and pinched at every twist and turn, as I certainly was, unnoticed of course by Bunty.

We arrived at the bazaar in what was now the middle of a body of Turks, and seeing a jewellery shop with some beautiful turquoises in the window, I signalled to him to go in, as apart from anything else I wanted to get away from the crowd, and thought stupidly that they might all go away if we sheltered inside the shop. How wrong I was, the Turks were not going to let a sight like me slip past that easily, and they all gathered in a vast crowd outside, some pressing their dirty noses against the window.

The shopkeeper was delighted to see us, bade us sit down, and I was then introduced to a compulsory Turkish custom. It appears that until everyone has drunk a ghastly cup of mud known as Turkish coffee, out of ornate gold cups, mercifully tiny ones, no conversation or business can take place. He obviously thought I was there to buy something expensive, and that no doubt Bunty was my 'sugar-daddy' into the bargain, ready to lavish any rich bauble on me which took my fancy.

Having braced myself to swallow the awful concoction, I then began looking at various lovely gems, again to the delight of the shopkeeper, indeed he became so excited at the prospect of a purchase he suddenly reached into a drawer and pulled out the most vulgar looking diamond solitaire ring I have ever seen. It was then interpreted to me happily, that today was some sort of anniversary and he was giving away these monster trinkets as gifts. I thanked him, but inwardly thought what a terrible copy of the real thing it was, it was so large, the only place I *might* be able to wear it I figured would be on stage. We carried on perusing, and finally decided it was time to go, especially as the crowd outside had now become even thicker and we were going to have a battle trying to get a taxi. I signed my autograph on several bits of paper, shook hands all round, was courteously bowed out, and then the fun began. Struggling through the mob was almost impossible and we literally had to fight and punch our way along. As we drew near the exit to the bazaar, there was a terrible shout and the two men from the jewellery shop came tearing towards us, eyes bulging, and white as ghosts, which under their dark Turkish complexions was quite something. The ring which the owner had so flippantly given me as an anniversary gift, had been his idea of a little joke, and was not a tawdry piece of rubbish as I thought, but actually the real thing, valued at one hundred and seventy thousand pounds. It seems in the excitement they had forgotten it was still on my finger as I left, suddenly made the discovery, and naturally panicked. I meanwhile was blissfully unaware of its worth, and indeed felt rather ostentatious wearing it, but had they not reached me, to this day it would probably be at the bottom of my jewellery box, with me thinking it was just a bit of Turkish delight! That or I would be languishing in an Istanbul prison still endeavouring to prove my innocence! Upon retrieving their diamond they ran back to their shop and we were left with the Turkish mob, now having reached fever pitch. I suddenly spied a taxi and yelled, 'Quick let's run for it over there'. 'You go on,' shouted Bunty as if he were in command of an army, and with true British grit, pulled out his sword and started swiping at the heads of the unfortunate Turks who were close at hand, crying 'Get back there' which sounded more like 'Gung Ho', as I breathlessly grabbed the taxi and sank into it. 'We can't go without Bunty,' I shouted to the driver, as I could see him trying to ward off further attacks and drawing closer to us. 'It's all right,' he cried leaping on to the running board of the vehicle, brandishing his sword and swiping at more heads, 'Drive on,' and so our taxi weaved its way through the milling throng, nearly crushing many in the process.

Bunty was still on the running board as we arrived at the hotel, and it must have made an odd picture for the visiting American tourists, 'What a splendid day,' he exclaimed, 'Let's go out again tomorrow and visit the Blue Mosque, perhaps I can have a stab at some more.' I thanked him for his kind invitation, but this time firmly declined.

Happily I left Istanbul, but did not see Bunty ever again which was the only sad part of it, as he was a marvellous character. He did telephone me once though a year or so later, inviting me to his birthday party. 'It's usually quite a romp,' he said excitedly, 'We fill the bath with champagne' . . . remembering the saga of Bunty's outing in Turkey, I politely managed to refuse his tempting invitation!

I is for ITALIANS

Now these are a totally different breed from the Irish, and their attitude to women is one which never ceases to amaze me. Whilst they make great lovers, as husbands they fall very short of the mark! The Italian male marries, and true to his religion stays that way for the rest of his life, but he proceeds to have a ball on the side, with as many mistresses as he can cram into a lifetime, whilst the wife dutifully waits at home ready with the spaghetti when he returns from a hard day's hunting!

One wife did not actually play the game this way however. She was married to Italy's number one heart-throb screen actor at the time, and far from waiting at home with the pasta, would lock her bedroom door and refuse him entrance until he had made amends by pushing a diamond bracelet or some other expensive bauble under it. She, of course, amassed a fortune over the years, and *he* merely suffered from old age and a surfeit of too much love-making.

J is for JAIL

The horrible experience of being jailed has never happened to me, although I sailed very close to being sentenced in Blackpool when arrested for a foolish prank. It *has* happened to my husband Alan though, and the circumstances by which it all came about were unfair and unjust. Alan and a friend pop singer Leapy Lee were sent to jail in 1970 just when both their careers were at their zeniths, but luckily our son Jason was only 12 months old and too young to understand. One Sunday the two of them were out for a drink at a local pub in Berkshire near our home, leaving Leapy's wife Mary and myself in the garden that lovely July summer evening. They had had quite a few drinks, as men will, and were playing darts. Whereupon two complete strangers, who were not locals, started making remarks about me (as they knew Alan and I were married.) Naturally this did not go down too well with him, and to make matters worse the resident landlord and his wife were away on holiday. So a temporary couple had taken their place. An argument started between Alan and the landlord's wife over the price of a drink which he had paid for, but she insisted he had not. She called her husband, who began losing his temper and the argument grew louder and worse. The two men who had been so abusive about me, seized upon this, admitting later that they liked a bit of trouble in a pub. Indeed it was proved later in court that both had criminal records, one for assaulting a policeman! Needing no second bidding they joined in the up-to-now verbal affray, and it was then that Leapy Lee made the big mistake of leaping up (which was how he got his name) and throwing a glass of beer over the landlord to try to quieten him down. From that moment everything went wrong.

The landlord, not at all pleased by this, seized a bar pump handle and went for Leapy like a raging bull, striking him on the head and felling him to the ground. The two strange men were by now fighting with Alan, and loving every moment of it, and as Leapy Lee staggered to his feet, he grabbed the first thing he saw which was a penknife lying on the bar. He struck out at the landlord, cutting his arm, and thereby, digging his grave, for in law the algebra is 'lethal weapon = prison'. At this point Alan was on the floor being kicked by the thugs, but both he and Leapy managed to get free, and fought their way out of the door leaving chaos behind.

Now I am not trying to defend either of them, but merely state the facts so that my reader may know exactly what happened, and why! The subsequent events were frightful. Leapy and Alan arrived home with blood pouring from the wound in Leapy's head where he had been struck with the pump handle, and about half an hour later the police arrived at my door and took them off for questioning as there had been a complaint lodged by the landlord stating Leapy had struck him with a knife.

In short Leapy was charged with grievous bodily harm and Alan, despite the fact that he was on the floor at the time, accused of being his accomplice. The case came up first in the magistrates court, and was then, as is the pattern of the law, sent automatically to the assizes. During this time Alan had acquired a sadly misinformed lawyer who kept insisting that the worst he would receive was a fine as it was his first offence. He then proceeded to advise Alan to plead guilty, since to be judged by a jury would slow up the procedure. Alan was due to begin a television series with me entitled *Queenie's Castle*, and did not like pleading guilty to something he had not done. But, assuming the lawyer knew best, he conceded, hoping it might speed matters up, thus enabling him to carry on with his work.

As is now known the world over, the judge glared at Leapy and sentenced him to three years, and lessened the sentence on Alan to eighteen months. So down they went.

I will not dwell on the misery and unhappiness of the next year which was the period Alan served. The loss of money, the humiliation for his parents, the heartbreak and sorrow, and my determined efforts to keep everything going, ready for his return to society, not to mention the trauma Alan himself went through as an actor who had suddenly been imprisoned with hard criminals *and* was married to *me*! This situation had to be sorted out physically when he was inside by the sort of punch-up he had been sentenced for. Only then did the baiting stop.

Lord Olivier and many other eminent show-business people had championed for Alan when his appeal came up against the imprisonment. But all to no avail. The 'powers that be' had an actor under lock and key, who must be taught a lesson, and made into an example for others to heed.

Everything no matter how tragic has its funny side, especially looking back when it is all over, and the tales which Alan now tells people about incidents which happened in jail, plus the characters he met, will fill his own book. But the most amusing thing that happened to me was on the day I arranged to take his parents down to the prison for a visit. Naturally it was a nerve-racking experience for them, a pilgrimage which they did out of necessity not choice. So it was with mixed feelings and trepidation that they journeyed towards Portland in Dorset. That was where Alan was in jail.

Of course I had been there many times by then, and knew a good hotel on the sea, literally a stone's throw from the prison. So as visiting time was not until two p.m. I organised lunch there. Now, my readers must bear in mind that here were two simple people from the North of England who under ordinary circumstances would have found adventure in a journey to somewhere they had never heard of. Added to this they were frightened and anxious to *do* the correct thing, yet at the same time full of foreboding at seeing their son a prisoner in jail! All in all, an extremely unpleasant ordeal.

Our car drew near the hotel and the grimness of Portland loomed up in front of us. My in-laws looked aghast at the sight. Upon entering, we were welcomed by the manager, who by now knew me well, and ushered into the cocktail bar, a grand looking place with a view of the sea. Music played softly in the background, and a smartly uniformed barman awaited our orders.

I asked my mother-in-law what she would care to drink, and then turned to my father-in-law who was staring round, eyes popping, almost open-mouthed. 'What will you have, a pint?' I enquired. His face was rigid and he could barely answer me, muttering furtively '*Can* we have a drink then?' 'Of course,' I said, 'What do you think I'm asking you for?' 'Well I never in all my life thought it would be like this,' he announced finally settling back with a beer happily in his hand. 'Like what? What do you mean?' I enquired a trifle curiously. 'To think I've worked all my life, and led an honest existence,' he rambled on hardly listening to my question. 'They say crime doesn't pay. Well if that's the way of it, I wish I had my life over again. I wouldn't be so honest!' Suddenly the meaning of his words struck me, and I burst out laughing. He actually thought he was inside the jail itself! The expensive furnishings and decor, not to mention the sophisticated cocktail bar with its music and choice of dozens of drinks displayed along the shelves, presented an overall picture of ultimate luxury to the old man. He imagined *that* was how prison life was, and wondered why he had fought to stay on the straight and narrow all his days.

J is for JONES

Tom, the sexiest singer ever to come out of Wales, and after all the awful things my mother had told me about the place (due to Grandma Dors' philanderings), it's a shame she did not stop there for maybe I would have been born in Pontypridd too, and could have caught Tom as he popped up from the coal mine covered in dust, and fresh as a daisy — for me anyway! Actually I preferred the early Tom Jones, even though he had rubbed the coal dust off by the time we met. He was and *is* a simple nice lad. Not too much of an intellect, with a rather limited sense of humour, but a straightforward, natural person. Today when I see him in photographs with a big fat cigar stuck in his mouth and trying to appear like a tycoon (he could never look like Lew Grade), I find the image has tarnished a little, and the Jones boy's sex appeal not as attractive as it was once.

Oddly enough one of my uncles (who is a bit of a rebel and still wishes he had been one of the Great Train Robbers, in spite of the sentences they received) worked with Tom's uncle at one time somewhere near Cardiff. They both got into such a scrape over some electrical wiring job that they were sacked on the spot!

My first confrontation with Tom was one night after a television show called *Ready Steady Go* back in 1964. We went extremely well together, and our obvious attraction for each other was very evident to the watching viewers. He had just made his first hit with the song 'It's Not Unusual' and was new and ready for the big time and all the fun and trappings that went with it! I had been in the business a good few years by then but I knew a good thing when I saw it — and I had seen nothing like him *anywhere*, not even in Hollywood where there are more gorgeous men to the square foot than anywhere else in the world. I invited him back to my flat in London where I had organised a big party.

There were two drawbacks to what could have been a big romance. He was married and although Dickie and I had been separated for two years by then, but in my usual fashion, never wanting to be alone, I had a rather unsuccessful pop singer boyfriend who watched us like a hawk that evening. Time went on and so did Tom, from strength to strength, and one night, quite a long time after the party, we all met in a late night club in the West End which was run by singer Annie Ross. Tom was alone, and I discovered later that he hardly ever took his wife Linda with him, but that seems to be the custom with Welsh husbands! I of course was with the aforementioned boyfriend and a couple of others and we all sat together to watch the cabaret. Tom sat by me, and during the performance held my hand under the table (not unnoticed by my companions I might add) and after the show had finished he asked me on to the floor to dance. Dance we did, but whether Tom had had a few drinks too many I do not know . . . . . We eventually all bade each other goodnight leaving Tom standing by the door staring at me with what looked like disbelief that I was not going to go with him.

A year or so after this episode we met somewhere and he invited some friends and I to dinner at a hotel near his home in Shepperton. This time he actually brought his wife Linda with him and we went back to their home for drinks. She was a quiet, sweet and typically Welsh girl who kept her house spotlessly clean, again typical of the Welsh — a trait that I am very much in favour of. I felt sorry for her as, for although he was making a lot of money and had things she never dreamed of, she seemed lonely and out of her depth. There was, I felt, almost an atmosphere as if she wished they were still back in Pontypridd living like an ordinary couple.

Once again a party rolled round at my house — I think it was Halloween Night — anyway I could always find an excuse for celebrating and I invited Tom and Linda. It was a good party — mine usually were — and during the evening Tom followed me out on to the terrace where we were barbecuing. His eyes glowed at me in the firelight and we stood looking at each other for quite a long time without speaking. 'Have you ever had the feeling everyone is looking at you?' I joked as I could see Linda through the big glass window looking a bit lost and out of it. Tom did not even smile, but then I said earlier he was not gifted with a big sense of humour. We started to talk about his marriage and he explained a great deal to me that night about his association with Linda, which was and always will be private. At the end of it all I said, 'It's a pity really Tom, we would have made a great couple.' 'I know,' he answered, 'But I would always be afraid to make love to you.' 'Good heavens why?' I gasped, remembering that time years before on the night club floor. 'Well you always treat me like a child,' he said, 'and I'd be frightened that you would laugh at me.'

It was suddenly obvious to me that my sense of humour and ability to laugh at almost anything had given one of the world's top sex symbols cold feet in the love department. For a long while I tried to become a more serious person, but a leopard never changes its spots, so they say, and I am still laughing to this day — not only about life, but also when I see the Jones boy swivelling his hips and acting the great lover.

K is for KAY KENDALL

The late sophisticated and glamorous star who died so tragically of leukemia, and whose delicious sense of humour endeared her to everyone including me . . . I met Kay in 1951 when she and I were appearing in a film together. We were introduced by a fellow actor who informed me that 'she was one of us,' the highest compliment one can be paid in the show-business world, for it means that such people care little for convention, are gypsies at heart, laugh at trouble and loathe hypocrisy.

Over the years we met at parties and premieres, and during the summer of 1955 we had dressing rooms in close proximity at Pinewood studios making different films. At the time Kay was having a love affair with Rex Harrison whom she later married. But at this point he was still wed to Lilli Palmer, so the whole thing was conducted on a very hush hush level, and Kay would always refer to him as 'my boyfriend', a somewhat incongruous name for a person of Rex's age and *savoir faire*. However, we all respected her privacy, and never actually mentioned him!

One day a certain actor who shall be nameless, but whose penchant for chasing the ladies was nothing short of male nymphomania, was running around the restaurant at the studios, chasing females and making good use of his lunch hour, when Kay came up to my table and said with disdain, 'Look at him, he's sniffing around here like a mangey dog.' I had to admit she was right! We laughed thankfully that he had left us alone, and it was then that she asked me if it was possible to bring her 'boyfriend' down to my house at Bray the following Sunday for lunch, as they fancied a day in the country.

I happily agreed and on the appointed Sunday they arrived in a chauffeur-driven Rolls Royce.

I had never met Rex before and was a little in awe of him, as his general manner seemed to be rather pompous and lofty, but Kay with her irrepressible personality soon had us all chatting away as though we were old friends.

Dennis and I reserved a table for lunch at an extremely good and rather dignified hotel at Cookham which dated back to the fifteenth century. And so we set off in our Cadillac. During the journey sparks began to fly. Rex and Kay were sitting in the back, and she alighted upon the subject of marriage — a thing, I immediately detected from his tone, was the last thing Rex had in mind. 'Oh come along Mousey,' (for that was his nickname for her) he said a trifle irritably, 'for God's sake don't let's start all that bloody nonsense again.' This rattled Kay, who persisted. And despite his obvious annoyance she made matters worse by fawning around his neck begging him to at least say he loved her. This was all done with a general air of half amusement, but the conversation came to a very unamusing and sudden stop when Rex who by now had had enough, clouted her in the ear! I could not quite believe what had happened and still wondered if they were play-acting. I stifled my surprise, cast a glance at Dennis who seemed to be finding it all very funny, and stared at the road ahead. We reached the restaurant and were duly bowed in by a dignified Maitre d'. The room was full of people lunching who all went rather quiet as we entered, for it was not every Sunday they saw a handful of film stars walk into the place.

Both Kay and Rex had become extremely noisy by this time and Kay was still holding her ear, with Rex telling her in his best 'Professor Higgins' voice to 'shut up', bitterly complaining that it was like being out with 'an untrained puppy dog'. Lunch was ordered, and the argument between the two seemed to grow worse, when finally having been told to 'shut up' for the hundredth time, Kay lost her temper and screamed at Rex, calling him a very unladylike name. As is usually the way when something like this happens, it is at the moment when a room becomes silent, so her rich, colourful adjective rattled round the sedate restaurant with great clarity of diction. Rex squirmed in his seat, yet made no attempt to silence her. The restaurant customers resumed their equilibrium, and mercifully the lunch came to an end. We paid the bill and left, amidst some disdainful glances, and proceeded back to our house. As we lived on the river, and owned a lovely motor launch, we suggested a quiet river ride to our guests, which they happily accepted. All went well until Kay began her 'when are you going to marry me?' dialogue, again, and Rex resumed his stubborn refusal to discuss the matter. Suddenly in a fit of madness, Kay threw herself into the water, which left Rex with no alternative but to jump in and pull her out as she could not swim. There was a terrible scramble back on to the boat, and we made for home as quickly as possible, with Rex demanding hot baths at once for fear they both caught cold.

Later, as they sat around, draped in towels, Kay exclaimed, 'I know what would amuse Rex, Diana. Tell him that story about the time you were arrested in Blackpool.' It was almost as if she was continually trying to please him, or at the very least endear herself enough to make him propose.

Seeing her excitement at the possibility of the story

delighting him I launched into the long tale and told it so amusingly that Kay fell about with mirth, but Rex did not even smile. Suddenly to my utter amazement, he stood up, looking anything but dignified without trousers, his rather skinny legs poking from underneath my bath towel, and announced pompously 'I refuse to listen to any more of this disgraceful story. My brother is also a very high ranking personage in the legal field, and he would not be amused either.' With this he stalked off in search of his clothes, leaving us mystified. Kay was horrified as she had never dreamed the tale was going to be taken in this manner. 'Oh I'm sorry,' she stammered, 'he gets a bit funny at times over certain things.' So saying she rushed off to find him. Dennis's remarks about the absurd pomposity of it all would be unprintable, but suffice to say they hurriedly dressed, climbed into the waiting car, and drove away without so much as a 'Goodnight'. When I saw Kay at the studios a few days later, she half-heartedly apologised, but looked embarrassed and hurried away. This was the last time I ever saw her. Afterwards Rex went to Broadway and stormed them with *My Fair Lady*. So happily he was once more accepted back into the bosom of America. Kay eventually married him, and they stayed that way until her tragic death, which it seems she was fortunately oblivious of right up to the end, as Rex had commendably kept the terrible secret from her.

K is for KEY PARTIES

I was not familiar with this game until I went to South Africa once to appear in cabaret, although it had been going on in England, and for that matter everywhere else, for a long time, so it seems.

For all those who are as ignorant as I was, the rules of the game go as follows. At the end of an evening's drinking and debauchery, all the husbands and wives who are bored stiff with each other, and wish to indulge in a bit of swapping, merely throw their car keys into the centre of the floor (this section of the game is done by the men I hasten to add), and the fun commences when the women select any key at random, and hopefully, if it is not their husband's, go off with the lucky owner! It is a kind of adult 'post office', except that in this case, one does not simply go outside the door and 'neck', as done in my teenage days, but spend the entire night with the owner of the key at his or her home depending of course whether their partner has made arrangements to suit the situation.

I could think of no worse fate that night in South Africa than to be sent off with a key and a man whom I did not even know, let alone fancy, so I did not indulge in the game, but everyone else had a whale of a time! My only other recollection of something similar, was a 'freaky' story which Sammy Davis Jr had told me about a party he once attended in Rome, when instead of keys being thrown in with abandon, someone, who was well stoned, decided that for a change they would do something quite original, and all throw their passports into a fire which was blazing away in the room, and watch them burn. Sammy realising he was obviously with a bunch of loonies, panicked and ran out of the house, and all the way back to the centre of the city, for the party was being held somewhere on the outskirts. He told me the journey was terrible for he did not know where he was, and in his anxiety to get as far away as possible, lost himself many times before reaching his destination, long after dawn. However I do not imagine the book entitled 'What makes Sammy run' was inspired by his harrowing experience.

The oddest tale concerning parties though, key swapping or otherwise, was told to me, again in South Africa, during my stay there. It appeared that a certain wife did not approve of this sort of fun, and also suspected her husband was being unfaithful when he insisted on attending them, despite his denials of ever taking part in the key throwing activities. One night unable to contain herself any longer, she disguised herself in a wig, and went along to where the husband was already well inebriated and thoroughly enjoying himself, believing his wife to be tucked away safely at home. Totally unrecognisable, she was approached by him, and he happily proceeded to 'chat her up'. This finally culminated in her agreeing to go outside and get into the back of his car for a love-making session. Once spreadeagled on the back seat, the infuriated woman pulled off her wig revealing her true identity to the horrified husband, and at a later date brought a divorce action against him, winning it on the grounds of adultery with an unnamed woman.

K is for KICKING

I think it is fair to say that if a girl has never had her bedroom door kicked down by a jealous, or zealous lover then she most certainly has never lived!

Richard Burton once kicked down the door of an English actress with whom he had been working, and having an affair whilst her husband was away, but the romance came to a sad end. However that was *before* he met Elizabeth Taylor. Whether he ever paid Liz the compliment of doing the same I do not know,

It is very flattering to have one's bedroom door kicked down. However I am at an age when I no longer find it exciting, and I know I must be growing old, for where I would once have been thrilled and complimented, now all I can think about is the expense of having the damage put right!

K is for NAT 'KING' COLE

When Nat 'King ' Cole died I think the world of music lost one of the greatest singers it has ever known, and to this day I *still* cannot believe he has left us; his voice is immortal. Way back early in 1952, for the first time since the war, British bands were beginning to invade America, and our best was undoubtedly Ted Heath. They had been booked for a big performance in Georgia and starring with them was Nat 'King' Cole. The hall was packed to capacity. Ted Heath and his band played for the entire first half, storming the audience and no doubt feeling very pleased with themselves, quite rightly! After the interval the 'King' began his act and all went well until suddenly two men (possibly Ku Klux Klan members) rushed onto the stage and knocked him down. Pandemonium followed, fighting breaking out everywhere. The Ted Heath Band sat frozen on stage not knowing what to do. Suddenly Ted had a brainwave, or so he thought, and shouted, 'Play God Save the Queen!' They obeyed instantly. But with all due respect, our National Anthem was hardly going to quell a race riot in Georgia! No-one was listening. As the strains of 'God Save Our Gracious Queen' pervaded the hall, Nat's terrified manager who was hiding in the wings, screamed out to the British band, 'Fuck the Queen, the King is on the floor!!!'

L is for LAWYERS AND LITIGATION

Litigation is a total waste of time and money, and although I know it is often essential, I can state through sad experience that it never works out successfully, except for the lawyers. I once had a law suit going on with an agent who owed me money, and at the end of the proceedings, even though I was in the right, my lawyer carefully explained (after ensuring *his* bill had been paid of course), that settling the matter out of court and paying the wretched man many hundreds of pounds to which he was not entitled, would cost me far less than if I went to court and won the case!

I once knew a lawyer whose charm and courtesy was only surpassed by his brilliance at totting up your bill. If he walked you personally to the lift at the end of a consultation, bowing you out and kissing your hand, you knew it would put at least an extra fiver on his fees.

Actually, the futility of litigation was best summed up to me by a crafty rogue who made millions, and then fled to Peru where he is now living in exile. The story goes thus: two farmers were arguing over a cow, one farmer was pulling the cow by the horns claiming it to be his, and the other pulling it by the tail, whilst the lawyer was underneath getting all the milk!

L is for LENNY

They made a film about him; he wrote his book which shocked many people. But that is how he spent his life, shocking people — usually hypocrites who did not like what they heard him say, for it was always the truth. I am speaking of course of the one and only Lenny Bruce, my dear friend who killed himself due to a tragic hang-up on drugs — a state brought about through no fault of his own. Like many ex-servicemen fighting for their country, having been badly wounded, he became hooked on morphine given to ease the pain.

My first meeting with Lenny was in New York where he was appearing in a small dark nightclub, and I thought his was the most brilliant comedy mind I had ever heard. Lenny's scene, his comedy and thinking, was totally different from anyone, and most of it was drawn from his experiences of life. I was in New York doing one of their top television shows — *The Steve Allen Show* — and Lenny had been booked by Steve, a shrewd judge of talent. Everyone thought Steve Allen had lost his mind by doing this as Lenny was unreliable, completely impossible to rehearse, and used material which was wickedly humorous involving the use of many four-letter words.

Lenny was far from being an idiot though, and he appreciated and respected Steve's trust in him so the show thankfully went without a flaw.

He attempted to enter England around the time of the Christine Keeler affair but the powers that be would not let him in. His escapades in cities like Chicago, where he was threatened with being found in an alley should he dare to come there again, were as famous as his act. The number of places he was allowed to perform in grew less and less, and the wine of success began to turn sour.

However, one incident did occur in a Las Vegas hotel when I was present. I was not with his party but sitting in front of him watching a very funny comedian, Shecky Greene, doing his act. Lenny got very exuberant and although his wife tried to shut him up let forth a stream of four-letter words loudly to Shecky, who defended himself well and the whole evening was extremely funny. The management were not so amused, however, and by tricking him to the telephone saying there was a call, they ordered him out of the establishment for ever! No doubt angry about this affair, and high on drugs, Lenny then went on to another hotel, the *Flamingo*, where Pearl Bailey was performing. Unable to stand her 'Uncle Tom' style of entertainment he leapt onto the stage, grabbed a fire extinguisher and, pointing it at Pearl, let her have it right in the face! 'Oh my Lord, my Lord,' cried Pearl, and as pandemonium broke out he was led away. I believe he actually sat down and wrote her a letter saying how disgusted he was with her act. He could not abide her 'shtick', as he put it, which involved pushing parts of her body into customers' faces. He had his opinion of what was right and wrong on stage and in life, but nevertheless he was escorted to the Las Vegas border by a gun-toting sheriff and told never to enter the state of Nevada again.

I loved him, and my fondest memories were not of the Lenny who shocked and stormed audiences on stage, but the quiet, almost elfin-like person who would turn up at my Beverly Hills home in jeans and whizz me off on the back of his motorcycle to proudly show me his brand new home with the swimming pool, no furniture, and a large orange pumpkin standing by the fireplace. Lenny, you are sadly missed, and today no-one would be startled by your antics — but like many great talents you were born before your time.

L is for JERRY LEWIS

One of the zaniest and most brilliant comedians of all time in my opinion, and according to his box office receipts I was obviously not the only one who thought so. But sadly this comic genius is also possessed of a manic ego. He and I got off to a bad start, it was not my fault but his enormous ego working overtime.

I first met Jerry when he was partnering Dean Martin at their debut appearance in London at the Palladium way back in 1953, and then again many years later in 1958 when he and Dean had split up and he was working alone. Once more there were pictures taken of us together in the star dressing-room. Afterwards during conversation I first saw the big power complex at work. 'You see this?' he announced shoving a bell type contraption attached to a long wire at me, 'This is the *Panic Button* and when I press it *everyone* comes running 'cos they know the big chief wants a pow-wow!' I expressed my compliments on the electrical wizardry of the gadget, but felt secretly very glad that I was not working with him or under him in the show as I cannot bear the kind of sycophantic behaviour which goes on around a superstar, expecially American ones who surround themselves with a retinue of people ready to bow and cater to their every whim. It reminds me of medieval days (not that I was there!) when the court circled around King Henry VIII. If he laughed they all broke into hysterics even when they did not understand the joke, but if he was not amused they all looked glum.

Our next meeting was to be much more significant. It was now 1960 in Hollywood and Jerry Lewis was making another of his highly successful films, this one called *The Ladies' Man*. He had expressed a desire to see me and my agent about a star role in the picture, so we presented ourselves at Paramount Studios to find the trademark of Jerry Lewis everywhere. Hal Wallis who used to run the studios had been put out of business by King Jerry, who also bore hatred towards him for the days when Wallis used to hit his desk with a large whip shouting to Dean and he, 'Be funny'. Jerry Lewis's name was everywhere — there were even little electric run-around trucks like golf course carriers painted pink, with drawings of him cartooned on the sides. I thought to myself what a marvellous feeling of power it must be to have lifted himself up into that illustrious position after years of oppression and being kicked around!

We were ushered into the main block of offices and eventually taken into the holy of holies — namely his large office which of course had once been Hal Wallis's. There sat Jerry behind the desk (which Wallis had whacked so often during the days when Jerry and Dean had been hauled up in front of him for a lecture), and I also noted the window behind him where it is reported that Burt Lancaster once, in a fit of uncontrollable anger, unable to stand any more tyranny from Wallis, had tried to strangle him and push him through.

Jerry was charm itself that afternoon, anxious to impress with all his gadgets and jokes and I noted that the *Panic Button* was still there too. When we finally got round to discussing a deal, he asked my agent, who was sitting timidly in the corner, what sort of money he wanted for my services. The agent gulped and asked what he was prepared to pay, at which Jerry looked stern and repeated his former question in a manner which Hall Wallis might have done.

'Er, well, as it's only a small guest role,' began my agent, 'Perhaps you would agree, to, well shall we say seven thousand dollars?' 'No, we will not,' said Jerry, 'I will definitely not pay that to Miss Dors.' 'Oh well,' drooled the agent nervously, 'Then whatever you think is best.' 'You have not asked me *why* I will not pay seven thousand bucks yet,' came the reply. 'Oh well Mr. Lewis, why not?' asked the now totally demolished agent. 'Because I think she is worth more than that and you are underselling her,' shouted Lewis, who was now squirming in his seat as he excitedly played the power game with the grovelling man in the corner. 'I will pay her *ten* thousand dollars,' he announced striking the desk with his fist, and looking as though he wished he had a whip in the drawer. My agent's face was a study — the poor man was utterly wiped out with the situation, but a deal was done and we left the studio, confused but happy.

The film was due to commence a month or two later, and during the interim period an offer was made for me to appear with comedian Danny Kaye in a film he was making, *At the Double*. There were a great many British stars in it as the action was mainly supposed to be in England, so I was a natural for the part. I completed my work with Danny and then sat back and waited for my call to begin Jerry's film. Time went by and no call came. The movie started and I had not even received a call from Edith Head, the wardrobe designer, to discuss my costumes. I began to worry as to what was going on and my agent proceeded to negotiate with the Lewis Production office as to what was happening.

We eventually learned to our amazement that Jerry had gone into a fit of jealousy because I had done the picture with Danny Kaye first. I suppose he looked upon him as a rival — though I find it hard to believe with his enormous ego that he ever truly regarded anyone as that!

Harsh words were exchanged between the studios and my agents. We had a contract and it held good, so whether I appeared in the film or not, I had to be paid! One day I suddenly received a call to be at the studios the next morning at seven a.m. I duly presented myself in the make-up and hairdressing departments, who all expressed great surprise to see me as my name was not on the callsheet. As they were unable to do anything to me, I went and sat in a dressing-room trailer on the set, and waited. It was a very strange situation. Other actors I knew who were working on the film kept coming in and saying, "What are you doing here?". The camera crew also nodded welcomes, but I was just left sitting in there all morning, rather like a prisoner waiting in the cells under the court for his time to come to go into the witness box.

At one point during the morning I saw Jerry go by, with not a glance at me although he obviously knew I was there. I had seen no script so if I had been called on to the set I would not have known what to do.

Finally, as lunchtime drew near, the assistant director came into my trailer looking rather embarrassed and said, 'Mr Lewis has sent me to say he cannot stand it any longer, and that he is sorry he has treated another artiste this way — you are free to go home.' I left, was paid the money, but never appeared in the film, and was told, as much as a year later by a girl he knew, that she thought it was terrible the way I had treated Jerry, and how sorry she felt for him.

I think the only occasion when he was actually stopped dead in his tracks was due to a very funny gag played on him by another comedian, Phil Silvers of *Bilko* fame. It seems, back at the beginning of their success, Martin and Lewis were playing the *Copacabana* club in New York and ripping it up every night. The *Copa* was situated on the ground floor of an enormous skyscraper building of apartments, and right at the very top, in his bachelor days, lived Phil Silvers. One night, around one a.m., as the comedy team were paralysing the audience, Phil could not sleep. So up he got, put a dressing gown over his pyjamas and went down in his private lift some twenty floors below to ground level where the *Copa* was. Without any warning he marched straight into the club and on to the nightclub floor, much to the amazement of the audience, grabbed the microphone, and said 'Keep it down will you fellows, I'm trying to get some sleep,' — walked right off the floor and into his lift leaving the audience, and Martin and Lewis, completely dumbfounded.

L is for LIBERACE

Let me say straight away that anyone saying anything against this highly professional star regarding his public or personal life, will be in danger of having to deal with me as a result.

If someone is fortunate enough to know Lee, when the tinsel wrappings and gimmicks are swept away, then underneath they will find a genuine and unbelievably kind man. Though he revels in performing on stage, he rushes through life at break-neck speed, appearing wherever they will let him tickle the ivories. He is only truly happy when he is working, he also likes nothing better than staying at home with friends, eating and playing games. Now I am not trying to persuade my reader that lurking beneath Lee's extravagant exterior is a quiet soul who prefers a hermit's existence with pipe and slippers, quite the contrary, but he once confided to me that during his hectic and busy year of work, the two occasions he insists on being at home are Christmas and in May when the lilacs are blooming on his birthday.

When I went to Hollywood in 1956, I first met him at a rather smart, but dull, party, leaning against a wall looking somewhat sad. When I asked him what was wrong, I found out something which is a key to his real character. It seems that two nights before he had given a concert for charity in the Hollywood Bowl at the request of the *Los Angeles Times* who, after packing the place thanks to his name and making a great deal of money, had turned around and lambasted his performance the next day in their newspaper. This was of course a terrible thing to do, but where was the man who reputedly shrugged off all his critics with statements such as 'Let 'em knock, I laugh all the way to the bank'?

That night I realised he was only human like the rest of us, and did care very much when people attacked him, it wounded him deeply. I tried to boost his morale a little by telling him that when he came to England for the first time, which he was going to do a few weeks from then, the British press would love him, and so would the British public. It turned out I was wrong about the press, as secretly I feared I would be. During his first visit, despite the enormous success he enjoyed at the London Palladium and everywhere else he went, the press carved him up badly. One columnist, now deceased, saw fit to write the

most scathing article ever written about anyone, criticising his clothes, sex life, and many other private things. Lee created a precedent by suing this particular paper, much to the delight of all show-business people, for no-one had ever dared to sue the press for fear of losing, and thus gaining bad publicity from all quarters. Lee not only sued, but won, although it cost him a fortune, much more than he was awarded. But he did it as a demand for respect and the truth despite the most horrible publicity any artiste was ever forced to receive as the trial unfolded, and the grisly facts were analysed over and over again in court. I have known him closely for twenty-two years and he is a godfather to one of my sons, Gary.

Of course his life-style is flamboyant, and there are many show people I know who sneer at me for being his friend. 'What's with that guy?' they say. 'How can anyone live the way he does with a piano-shaped swimming pool, and bed, plus all the pictures, trophies and trappings of his career spread out in rich splendour all over the house?' Well, the answer is simple. None of these things are really Lee. Yes, he revels in being Liberace and all the early homes and gimmicks were done for a purpose, to make him a millionaire which he is today several times over, and if the knockers were honest they would admit that they too would have done the same if they thought it would result in the kind of wealth and luxury Lee enjoys.

I have spent Christmas at his home, a showplace overlooking Hollywood which is now open to the public, and watched him open all his presents excitedly like a small boy, amidst the *five* Christmas trees all in different colours and lights decorating the drawing-room.

On my last visit to his beautiful, new and very private home in Palm Springs, Alan and I were treated like royalty, but then I suspect Lee lives better than royalty! The house, unlike all the others he has owned with their gimmicks and star-style decor, is so tastefully furnished and elegantly designed, it is fit for a prince. The dinner he held in our honour was second only to a meal one might expect at Maxims in Paris, with gold and silverware, crystal glasses, candle-light chandeliers, and superb cuisine. Typical of Lee, under each guest's plate, he placed a little gift which he had shopped for all day, and derived more pleasure in watching people's faces as they opened the packages, than ever he would have done if we had all brought gifts for him. He actually owns three other homes in Palm Springs; one which he bought, designed, and styled for his mother as a present which she refused to even go to see; and the other two just as 'fun' homes, as he describes them. In the past Lee had a whale of a time dressing flamboyantly, and wearing outrageous clothes and jewels, which back in the Fifties created a great deal of excitement. But when the Sixties began really swinging, and everyone freaked out with their clothes, Lee who was here on yet another tour, told me rather worriedly that he did not know what new gimmick to pull, as by then the public had seen everything. To use his words: 'I just cannot keep up with the game like I used to, there are so many "way out" clothes in the shops now, I've got to think of a different gimmick.' For several days he racked his brains as to what to give the audience on his opening night at the Palladium and finally announced that he was coming up with something special, but refused to reveal what it was to anybody including me.

The opening night arrived, and I sat in the audience waiting and wondering what he could do which had not already been done by countless, far-out rock groups and singers who were also much younger than him. As usual he went through his act, playing the piano, showing off his jewels and taking the mickey out of himself, while the audience cheered and applauded. His suit was glittering and styled in the usual fashion, and he also managed to get off and make a change, appearing in another suit of even more stunning proportions. Even so I could not help thinking that all these things had been seen and done before, and he was really going to have to pull something big out of the bag to make the audience sit up this time.

Suddenly at the end of his show he did it, and once again the Liberace we had all come to know, and either love or despise, blossomed forth. Standing centre stage and taking his last bows graciously, I noted he seemed to be holding one hand behind his back and wondered why. . .then it happened, unknown to us he was clutching a small electric box, complete with switch, and just as he was bowing for the last time, his entire suit lit up like one of the Christmas trees at his house in Hollywood. He was covered from head to foot in lights which had been sewn all over him for the occasion.

It was very spectacular and the audience went wild, but afterwards in the dressing-room he confided to me that it had been 'sink or swim', for he was in danger of blowing himself up in the process and regardless of his desire to have a big finish, this was not the way Liberace truly wanted to go!

L is for LIFE

I love life, and cannot think of anything worse than not being around to see what is going on, but that is probably because I have such a curious nature, and hate to think I am ever left out of anything.

Since my near bout with death when I contracted meningitis some years ago, life has taken on a new meaning for me, as apart from anything else, I am really here on borrowed time! I no longer get worked up about the petty things in life as I did before. People do not bother me as much, their opinions and criticisms of my behaviour which used to mean a great deal once, no longer even interest me, and I try to live each day as it comes without worrying too much about things. This is difficult for someone like myself, even now, for I am by nature a worrier, and do have responsibilities and codes of behaviour which cannot be broken even if I want to.

Thanks to my religion I am no longer afraid of dying, and age as revealed under the letter A far back in this book does not bother me in the least. The only thing I do feel about age is that I would, like most of us, be delighted to have my time over again in order to change certain things, but that is a hypothetical situation! I would hate to go through the rest of my life wishing I had done this, or not done that, and really I have enjoyed everything tremendously, with the exception of making and subsequently losing a lot of money through merciless manipulation and managing by other people, such as accountants, advisors and general 'hangers on'.

No, my two regrets about growing old and eventually dying are, firstly, that I do not want to miss anything. If I was younger in years now I could obviously be around much longer, and secondly to be with my sons, for I will be sorry to leave them behind.

One of the worst words I ever hear is 'bored'. There are so many wonderful things to do in this world, and if a person is very rich yet bored with everything, then it is always possible to go out and help someone else who is less fortunate than themselves. There is no reason for *anyone* to be bored in this life, and all too sadly one hears this word coming from the lips of the young, more than anywhere else.

Actually comedian Bob Monkhouse summed up my zest for life one night at dinner, turning to me he said, 'Diana, you are indestructible. When they finally explode the H Bomb, only you and Lew Grade will be left standing!'

M is for JAYNE MANSFIELD

It would be silly of me to try and write any kind of book without mentioning Mansfield, or indeed Monroe. The latter I never actually met — we passed in mid-air over the Atlantic in 1956. I was on my first trip to Hollywood to do a film there and she was on her first trip to England to do a film with Sir Laurence Olivier. We were both received at our destinations like the coming of the second Messiah, though she was not in such a difficult position as me, for everyone knew her films here, whereas no-one had seen anything I had done in America, and I had to have a stock answer ready for all the press who continually asked me why I had aped Monroe. Luckily I was able to show them a press cutting of many years before when she had been seen in her first film here, *The Asphalt Jungle*, and a columnist had written 'How much like Diana Dors this new Marilyn Monroe is', but it did not help much over there as they were convinced I was cashing in on her publicity as 'England's answer to Marilyn Monroe'.

It did not help that there was another blonde also making headlines as fast as she could get in front of a camera, but this was one of theirs, namely Jayne Mansfield. I met her in Hollywood with her husband, muscle-man Mickey Hargitay, and could not believe that this sweet cooing dumb blonde from Texas was really as dumb as she pretended to be. The ruthless activities of her determined bid for stardom did not go with her sugary voice and attitude. But in all the time I knew Jayne she never let the mask fall once, until at the end I finally believed she really did speak and think like a Kewpie Doll.

Our next meeting was in England, in Wakefield of all places, a far cry from Hollywood in the fifties. But like me she was doing a cabaret tour, and cashing in on her screen name for money. Ironically we were both staying in the same hotel and I knew she was due to arrive when I saw all her pink luggage in the lobby. Jayne had a 'thing' about the colour pink — her house in Hollywood was pink, so was her swimming pool. Autographs would be signed with a pink pen and a little pink heart drawn over the 'i' in Mansfield instead of a dot. On one occasion she actually got her hairdresser to shape and colour her pubic hair into a pink heart — this was probably the only part of the Mansfield anatomy the public never saw in photographs!

The press went wild when they found out that two sex goddesses were shacked up in a hotel in Wakefield. Publicity sessions and pictures were organised at which she and I presented ourselves like two gladiators squaring up for a fight. When the flash bulbs stopped clicking and the press had finally scuttled off with their spoils, Jayne and I became quite good friends. She was having a 'ding dong' affair with the American lawyer Sam Brody who was eventually killed with her the following year, 1967, in a tragic car crash. It was a tempestuous relationship — they would lie in bed all day making love, then she would stagger on to the night club floor, go back to bed and resume, have a fight, and he would fly off in a temper to Los Angeles leaving Jayne in tears. Then a series of hour long transatlantic phone calls would carry on until they eventually 'made up' and he would come flying back. No expense was spared in their affair and I think it probably took all the money Jayne was earning on her tour to keep it going. She was in the middle of a divorce from her third husband, and had one of her five children with her in case he tried to snatch it back. Sam Brody was also going through a divorce, so there was legal trouble on all sides. She had a large retinue of followers, managers, agents and the like, and a passion for animals, especially little chihuahua dogs. But during the week in Wakefield she developed a desire for a great Dane, and so all day and every day, great Danes were being brought to the hotel for her appraisal. Jayne could not resist any of them and wound up with two, instead of merely one as planned, which did not please the management as the place was beginning to look like a kennel.

Each night after we had finished our respective shows we would gather in Jayne's suite, eat, drink and talk until the early hours. I used to find conversation with her a bit limited, especially as she was on the telephone to Brody in America for hours at a time, so instead I found good conversation with comedian Max Wall who was appearing in Jayne's show.

One night just before Brody returned from yet another flight to Los Angeles Jayne showed me a diamond solitaire he had given her for her birthday. It was obvious she was madly in love with the fellow. She asked me a question which at the time I did not understand. 'Do you believe in monogamy?' she inquired. I was unable to answer coherently at the time, but stammered something out as I am never at a loss for words, and whatever I said obviously appeased her for she went on gazing at her diamond happily. I made a mental note to find out immediately what monogamy was, and am now thankfully quite conversant on the subject.

I never saw Jayne again after that week. She went back to America in her usual blaze of publicity with Sam Brody being sued at Uxbridge magistrate's court for illegally bringing in two chihuahua dogs as a present for her. One of her last statements to me was something that I just could not believe or accept. We were discussing her sex life with Brody and in her funny little-girl sugary voice she said, 'You know Sam is a very demanding man. He makes love forty times a night.' When I expressed total disbelief that even *superman* was capable of making it *that* many times, she insisted that he was extremely over-sexed and there was no satisfying him! I related this story to actress Angela Douglas, Kenneth More's wife. She too was astounded and ran home to tell her husband that there must be something lacking on his part. Kenneth replied, 'Rubbish, that woman is so dumb she thinks forty times a night is just in and out.'

M is for FREDERIC MARCH

The late and great American Oscar-winning actor who gave so many wonderful performances during his life, but whose unfortunate passion for the ladies often got him into trouble, especially with his wife, actress Florence Eldridge. I was sixteen and making a film at a studio in London when he arrived to star in *Christopher Columbus*, heavily guarded by his long-suffering spouse who had craftily got herself a role in the picture so she could *really* keep an eye on him. Frederic would be seen walking along the studio corridors looking distinguished in his Columbus wig and costume. He had already cast a lecherous eye at me and one day as I was passing his dressing-room an arm shot out and hauled me inside. I found to my dismay that Frederic March was on the other end, and he proceeded to try and make it with me then and there. I struggled free and ran out of the door much to his chagrin, and ever after he became extremely sullen, glowering at me whenever we passed each other.

I was naturally not the only target for his activities. The female hairdresser whose job it was to put on his wig each morning was repeatedly embarrassed by his unsubtle 'groping up her skirt'. One day she could stand it no longer. Throwing down her comb in a rage she exclaimed, 'Mr March, if you don't stop doing that, I am going to put a goddamn rat-trap up there!'

M is for MARIJUANA

I do not smoke ordinary cigarettes, therefore to smoke 'pot' holds no attraction for me, thank goodness. I suppose I am one of the lucky ones who do not need drink or drugs in order to enjoy life — on the contrary I can get 'high' on people or situations quite naturally. When I was seventeen, a film starlet, and in with a group that included several well-known celebrities of today who were then just getting started too, we bought some marijuana once for kicks. I remember all of us sitting round in a circle puffing away (which of course was our first mistake as we should have been inhaling) and waiting for something fantastic to occur. Naturally nothing did, and we were not only very disappointed, but rather upset at how much the stuff had cost as we were not too well off. Then one night someone suggested at a party that we should put aspirins in Coca Cola to get high, assuring us it would definitely work. Again we tried but nothing happened except that disc jockey Pete Murray came out in lumps the next day and was most displeased as, being an actor then, he had to miss a very important interview.

Amyl nitrate was also experimented with around that time. One could purchase it at any chemist by saying it was for someone who had palpitations of the heart. As we all broke the sachets, sniffed the aroma up our nostrils, and jumped up and down like scalded cats for twenty seconds or so, we felt we were really living — eventually to discover that unless it was a desperate measure to prolong the excitement of love-making (as was the case with one friend of mine who would not be caught dead without a sachet or two under the bed during his sexual activities), it really was not all that good and left an appalling smell in the room after everyone had finished 'turning on', as they say.

All this teenage nonsense ended — as far as I was concerned. Drugs, pills, or pot had no place in my life at all. I was not against them, and did not rush from the room if offered a 'smoke', which was much in fashion in Hollywood in the early sixties. Frankly, it had actually become a bore to me as everywhere one went people just sat smoking and gazing into space, thereby killing conversation. It was considered the 'in' thing to do and if you did not do it then you were 'out'. It is still, we know, illegal, yet I hope one day it will be legalised for I think and know from experience that it does not do half as much harm as drink. People are less violent on 'pot', boring maybe, but nowhere near as maudlin and repetitive as a drunk. It is still a prisonable offence, and was certainly so in my teenage years when film star Robert Mitchum was jailed for ninety days for smoking the dreaded weed.

Fate was certainly in my corner one day in Hollywood back in 1963. A very handsome Italian-American boyfriend of mine, whose father was extremely rich and had bought him a New York nightclub with which to amuse himself, had come out to the coast for a short trip. He and a friend were staying at the swank Hilton Hotel on Wilshire Boulevard, and one day we all went for lunch at the Luau Restaurant, on Rodeo Drive. I had called for them first at the hotel as they had no car, and spent about ten minutes in their suite. After lunch we journeyed back to the hotel and they asked me to come in for a coffee. I declined as I had several important things to do, and in spite of strong pressure from my lover, who was extremely peeved at my refusal, I drove off promising to call them later. Thank God his usual persuasive charm had not worked that day, for when they got up to their suite two detectives leapt out at them and without further ado they were taken down town to a Los Angeles police station for questioning and held there for nearly two days! Had I been with them I would also have been arrested and by the time I had proved my innocence the publicity would have been fatal. I shudder even now when I think of the possible implications. It seemed my boyfriend smoked 'pot' and had concealed a 'joint' (as the cigarette is called) in a suit pocket and forgotten it. When the valet picked up the suit for cleaning he found the offending item in a pocket and immediately reported it to the police. If I had been sitting there in his suite when they pounced, it would have been very difficult to try and prove that I was not up there smoking myself, and I suspect I would have been held as an accessory. I have always had a strange knack of getting publicity without ever employing a press agent, but this was publicity I would *not* have wanted — and what an awful injustice when for *once* in my life I was not guilty!

M is for MARRIAGE

'Whoever invented marriage must have been some sadist in the barbaric ages,' moaned film actor George Brent when we were filming a thing called *Manbait* in 1951. As he had made it to the altar four times by then, I realised it was a sore subject, particularly where alimony was involved. I myself was on the verge of getting married for the first time and I figured in his experienced way he was trying to give me some advice. Whatever he meant to do he did not succeed and I went ahead and 'tied the knot' with Dennis Hamilton at Caxton Hall, after having only known him five weeks! What followed I have not time to go into under the letter M but sadly it turned out in the end that George Brent was right. One ghastly incident, which almost upset our marriage before it had even begun, was the American producer of the film arriving within a week of the ceremony and, having seen my performance on the screen, going completely crazy. To my agent's delight he offered me a Hollywood contract. I was nineteen years old and this had been my dream since the age of five, so I was over the moon with excitement. However, there *was* a hitch. The producer heard with horror of my marriage and instructed the agent that the deal would not go through if I remained so. My agent shook with fright and ventured to say I had only been wed a week or two. But the producer was adamant that he could not build me up into a sex symbol like Shelley Winters if I was married. 'Then what do you suggest?' asked my agent. 'Let her divorce him and marry him again later if she wants to. It'll make good publicity.' His ears were deaf to our pleas that we did not behave in this way in England, and that was that! Eventually, after a lot of upset between Dennis and I, we told him what to do with his contract (although within me I felt I had committed professional suicide). Dennis, however, with his flair for publicity, turned it into an incredible story. I had, apparently, refused a Hollywood contract in order to stay in England, the land I loved! This was one of the many publicity stunts he organised for me when he decided to turn me into a household name, 'a female Errol Flynn' as he put it.

I have been married three times in my life, and I now know, as the last one was in Church, that making vows to God as to what you are going to do with another person is well nigh impossible. At its best marriage is a very difficult state of affairs. Men and women were not meant to live together other than to create children, their likes and dislikes are totally different and I can honestly say that in the whole of my life I have only met one completely happily married couple who never fought, and loved each other until death did them part — strangely enough my second husband's parents, who were devoted. Marriage is beautiful, especially at first, but sadly it all ends up the same way. Of course we all need someone to love and live for and it is the greatest compliment a man can pay a woman to ask her to spend the rest of her life with him (though why most of them bother when there are out rushing around looking for fun on the side I cannot understand).

It all starts when we are children and every story ends with, 'And they all lived happily every after.' I am not bitter or cynical when I say that in ninety-nine cases out of a hundred this does not happen, but I suppose people will still go on doing it, and good luck to them.

I think it is all best summed up by a witty female friend of mine, one Pamela Mason — ex-wife of the actor James, who said, 'No-one should get married until they are sixty, because after sixty what the hell else is there to do?'

M is for VICTOR MATURE

The Hollywood star with whom I once had the pleasure of making a movie entitled *The Long Haul*. It received appalling notices but we had a lot of laughs filming it. It also made a great deal of money, which is always nice when you have been torn to shreds by the critics and can laugh all the way to the bank (as Liberace once so aptly put it). Vic had been laughing all the way to the bank for most of his career. He was the first person to say he could not act, and had two expressions which he numbered 'five' and 'eight'. These involved using his eyebrows in upward and downward positions, thereby looking as though he was giving a sensitive and intelligent performance, as in such films as *Samson and Delilah* or *The Robe* in which he had to look as though he was suffering and thinking at the same time.

I adored Vic and I adored his sense of humour. But many people, particularly women, could not abide him, which was strange since he possessed fantastic good looks, perhaps almost too good! He told me that when he first began in Hollywood he modelled himself on Clark Gable and always tried to conduct his life and career in the same way so that people would be very much in awe of him. Unfortunately Vic's zest for life and sex were way ahead of Gable's, and his sense of humour also got him into trouble, such as the time he described to me, when, under contract to 20th Century Fox, he had a leather jacket made

embroidered with the words 'I am the handsomest guy in movies' just to infuriate those who were already jealous of his looks, and very sceptical about his acting ability. Much later in his career he moved out of Hollywood to a ranch and openly stated that the only time he went to Los Angeles was to get a divorce!

I had met him some years before we made the film together and under quite extraordinary circumstances. In the early fifties, my husband Dennis and I were living in a beautiful house at Bray, on a backwater of the river. One day I looked out of the living room window and saw Dennis coming up the garden with Vic, a film director named Terence Young, and actress Katy Jurado.

Apparently he had seen them floating by in a rented canoe and hauled them on to our bank for drinks in the boathouse. Vic had had quite a few drinks before he got into the canoe so by the time he reached me in my bright orange hotpants, he thought he had actually seen the American cartoon Daisy Mae of Lil Abner for real. Katy Jurado was obviously well besotted with him and it seemed as though she was hoping to become the next Mrs Mature. Vic behaved himself with a certain amount of restraint, but indicated to Dennis, with whom he had become good friends, that he would like to return without Katy at some later date. The invitation was extended the following Sunday for lunch, and eventually they left. Sunday arrived and Dennis and I went out to visit some friends nearby for a late morning drink, before our guest was due to arrive. But what we had completely forgotten was that we had invited a rather staid elderly Colonel and his prim wife for lunch that day also. By the time we remembered, the worst had happened. Whilst we were out, Vic and his director friend had arrived and Vic had taken an immediate fancy to one of the Spanish maids we employed. To make matters worse, the Colonel and wife had also decided on an early arrival, and receiving no reply to their ring at the front door, proceeded round to the back of the house, where to their horror they saw Vic and the Spanish maid in an extremely intimate position on the kitchen table . . .

We never saw the Colonel and his wife again who, after giving us the benefit of their feelings over the telephone, decided it was probably best to keep well away from those 'awful show business people'.

Vic's capacity for the ladies never ceased to amaze me. Every morning during the filming of The Long Haul, his limousine would arrive at the studio at 8.30 a.m. with a sleeping Vic in the back. There they would leave him until the very last moment, when his various stand-ins and doubles had done everything possible for him without actually playing the scene. It was a well known fact that Vic never did any of his own danger action, fights etc. and I think his stand-in Harold Sanderson was probably seen more in Victor Mature's movies than Vic himself. I remember on one occasion he decided that he did not want to be made up for a scene we were doing in a lorry. It was an integral part of the film. There was a long harangue between him and the director, Ken Hughes, with the make-up man hovering nervously about with his sponge covered in Max Factor Pancake Base. Finally Vic relented to the extent that he would only let the man make-up *one* side of his face, the side facing the camera. The scene had to be played with him not moving a feature (not even his famous eyebrow acting) for fear the un-made up side would show. There were many funny moments on that film, and if they had filmed the 'goings-on' between takes, it would probably have had much better notices! Vic had what he called his 'shit list' marked on the dressing room wall and anyone who transgressed during the day was immediately included on it with a certain number of marks. If they were in favour, their former errors were erased. What his price for coming off the 'shit list' altogether was I do not know, although if the person were female I can hazard a pretty good guess!

The last I saw of Vic was in a film in which I think he gave his best performance, *After the Fox*, with Peter Sellers. He portrayed a faded film star, really taking the mickey out of himself for the first time on screen; and he was extremely funny.

M is for GROUCHO MARX

One of the all time great comedians who along with his equally famous brothers created comedy in films way back in the thirties which was so ahead of its time and still has present-day audiences falling about — the supreme test of brilliance. Groucho's success has been proved by the fact that he lasted longer than the rest. I met him in Hollywood many years ago when I appeared on a television show he was doing which was a form of 'chat' show with more 'ordinary' people appearing on it than celebrities, but all withering under the incredible Groucho wit and wicked cynicism. I had just read a book which had been written about him by his son, describing highly entertaining events in his father's life. One hilarious moment occurred during his second wedding, when he was asked by the presiding judge if he would take this woman for his lawful wedded wife. Groucho remained completely silent. Again the judge asked the question and was met with the same silence. Finally someone nudged him and the judge repeated the question yet again, only to be given this answer from the irrepressible Groucho, 'I'm thinking it over.'

I met him again at a New Year's Eve party, given by the late Jack Benny. This was an annual and very pleasant Hollywood affair to which everyone who was anyone always went. I noticed Groucho with his famous cigar going round to different groups and staying with them, until his rather beautiful third wife arrived, then he would immediately move off. He joined my group once or twice and the same thing happened. I did not wonder too much about it as I had met one of my favourite actors, Marlon Brando, who had been extremely complimentary about some film he had seen me in, so I was rather lost in the pleasure of his flattery, a situation totally foreign to me in those days, as no-one there in the film city had ever seen any of my previous work. As midnight approached I was standing talking to a bunch of people when Groucho appeared again, and I quickly looked to see if his wife had managed to catch up with him this time and hold on, but he was alone. He regaled us with jokes and inevitably we lost track of the time. Suddenly we realised it was twelve o'clock and everybody cheered, 'Happy New Year', 'Auld Lang Syne' being played by the hired orchestra. At this moment Groucho's wife arrived and touched him on the arm. He quickly looked around to see who it was, but on finding that it was his wife, snapped 'A Happy New Year to you Madam, whoever you are,' and ran off.

M is for MOTHER

I suppose everyone thinks their mother is beautiful and I was no exception. I did not arrive until my mother was forty-two years old, and I was something of a shock, as she and my father had been married thirteen years and had given up all hope of having children. My parents met during the First World War when my mother, who had been married before to a gambler, had been widowed due to his being killed in the war. Prior to this marriage she had worked in a stately home as a lady's maid, and there had been some scandal as the son and heir had fallen in love with her and had been sent to Australia to 'outgrow' his infatuation. She held the distinction, of which she was rather proud, of being one of the first *postwomen* during the Great War. She had long hair which she could sit on, dark blue eyes, and a beautiful singing voice for which she took lessons.

I think she secretly wanted to go on the stage, but then she met my father who was a handsome dashing Captain with two or three girls always hanging on his arm. They were married in 1918. My father had served in India, France and Germany and was invalided out with an eye injury when a grenade exploded in the trenches. He also had a weak heart due to catching malaria in India. In fact the doctors told him he had only ten years at the most to live, but he outdid them, and with my mother waiting on him hand and foot (no women's lib then) he lived on for fifty-one years. When my mother cut her hair in the twenties' bob fashion, he did not speak to her for three weeks — and was I suppose, in his way, rather Victorian in outlook. He played the piano splendidly and he and my mother were very popular, living a carefree social life until my arrival. Then as my mother put it, 'Everything changed' — there were no more parties and she devoted her life to me, whilst my father went on living his usual life, drinking his beloved beer, playing cards at the club, and accompanying visiting singers at the local theatre on the piano.

My mother and I were great pals and we played many an

unsuspecting trick on my father. He did not stand a chance really poor man! We would sneak off to the cinema many afternoons when I should have been at school, which I hated, and that was how I got my first love of films. It was when I was thirteen and we were on our yearly holiday to Western-Super-Mare — my father's favourite seaside resort — that unbeknown to him, and with my mother's help, I went in for a beauty contest at the Lido swimming pool. Giving my age as seventeen, I came third! My father sitting on the beach, happily reading his *Daily Telegraph*, would never have allowed it. But I think he was quite proud when we came back with the news — little did he know this was just the beginning. The next step was my mother persuading him to let me go to London at fourteen and study at the London Academy of Music and Dramatic Art. He fought like a tiger, at first stating that the theatre was a lousy profession. But finally he relented when I said I would try and get my diploma and come back home to teach. He paid up the fees and off I went. I also got my diploma, but had *no* intention of returning and indeed by the time I was fifteen was under contract to the J. Arthur Rank Organisation and earning more than my astounded father.

My mother was delighted, and her dream about me had been fulfilled. It was sad that she, above all, did not live to see me attain really big stardom for she died in 1955, just as I was climbing to my peak. She had championed, cared for and defended me all my life, and I think that until you lose your mother you do not truly understand the saying in this life, 'Your mother is your best friend.'

M is for MOTHER-IN-LAW

It is possible to acquire several mothers-in-law during a lifetime: I have actually had three. No matter how lovely your mother-in-law happens to be, she never really thinks you are good enough for her son. I am dreading the time when it is my turn to be one for I know I will feel the same about *my* sons, but will have to smile graciously and put up with whoever is dragged in as their choice of wife.

My first mother-in-law was a dizzy sort of lady who had reached a stage in life where she kept buying frilly, silken underwear and showing it to her son, my husband, with delight and glee. I don't know what Freud would have said, but after thirty-odd years of marriage she ran off with a much younger man and that was the last we ever heard of her.

My second mother-in-law was a darling. In fact she and I got along better than I did with her son.

My third and present mother-in-law is also a dear and kindhearted soul — a very blunt Northern lady who is usually right with her opinions and advice. She has a good sense of humour and would do anything for anyone — but she will always try to keep up with the Joneses whatever happens, and when the press asked her about Alan's forthcoming marriage to me, wishing to keep the family's end up she told them that they were the only house in the road with a bay window!

Millie (for that is her name) always fought hard for her family and when she enrolled Alan, then 18, at RADA she took him to the bank to open an account. The manager asked if he was a minor. Millie, affronted, snapped back haughtily 'he is *not* — he's a student.'

The first time my parents-in-law came to see us after our marriage we took them out to a very exclusive restaurant. Millie was clearly on her best behaviour and anxious not to let the side down. She eyed the 'stiff and starchy' waiters with suspicion, and noted the cocktail-drinking people with their 'posh' Berkshire accents as she put it. Someone in our party was buying a round and asked me what I wanted. 'I'll have a Bloody Mary,' I said gaily. I saw Millie wince slightly as the host turned to her, 'What will you have?' he asked. Not wishing to appear out of place and thinking this was the way all the 'toffs' behaved, Millie threw back her head and said with a deep breath, 'Oh, I'll have a *bloody Scotch!*'

N is for NEON

To have one's name in lights in London's West End, or on Broadway as the case may be, is naturally every actor's ambition, but the real reason I have picked on this particular subject is just an excuse to tell a silly little story which is reputed to be true, regarding two actors who met one day in Piccadilly. Each enquired what the other was doing, if anything. One actor proudly announced that he was working in a current West End play entitled *I Killed the Count*. The other sadly could not boast of an acting job, but he *did* have a position with an electric light firm, who had ironically been responsible for the neon sign advertising *I Killed the Count*. 'What do you actually do?' asked his actor friend curiously. 'Oh, it's quite easy work really,' came the reply. 'I'm an "O" watcher for the neon light company!'

N is for ROBERT NEWTON

The most controversial and colourful character England has ever produced, and a brilliant actor in to the bargain. The stories about his professional and private life are unending, and when a group of people who knew him sit down for an evening, they can usually exchange so many tales about him there is no room for other conversation. His drinking was, I suppose, the thing that triggered off most of his escapades, such as the occasion when he staggered into Dame Anna Neagle's dressing-room exposing himself in front of a group of ladies as she was serving them tea, or the night in Rome when he threw a party in a nightclub and bought champagne all round, knowing full well he could not pay the bill. Long before the management could settle the matter, he pretended his wallet had been stolen and sneaked away to the airport where he was catching a plane to England.

He starred in a film I made in 1947 entitled *Oliver Twist*. One morning he did not arrive on the set as usual, and the production department telephoned his house anxiously to see if he had overslept. His wife assured them he had left in the chauffered car at the correct time, and the driver had been given explicit instructions *never* to stop at any public house on the way to the studio no matter how much pressure he was under from his passenger. The film company were at a total loss as to know what had happened to him. The hours went by, and as is the case on a film, time and money were ticking by too. Around midday everyone was assembled on the set in desperation trying to figure out what to do, when suddenly a mischievous voice from up in the gantry called out, 'Yoo Hoo'. There was the missing rebel, waving an empty bottle of whisky, having sat up there gleefully watching their panic for hours.

Newton left this country years later under a terrible cloud and never returned. He had nearly come to the end of a film entitled *Trilby and Svengali*, when his marriage problems got the better of him, so he grabbed his baby son in a carry-cot and left these shores, vowing he would never come back. He must have known that he was committing professional suicide, for no film company would ever insure him again. As it was, the entire film of *Trilby* had to be recast and shot at unbelievable expense. Right or wrong, I admired the man, for at least he had the courage of his convictions. Many actors *talk* about doing things, but that is as far as they ever get!

Probably the funniest story about Newton happened many years before he had attained stardom. He was touring as the Duke of Buckingham in a Shakespearian play with another fine actor and drinker, the late Wilfred Lawson. Naturally the pair got on very well, and did a great deal of heavy drinking together, but it never affected their performances. One day, however, the worst happened. Both drunk as monkeys, they staggered along a street and upon seeing a fishmonger's shop with all the cod's heads laid out on the slab, Wilfred was reminded that they had a matinee that very afternoon. 'My God, Robert. We've got a matinee!' he exclaimed and pulled Newton off as fast as he could.

On arrival at the theatre they rushed headlong into their dressing-rooms, and proceeded to try to climb into their costumes. Wilfred was in such a state he put his tights on twisted round the wrong way, thereby making his codpiece look like a diseased hip, but undaunted he hit the stage just in time for his cue. Owing to his inebriated state he began reeling off the lines in such a way they made no sense whatsoever, and it was quite apparent that he was tipsy! Unable to stand the performance he was giving any longer, someone from the gallery shouted out, 'You're pissed!' Wilfred stopped dead in his tracks, looked up into the darkness and remembering that his friend Newton had not yet made his entrance, snarled, 'You think I'm pissed? . . . Just wait until you see the Duke of Buckingham!'

N is for NEW YORK

Speaking of lights and theatres immediately brings this particular city to mind, for New York was once, in my opinion, the most exciting and colourful place in the world, but has now deteriorated into a ghastly concrete jungle, where it is no longer safe to walk along the sidewalks in broad daylight. When I first arrived there in 1956, it took my breath away, I had never seen anywhere so wonderful in my life, there was so much going on all round the clock, the theatres and clubs, the fascination of Chinatown, and the hurly burly of Harlem.

I have been back many, many times since, to work and play. I have also fallen in love there and once I actually got married in a friend's apartment on Park Avenue after appearing on a big television show.

Each time I returned to the city I noticed it changing, the gradual decline and fall of somewhere that had been great, the rise of the crime wave, which at one point was restricted only to small back streets and alleys, becoming so alarming that no longer was it possible to stroll peacefully in Central Park, or even feel safe in one's own hotel suite.

This last situation was really brought home to me when I appeared in cabaret once at a smart nightclub, and stayed nearby at the Hotel Americana. There had been a series of robberies in stars' hotel suites, where thousand of pounds worth of jewellery had been stolen, plus one daylight assault on film star Zsa Zsa Gabor in an elevator, when she was relieved of some diamonds! The New York police department decided it was time to act *before* the criminals, and so, one night just before I went to the club to perform, I received a call from them asking if I would allow two of their men to stay in my hotel suite for the night whilst I was working, as they had reason to believe I might be next on the list. I readily agreed, and before I left a kind of Starsky and Hutch pair presented themselves at my door, I was rather reluctant to leave them as I found it all quite exciting, and far more interesting than going off to do my show, but I told the policemen to make themselves comfortable, and went to the club. I did not return until nearly four a.m. when I found the detectives still crouched in uncomfortable positions under the bed and behind the curtains, no doubt they had been hiding in wait like this all the time for the prospective burglars. Such was their excitement as I made my furtive entrance they nearly grabbed me! Apologising profusely, they shook hands and left assuring me that everything would be all right, but to keep my door well locked just in case. I can honestly say that it was the first and last time I had two men in my hotel room all night, and was unable to do anything about it!

N is for NUDES

At no time in my life have I ever been photographed in the nude, always there was some discreet form of cover be it fur, G string or flesh-coloured leotard.

I feel sorry for young actresses of today who, in order to begin, have to frolic around in the nude and appear in pornographic type films.

Way back in my early career though I was approached by a photographer to pose, seemingly nude, but with the essential parts of me covered up, for a picture book he was compiling in '3D', a technique devised to entice flagging audiences back to the cinema. Each customer received a pair of cardboard spectacles, one lens red, the other lens green. This was supposed to reveal the action in fascinating closeness.

All the 'peeping Toms' naturally thought they were going to see more than they normally did, but audiences soon realised it was an unsatisfactory way of viewing what was usually a load of rubbish, and so it died a natural death.

However it was all the go at this time so, for a large fee I posed for two weary days, in reclining, glamorous positions around my home, lying on tiger skins, satin bedspreads and the like, all to give the book a sensual and erotic flavour.

The book had the usual cardboard spectacles for certain anxious viewers to study my anatomy from all angles and hopefully spy something which they would not normally see with the naked eye. But like the films it actually revealed nothing.

A year or two later I was chosen to star in *A Kid for Two Farthings* directed by the late Sir Carol Reed. This was most important for me and it was like being chosen to appear at Buckingham Palace — but, as usual, my past caught up with me.

Certain magistrates in Halifax had decided that the book *Diana Dors in 3D* was obscene, and having announced this fact to the press, retired for a month to read it, (thereby having a damn good look through the cardboard spectacles) in order to consider it.

'Halifax Magistrates Declare Diana Dors Obscene' screamed the newspapers, once again I was at the centre of a 'storm in a teacup' and hating every moment of it. They finally returned a verdict in my favour, it was truly a harmless book, but because of their month of leering and looking the damage was done and I was labelled with the tag of posing for obscene pictures.

One may think time heals all, but some ten years later, after several respected films, a trip to Hollywood, and having become a mother, a rather aristocratic friend introduced me to his aunt one day. After I left, the old girl was still in the dark as to who I really was. 'She is Diana Dors the film actress,' my friend explained. 'Oh yes,' came her eventual reply. '*That's* the one who posed for those dirty pictures once isn't it?'

N is for RUDOLF NUREYEV

Like everyone else, I am a great admirer of this fabulous ballet dancer, but unfortunately the occasion I met him was not as artistically choreographed as his theatre productions.

Nureyev was brought to my house one Sunday afternoon quite unexpectedly and had I known of his impending arrival I would have made arrangements accordingly, for it was not every day I had an international star of such magnitude gate-crashing my home on the off-chance of a cup of tea.

From the start things went wrong, his entrance, swathed in white leather from head to foot, looking rather like Marlene Dietrich, was obviously intended to be somewhat spectacular and get us all going, but unluckily for him the whole thing was marred by bad timing. An old flame of mine with whom I have stayed friends all these years, namely 'Dandy' Kim Waterfield, chose quite coincidentally to make a descent into the garden in his gleaming new blue and white helicopter, which was a very difficult arrival for anyone to compete against. As everyone milled around Kim and his aircraft, admiring it, asking what it was like to fly around in, and pop down to friends' houses miles away for a drink, Nureyev quietly slunk into the drawing-room, white leather and all, and hunched in an armchair looking extremely sullen.

Surprisingly enough no-one really took very much notice of him. Indeed the only ones who showed him any attention at all were my two boxer dogs, who leapt all around him with their usual high spirits, looking somewhat like canine Nureyevs themselves!

Relations between East and West were not entirely improved when a boyfriend of mine who happened to be in residence playing host that day, asked him what he would like to drink, and received the rather haughty reply, 'I only drink Russian Vodka.' My boyfriend, taken slightly aback by this statement on a Sunday afternoon in the country, and a trifle worried as he knew there was none, jokingly replied, 'I'm sorry we don't have any of that, but if you fancy it there's a bottle of Tizer in the fridge.'

An hour or so rolled by and still only the dogs and Nureyev were making contact. Actually thinking back to some of the people there at the time, he was probably happier to remain in the company of canines than humans, for not another word passed his lips after the Tizer affair.

During the afternoon however I saw Nureyev slip through the French windows when no-one was looking, and presumed he was merely going to accompany his doggy friends on a stroll around the garden. Some minutes later I perceived the dogs joyfully 'cocking their legs' in the rhododendron bushes, but Nureyev decided to go one better! Having slyly surveyed the offending aircraft which had stolen his thunder, he got his revenge by relieving himself against the tail!

I can assure my reader it was not the sort of performance for which he usually received great acclaim from a Covent Garden audience, and it certainly would not have been artistically appreciated by Kim either, who at that moment was blissfully unaware his machine was being defiled.

Finally it was time to go, but his exit was eclipsed by the sudden and once again unwitting decision on Kim's part to leave at the same time. As Nureyev crept out of the door, the rest of the party did not even see him go, for they were all too busy waving goodbye in the heavy downdraft of the helicopter.

If all this seems like a rather rude reception for so talented a person, then it is with sincerity I extend my belated apologies to Rudolf Nureyev and promise that next time he ever graces my home, I will be sure to have more than a bottle of Tizer put aside for him.

O is for OEDIPUS

It came as a great surprise to me to be asked to appear at the highly artistic Chichester Theatre opposite Keith Michell, who was Director of Drama there, in the 1974 summer production of the classic play *Oedipus*, by the Greek playwright Sophocles.

We rehearsed the play for five gruelling weeks under a mad Armenian producer named Hovannis Pilliakin, and opened one warm summer evening to fairly good notices. Keith looked resplendent as the tyrant Oedipus and in case anyone is not familiar with the story, I played his mother with whom it is found out, as the story unfolds, he is having an affair! This was all written five thousand years ago in Greece, and naturally one had to rely on a great deal of imagination as to what the characters were REALLY thinking about it all. Whether this sort of thing happens there today, perhaps only a true Greek descendant, like my old friend Telly Savalas could inform me of and with his gift of the gab he could make anyone believe anything! However the play grinds to a ghastly halt with Jocasta (that was me) hanging herself and Oedipus gouging his eyes out on stage after the terrible discovery that he had been making love to his mother, and not his wife, as he thought all along.

As one may imagine there were some pretty serious emotional scenes between us, especially the final one when I am on my knees crying and begging him not to be too upset, and he is crying and tearing his hair out in handfuls, swearing dreadful oaths as to what is going to become of us both.

Now I do not know if it is widely known amongst people who are not in the theatre that actors, after a very long run of say months, or sometimes years, do tend to have their lines off 'parrot fashion' when a certain time has elapsed, and they have all settled down to a monotonous run of six nights a week and two matinees. The mind does seem to wander on stage at times, and though one is speaking the lines, one's mind is elsewhere. It is a dangerous course to

175

take as suddenly, when you stop thinking about whether you have remembered to phone the butcher and order the weekend joint, or if the laundryman is calling that day, you suddenly realise where you are and what you are doing — and nine times out of ten forget your lines completely in the panic of the moment. This had happened to me several times in the West End, but luckily it did not happen to me *exactly* like that at Chichester, although the resulting panic was just the same.

Before I left home one day to perform a matinee, I had asked the nurse, who was looking after my son Jason, to turn off the oven, where I had placed a turkey, at a definite time in the evening. I reminded her again before I left saying that if she forgot we would have no Sunday dinner as the bird would be burnt to a cinder.

The matinee commenced, and Keith and I reached the last tragic scene with me on my knees looking pleadingly up into his face. He had, amongst other clever make-up tricks, built himself a putty nose in order to look more like the character. This transformed his features completely. As I spoke my lines and begged him not to think badly of me, with tears rolling down my face, he suddenly looked remarkably like the turkey I had left in the oven. I think it was the putty nose that did it as that afternoon his hands must have slipped a little, and it looked more like a beak! Immediately I started wondering and worrying whether the nurse, who was a rather dozy Welsh girl, *would remember* to turn the oven off, and what would I do about food for the next day's meal if she did not. All this time of course I was acting my socks off, and the audience were not aware that such mundane thoughts were racing around in my mind, so lost were they in the emotion of the scene.

Eventually, as Keith leapt into the air disowning me as his mother, I came out of my reverie and realised where I was. Of course the worst happened and I could not remember the next lines for the life of me, I think I covered up by screaming and raving louder than usual — the words being wholly unintelligible to the audience thank goodness.

O is for OLIVER

Now I personally know only two Olivers, namely Twist and Reed. I had the good fortune very early on in my career to appear in *Oliver Twist* which they were making at Pinewood Studios. It was a very classy production with a host of illustrious stars like Alec Guinness and Robert Newton, and an even more illustrious director — David Lean, who has made some wonderful films — such as *The Bridge over the River Kwai*. The fact that he made overtures to me in the drawing room one day and then got frightened, as I was only fifteen, and gave up the idea, taught me one of my first lessons that even genius directors are men when it comes down to the nitty gritty. I was so heavily made up as the slut Dickensian maid, Charlotte, in

the coffin maker's shop, that not many people even to this day know I was in the film. One person who recognised me and memorised some of my dialogue (I've never known why) was Sammy Davis Junior. He was so tickled by my rough treatment of Oliver and my indulgence of the horrible character Noah Claypole, that when I first met him many years later he chanted my lines, 'I've saved a nice bit of bacon from the master's supper for you, Noah dear.' I was amazed he had remembered them for I had certainly forgotten. On one occasion when he was opening in cabaret in Hollywood I sent him a first night wire with the words, 'I've saved a nice bit of bacon from the master's supper for you Sammy dear — provided you are a success tonight.'

Oliver was played by a little eight year old cherub of a boy named John Howard-Davies. Some days David Lean who was patience personified with him, would have to bribe him with chocolate to do a scene if he didn't feel like it. Anthony Newley was also in the film and marvellous as the Artful Dodger. He was the same age as me and now we are all grown up and much, much older! Our little Oliver is a producer in television, and amongst other work was responsible for the highly successful *Steptoe and Son* series.

The other Oliver (Reed) I never actually met but have followed his career and frantic attempts in real life to be a hell-raiser, drinker, and womaniser with great amusement. He is attractive of course. But I do not like the way he knocks his fellow actors in print, and I was surprised when once he even turned upon poor Raquel Welch saying she was not as sexy as him. In her defence I must state that Oliver Reed has not always been the strong, masculine hunk he is seen to be on screen. Way back in 1955 when I was starring in a comedy film called *Value for Money*, who should come mincing on with one line as a fairy chorus boy, but our hero Oliver! I realise of course that all actors have to start somewhere and I often look back and shudder at many of my old films on television. But at least I have never appeared as a butch lesbian!

O is for SIR LAURENCE OLIVIER

This noble knight, I consider to be the only actor in England to really warrant a title. He is now of course *Lord* Olivier, but when I first met him he was still a *Sir*.

My heart beat excitedly when I was told that he was in the audience at a theatre where I was enjoying a fantastic success in a revue back in 1952. He had come to 'look me over', as they say, for a film he was about to make entitled *The Beggar's Opera*, but it never came to fruition for I had so many offers on the strength of my success that for the first time in my career I did not know which one to accept, and I was just twenty years old.

The next time we met was at the premiere of my best film *Yield to the Night*. He was there alone and after the performance he came up to me and said, 'Bravo.' One word from an actor like Olivier is worth a thousand more from others.

The years went by and my career went steadily down and down, until by the middle sixties I was forced to leave my children in Hollywood where we had all been living, and come home to England in order to make money by trading on a screen name that had once been big. I started doing cabaret in working men's clubs all over the country, cracking jokes about my former sexy image, and putting up with all the shouting, leering and in some cases bottle throwing that went on whilst I was on stage.

On one occasion I was due to appear in Newcastle at a club, and as it was Good Friday the manager had been refused a licence to open, so I was left with an evening to spare. The stately drama theatre was boasting a production which starred Michael Redgrave and Joan Plowright, Lady Olivier, as she was by then. Sir Cedric Hardwicke, a marvellous actor of many Hollywood films, had a son named Edward, and he invited me to see the play that evening.

Afterwards he insisted we go back stage to congratulate Joan on her performance. I did not know her, but he assured me she knew we were going to be in the audience and wanted to meet me. Sure enough she greeted me with

180

great warmth, and after an amusing half hour in the dressing room, invited us both back to the hotel where she and Sir Laurence were staying. I declined at once, muttering something about 'his not wanting to see *me* at that time of night', but she refused to listen and ushered us into her waiting car and back to the hotel for supper.

Sir Laurence greeted me with the same warmth his wife had shown, and as we talked my eye caught sight of a salad supper for two laid on the table in the corner. 'Heavens,' I thought, 'they were going to dine together alone, and now I'm here.' Knowing English hotels I also realised that after a certain time there was no chance of an added order or two being sent up.

I chattered on and eventually Joan said, 'Come on Diana, sit here with me and let's eat, you must be starving.' 'But what about you?' I asked Sir Laurence. 'Oh never mind,' he answered gallantly, 'I had something earlier on, just tuck in.' I knew he was merely being courteous and Edward Hardwicke who probably felt as embarassed as I, hastily said he had eaten too, which I knew was untrue for he had been with me all evening.

Desperately I tried not to steal Sir Laurence's supper and continued to argue, but he finally pushed me into his chair at the table and *made* me eat.

As the night wore on, and I began to relax, we became great friends, sitting there until four in the morning telling stories and jokes which had us all crying with laughter. I also found his language as salty as mine which came as a surprise, but a nice one, for I remember thinking that here was probably the greatest and most respected actor in the world — and he was as natural and human as it was possible for anyone to be!

Long, long after that night in Newcastle, which hardly sounds as glamorous as say 'that night in Monte Carlo', I was making a film at Pinewood and lunching in the studio restaurant heavily disguised with a red wig. Suddenly, there was a flurry near my table and up came Lord Olivier, as he was by then, arms outstretched, uttering cries of welcome.

I do not know how he knew it was me under all that

make-up, for he was the only one in that restaurant that did, but the incident touched me. It also impressed everybody else there too, for the film's publicity man came up to me later that afternoon and informed me the whole studio was buzzing with the news that Lord Olivier had actually seen fit to come to my table. Such is show business!

O is for OPAL

This beautiful precious stone is not the only kind of Opal in the world. Years ago when Dennis and I were first married, living on air and the occasional water softener which he used to sell for a firm he sometimes worked for, we found it necessary to purchase, out of our limited funds, a very cheap tiny car which boasted 'Opal' as its trade name. The man who sold it to us was also very broke and he let it go for fifty pounds. So we were delighted about the deal until we got it home and found out what an error we had made. Obviously if we had had the time to consider the situation, we would have realised that the wretched thing was useless mechanically, but we were stuck with it, and at every opportunity the Opal broke down — be it country lanes or busy London streets. It had no sense of discrimination at all!

Now when I say we were broke, I do not mean we were down to our last few thousand, I mean we often did not have the price of a meal. One may wonder why this was so, but I was only twenty, had been dropped by the Rank Organisation, was being offered no films or theatre work, and was, as Dennis so aptly put it, 'A has been before I had been anywhere.'

The same could also be said of him. He had tried acting in his early youth, but found it a very unsatisfactory profession, and so had drifted into all sorts of other areas, until he stumbled upon the water-softener market, and *me!* We got married at Caxton Hall in a blaze of publicity. But that was that. At this point in our lives we were living like hermits, miles away from London in a house for which finally we could not even pay the rent, and had to do a moonlight flit. It may seem incongruous to readers that the Diana Dors they have always followed in a world of luxury, glamour and big expensive cars, was really like so many other unfortunate actresses — penniless in the early part of her career.

One weekend Dennis and I drove off in the Opal, with our fingers crossed, to visit an old school friend of his. He was an extraordinary fellow who lived near Woburn, in Bedfordshire, with a vast family of brothers and sisters, and a father who once had been a Major in the army, but who had fallen on hard times and went around poaching rabbits. David's mother was related to the American film star Gary Cooper. I know this to be true for she showed me the photographs of their mutual grandmother, a Miss Cooper, who was the living image of the now late Gary. However when I met him in Hollywood years and years later, and informed him of his family connections in England, he merely looked quite blank and answered with his famous throaty gulp . . . To be fair though, he *had* consumed a large amount of alcohol at the time, and was probably not too sure of what I was saying anyway.

However, Dennis's old school friend was *also* a bit of a poacher. Indeed he would nick anything if he could find it, and was employed at that time in a tree-stump blasting project, which was not paying too well. He and Dennis went out shooting one day, but having bagged nothing came dejectedly back to the house leaving the dinner table sadly empty. Suddenly he had an idea. 'I know where there are some beautiful hens not far from here,' he stated. 'But how can you go and shoot them?' I asked rather stupidly. 'We don't shoot the buggers, we nick 'em,' he announced firmly, rubbing his hands together with glee. And so without further ado Dennis, who also considered it an excellent idea, bundled us into the car and away we went.

It was an appalling night, dark, windy and pouring with rain. 'This is it,' he announced as we drew near a small farm which could only just be seen through the waterlogged windows, at which point he and Dennis leapt out of the car, leaving me sitting there alone feeling rather like half the team of *Bonnie and Clyde*, and wondering whatever my father would say if he knew what I was up to!

After what seemed ages they returned triumphant with two sacks and got into the car, soaked, but pleased with the capture of six hens. Dennis tried to start the engine, but at that moment the Opal decided it was time for another breakdown. No amount of encouragement or threatening would shift her into action. As one may imagine there was now an awful lot of noisy grinding and wheezing going on under the bonnet. Naturally, the farmer, whose poultry they had just cheerfully pillaged, came out with a lantern to see what was going on.

'Hide the bloody chickens', ordered Dennis, winding down his window and giving the man a big smile. 'We seem to be stuck,' he said helplessly. 'I'll take a look for you,' replied the obliging farmer. So saying he hung up his lantern on a nearby tree and proceeded to lift the bonnet and peer underneath. Dennis got out, hovering by his side, but it was left to us to control the birds.

They were not dead as I had thought, but extremely angry at being disturbed from their roost!

As the farmer tinkered with the Opal outside, the storm became even worse, whilst inside were his prize hens which we had to try and bat down each time they poked their heads out of the sacks. All this was easier said than done, however, for some managed to escape and were now flying round the interior of the car, clucking and flapping their wings. Luckily there *was* a storm, for had it been a calm summer evening their owner would have certainly heard all the loud protesting cackles! Mercifully, the Opal merely needed some minor adjustment, and Dennis thanked the farmer giving him a small monetary sum, and drove off with the still flapping birds. It certainly taught us two lessons that night. Never steal chickens again, and *never* buy another Opal!

P is for PEERS

Whilst I am still on the subject of the aristocracy, foreign or otherwise, I may as well deal with a few of the popular English 'peers.' Four actually come to my mind straight away, and by an odd circumstance I know all of them well, probably because they associate with show business people and the masses, unlike many of their stuffier counterparts.

Lumping them together they sound rather like stops on a railway, Montagu, Lichfield, Bedford and Bath, but of the four, the oldest friend I can boast is Edward Montagu, for he and I go back to 1954, whereas my acquaintance with the others came later. The Marquis of Bath was the second peer I met, at a pop festival in his stately home 'Longleat,' which by then had been turned over to the public to view for half a crown a time! In those days, apart from installing ferocious lions to stroll around the grounds thus giving the place a jungle flavour, he also organised many pop festivals in order to cater for the teenage market. Henry is a marvellous character, tall and aesthetic, he and his sons personify the typical old feudal barons of England when it comes to their estates and heritage, but their general mode of behaviour was, and still is, far from ordinary and conformist, for all Henry's sons were forerunners of the permissive society.

The eldest, Viscount Weymouth, lives in a section of the magnificent palace at Longleat, sporting a beard, ear-rings, hair tied back in a bow, and painting as fast as he can get the canvasses on the walls. As he does not do much other than this, one may imagine his rooms are covered with them, certainly he never needs to buy wallpaper! Alexander is remote from the rest of the family, completely and delightfully 'nutty,' and of course he is the heir to the title and estate. The second son, Lord Christopher Thynne, is, amongst other things, a photographer. When I last met him at a party at Lord Montagu's, he tried to get me to help organise a series of nude pictures of up-and-coming actresses for *Playboy* magazine, which he seemed to think with my help would be a howling success. He was probably right, but the idea never got off the ground. I was

185

Bath and Montague

invited to Christopher's wedding a few years back, but as usual I was filming somewhere and had to miss out on a good time. Unhappily the whole affair hit a sour note when the newly weds arrived at London airport to fly off on their honeymoon, and were found to be in possession of a great amount of 'pot.' This hit the press, and subsequently the court, hardly getting the marriage off on a dignified start.

Henry's youngest son, Lord Valentine Thynne was really the first Chelsea drop-out and 'hippy' way back in the very early Sixties when long hair and all that sort of thing was still frowned upon, consequently his behaviour received a great deal of colourful publicity and criticism.

The Baths are an interesting family, and I am proud to know them. If Henry's sons hardly present a typically aristocratic picture, then who can be surprised when their father has openly described himself as an admirer of Adolf Hitler, possesses several water colours done by him, and also made a large bid on one occasion for the Fuhrer's lavatory seat? The mind boggles when one imagines the

Marquis of Bath sitting there performing his morning ablutions on a swastika covered toilet!

The third peer I do not know so well, but have met several times. He is the Duke of Bedford, who inherited Woburn Abbey somewhat reluctantly from his predecessor and proceeded to turn it into a grand funfair and side-show. Always ready to do anything for newspaper space, and an all round good sport, my first meeting with him was in Australia, and the second occasion was when he and his wife, the delightful Duchess Nicole, who had once been in show-business herself, came to Hollywood and were invited to just about every party there was during the season.

My last meeting was much more personal. I was appearing very successfully in a West End play entitled *Three Months Gone* for which I received fantastic notices, thus rejuvenating my flagging career again. Amongst all the other illustrious folk who climbed the rather dirty stairs to my dressing room, were the Duke and Duchess of Bedford themselves. The Duchess was radiant and sparkling with diamonds from head to foot, and both were extremely complimentary of my performance. This is the sort of moment when an actress's career suddenly seems worthwhile, and one drinks the wine of success and flattery with relish to make up for all the bad times.

The fourth and most handsome peer is Lord Lichfield, cousin of the Queen, until recently one of the most eligible bachelors in the country, and a very 'today' type person, whose main work is photography. I first met him on a television show way back in the early Sixties when he was quite young, very handsome, and about to launch an elegant clothes boutique in America called The Belted Earl. After this I ran into him at various parties where he usually had a famous beauty hanging on his arm, and in some cases, such as Britt Ekland, ex-wife of Peter Sellers, had quite a struggle to shake them off. On one occasion we judged a beauty contest together in Birmingham, and it was a most enjoyable night, for Patrick is a great raconteur, which enabled us to laugh the night away!

But back to my first peer, and dearest friend Lord Montagu. We met in 1954, when he was going through a crisis due to some scandal and persecution. Such was Edward's character, he knuckled down and made the best of what must have been an appalling situation to a man of his position.

Edward had inherited the beautiful stately home, Palace House, from his father, but at the time it was crumbling and nearly in the bankruptcy court. It is a tribute to his determination and business acumen that he lifted it right out of the doldrums, opened it to the public and, like the Duke of Bedford, was always ready for a new and good publicity gimmick or idea. I have sampled his hospitality many times, both at Palace House and also at the lovely beach home where he retreats for peace and privacy away from the prying eyes of the public who visit Beaulieu. We have sunbathed on beaches in Venice, dined in expensive restaurants the world over, and I have also attended some of his fancy dress balls which are always done on a highly spectacular level. Edward loves to entertain, mixing all kinds of different people together. His energy knows no bounds, which is why he has now transformed the crumbling old stately home into a million-pound business.

I have often envied him and thought how nice it must be to be born into such splendour, especially one day when we were cruising along the river in his smooth motor boat, which was being driven at quite a speed! Noticing other people in their boats, not to mention fishermen looking somewhat annoyed at the terrific backwash he was causing by doing this, I remarked rather cautiously that he seemed to be angering them.

'Well why shouldn't I go fast?' he observed casually, 'It's *my* river.' On the other side of the coin though, like anything else in life there are situations which are not always pleasant. One day his six-year-old son and heir, Lord Ralph, was viewing the enormous estate with Edward. Suddenly he stared up into his father's face and exclaimed gleefully, 'Just think, when you *die* all this will be mine!'

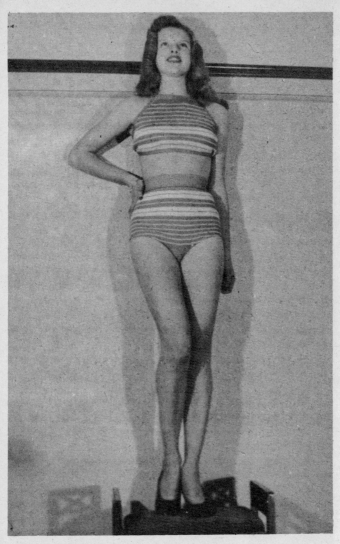

P is for PIN-UP

Aged 15!

P is for PISCES

Scorpios, such as I, do get along well with this sign, as we are both water ones, and indeed many friends of mine are Pisceans, including my present agent, who happily has not turned out to be like all the rest, as dealt with under 'A' for agents at the beginning of this book. Pamela Mason, ex-wife of the actor James, is a Piscean, and without doubt the most brilliant, amusing, and devastating friend I have ever had . . . ANY woman who fires the lawyer, and conducts her own divorce case as Pamela did because she was able to do a better job, could only be born under the sign of Pisces or Scorpio. I have never actually gone as far as that, but Pamela won herself a million-dollar settlement into the bargain!

Good people, these Pisceans, their only problem is those two damn fish swimming in opposite directions!

P is for POLICEMEN

Now I have nothing against these keepers of the peace, in fact truly I think they do a marvellous job, dangerous and poorly paid. Besides in this world you must 'fight fire with fire', which is a politer way of saying 'set a thief to catch a thief'. Policemen, all things considered, are not a bad group, though they do tend, like anyone else who climbs into uniform, to get carried away with power, but there are good ones and bad ones, and for the good ones I am grateful.

I have had a few brushes with the law, not always necessarily in court, as happily most of these have been confined to traffic offences and the like. But I can think of two occasions when my experiences were, to say the least, extremely odd.

The first was back in 1958 whilst driving my big American car through the borough of Hammersmith in London. I was not actually at the wheel, but a boyfriend who drove very well was, and obeyed all the signals given. It just so happened, that morning, there was a particularly bad-tempered policeman on duty and in a fit of pique he would not allow us to turn right as we wished, but irritably waved us on. We indicated that to go straight forward would have taken us away from our destination, and also there was no sign stating we should not turn right, but he shouted something officious and refused to let us go. I have always been a rebel when it comes officialdom, so I reacted angrily by saying, 'Go on, drive down there anyway'. As we did so, going at a speed of no more than five to ten miles an hour the constable obviously saw 'red' because we had disobeyed him, took a flying leap on to the bonnet of the car, as though he was trying to stop a getaway car after a bank raid, and lay there spreadeagled until we came to a stop. The crowds milling around the street all gasped, as they too probably thought it was a policeman doing his job and catching some gangsters. With this he blew his whistle very loudly, thereby summoning several more of his colleagues to come running to the scene of the crime as if he were in danger. By the time he had climbed off, and run to my side of the car window, hammering on it with his fist, and causing my pet poodle to bark hysterically, my boyfriend had got out of the car, and walked round to him.

He remonstrated with the constable, and asked him to stop pounding the vehicle, but made the mistake of catching hold of his arm to prevent him from doing it further (I say 'mistake', for later in court it was described as technical assault by the prosecution), and after a lot of fuss and bother, the policeman hauled us both to the local police station, where my boyfriend was detained in custody for several hours.

Amidst blazing publicity, as it is not every day a policeman goes for a ride on a film star's Cadillac, the case was brought before the magistrates, and after long deliberation they decided as magistrates do when they think that they do not like the look of someone, to fine my friend and take his licence away for a year. So much for British justice!

My other affair with a policeman, and I do not mean it in the romantic sense, was the case of a homosexual estate agent I once knew whose one ambition was to have an affair with a policeman, whilst he kept his helmet on a table at the side of the bed! One afternoon when I quietly sat in my drawing room the bell rang at my front door. My housekeeper answered, and came in looking rather nervous saying, 'It's the police madam', so I went to see what they wanted.

Instead of a couple of members of the flying squad, a young man stood there in plain clothes. He identified himself as being from the local police station and showed me his card, so I made polite conversation for a while, but was curious as to what he really wanted. Eventually, looking a trifle embarrassed, he said, 'I was wondering if you could help me Miss Dors, you see I want to leave the force and get a job as a male fashion model. I thought perhaps you might be able to advise me as to where to go and what to do?' I was, for once in my life, taken somewhat aback, as it is not exactly an every-day occurrence to find a policeman at one's door wanting to become a model. However I gave him names of several agencies I thought might help him, and away he went. I asked my estate agent friend, whom I suspected was the culprit behind the matter, what had become of him afterwards, and it appears that his modelling career did not go too well, but he was fortunate enough to meet an elderly widow, who died eventually and left him all her money, so his story ended happily.

P is for PRIESTS AND PRANKS

Regardless of the picture on the back of this book, and my references to Catholicism, I like to think that my sense of humour regarding the church is on the same par as comedian Dave Allen who never stops joking about religion, and getting a little harmless laugh here and there in the process. Most Catholic priests that I am fortunate enough to know, are marvellous people, with a great sense of humour themselves, and very modern up to date knowledge about today's world, unlike their former heads of office seemed to be in the bad old days.

The first and most unconventional priest I ever knew had better be nameless, as apart from his sense of humour, love of life, and many of the good things he did for people, especially boys' clubs in London, he overstepped the mark by allowing himself to be drawn into a big robbery which once took place on the Riviera at the home of film magnate Jack Warner. The last I saw of him was in Hollywood where he was living it up like a movie star. Fortunately most priests do not choose to go this route, and it has always seemed a sad thing to me that when a priest *does* leave the straight and narrow, for after all they are only human, then all the other ones are blamed and catalogued in the same way.

However this story deals with an actor who was merely portraying a priest on television, and who allowed himself to be brought back to my flat in London one evening after a cocktail party we had all attended in connection with the television company. He was still sporting the clerical costume and collar he had been asked to wear for press photographs, and I hasten to add at this stage two important points. One that he was a male nymphomaniac, and two, he was easily influenced by that Master of Tricksters and Pranks, actor Harry Fowler, who can usually talk anyone into doing anything.

It took no time at all for Harry to convince the actor concerned that I was at the centre of a call-girl racket along with some anonymous American, and if he came back to the pad, girls in abundance could be brought for his pleasure. Harry also insisted that he keep his priest outfit on as an extra bit of excitement to fool the girls and perhaps turn them on. What the poor misguided fellow did not know was that *he* was the one being set up for a prank, and that the girls in question arriving at Harry's command knew exactly who and what he was, despite his persistence in wearing dark glasses for fear of being recognised.

The fun commenced with two pretty girls giving the dumbfounded actor the 'works' in a spare bedroom, with a crowd of people including myself, Harry and many well

195

known stars and titled folk, all spying through the window from the balcony outside. The actor, safe behind his dark glasses, thought the girls really believed him to be a genuine priest, and solemnly took their confessions, whilst they played their parts to perfection, allowing him the courtesy of thinking he was incognito and obviously in his opinion acting the role as well as he did on the TV screen.

At length the game came to an end, and the 'priest' having had his kicks, ran off through the front door and as far away from the flat as possible before anyone became aware, he thought, of his true identity, leaving us all, girls included, helpless with laughter at the preposterousness of the situation.

The final irony of the entire scene came the following day, when sitting in a smart hairdressing establishment being shampooed, the aforementioned actor's wife, a rather snooty lady whom I had not seen for some time, loomed over me saying in a loud voice 'Hello darling, I only said to my husband the other day what a long time it has been since we met . . .' I managed to stifle a smile as I agreed with her, and wondered what she would have thought if she had caught sight of her spouse scurrying down the corridor away from his audience the night before.

P is for PUBLICITY

Publicity is the life-blood of showbusiness, and I have had, as everyone knows, more than my fair share of it, but oddly enough never by design. Most people at some time in their careers decide to employ a press agent, who, in return for their money, provides them with as much newspaper and general publicity as possible. But, contrary to popular belief, I have *never* had to do this. In the first place my husband Dennis Hamilton had a remarkable talent for creating publicity, and in the second, rather like the late Errol Flynn, things always seemed to have happened to me in such a way as to make sensational headline publicity without my courting it.

One typical instance happened years ago whilst living on my delightful fifteenth-century farm in Sussex. One afternoon as I sunbathed in the garden, I noticed an aeroplane circling round and round in the sky above me. Gazing lazily at it, I realised it was coming down lower and amusedly thought maybe the pilot was trying to have a better look at me, particularly as I was wearing a bikini at the time.

Gradually the plane came so low that I could see the pilot clearly and he waved his hand. I waved back not wishing to be impolite, but then an amazing thing happened. He landed there and then in one of my fields!

I left my sunchair and hurried towards the plane. As he climbed out smiling I noticed a bundle of letters in his hand. 'Good afternoon,' he said, 'I've brought some mail from your last address. You see I'm married to your ex-cleaner. Instead of posting them, she thought I should bring them personally.' I quelled my desire to ask how a charwoman's husband could afford to fly around in his own plane, and duly invited him in for tea.

Having delivered the mail, and consumed tea and biscuits, he announced it was time to fly off. Together we went to his little plane, where he took a photograph of me standing by it, climbed in, waved once more, and started up the field.

Now up to this point, aside from the rather unique situation of a charwoman's husband delivering my letters by plane nothing more would probably have been heard or thought about the matter, but as the propellor whirled and the engine roared for take-off, this plane left the ground and suddenly crashed into some telegraph wires running along on the other side of the field. There was an enormous bang, and I rushed towards the plane in a panic expecting to find him a mangled heap. To my utter astonishment the plane which was in a mangled heap lay there in pieces, but he was upright, untouched and walking towards me with a big grin on his face. 'Well that was a close shave,' he exclaimed cheerfully, as though he had merely dented the machine. 'Are you all right?' I gasped, and he assured me he was, if a trifle shaken. This event led to the sort of publicity which I am renowned for. Local police rushed to the scene of the accident, and before an hour had passed, the press were onto it. 'Pilot falls out of the sky trying to glimpse Diana Dors' went the sort of headlines connected with the story all over the country. Once again the die was cast, and show-business folk thought my press agent and I had been at it again! How could I explain that I was merely sunbathing in my own garden on a quiet Sunday afternoon . . . ?

Worse was to come for the pilot, however, for it turned out that the plane was not his after all, but a rented one that he often played with. Furthermore, and much to his chagrin I would imagine, it was rumoured there might be some sort of liaison with the wife of the airport's owner, and what the two of them explained to the unhappy husband afterwards I do not know!

By the same token though there is a saying, that 'all publicity is good publicity.' But it can seriously effect an artiste's reputation on occasions and I do not subscribe to this theory. The swimming pool incident in Hollywood ruined my career for a long while, despite the world publicity it created. And pop singer P.J. Proby, a great friend of mine, never made a come back after his accidental trouser-splitting affair. In fact to this day people still talk about it as if he had committed a serious crime.

My last word on the subject of the adverse effects of publicity concerns actor Tom Bell, who was unlucky enough to get a little too drunk at a luncheon honouring Prince Philip. When the Prince stood up to make one of his famous speeches, Tom, in a state of excitement, called out, 'Say something funny!' If analysed, it was not a particularly offensive statement, cheeky perhaps but worse things have been said to royalty in the past. But the result was that for many many years Tom was ostracised by many people in show-business, and, brilliant actor that he is, his career has only just begun to recover.

P is for PUNCTUALITY AND PRINCES

One of the first things I remember being taught at school was the saying 'punctuality is the politeness of princes,' and I am sure this is correct. Certainly the politest people I know are always punctual and I too make it a rule never to be late for an appointment, for as I loathe to be kept waiting myself, I do not like doing the same to others.

A bitter lesson I learned after arriving in Hollywood was that no-one is ever on time, especially for a party or dinner. To be first through the door there is to appear over-eager. It is also not casual enough and this is what everyone tries desperately hard to be, no matter what is at stake. When inviting people to dinner I would name an appropriate time, allowing for them to be a few minutes late, and then serve cocktails before dinner. This way I did not have to rush them to the table as soon as my cook announced that it was ready. In England this would have been fine, but not Hollywood. The first time I threw a dinner party there I waited at seven-thirty for my guests to turn up, the Martinis were iced and ready, but no one appeared. By eight o'clock I was growing a bit anxious, and at eight-thirty, positively alarmed, for now cocktail time had come to an end, and the cook was throwing a fit saying the dinner had been ready to serve for fifteen minutes, and it was all going to be ruined.

Having persuaded her to keep it simmering, I telephoned the guests who said blithely that they were just that moment leaving, no apologies were made for the delay, and when they did arrive I rushed them like Olympic runners to the dining-room with no pre-dinner drinks, which no doubt they thought was an odd British custom. After this disaster the cook handed in her notice and I realised there was a code out there which people used for dinner party invitations, so having made several more attempts, I finally got the hang of the game. If one wanted people to come at a certain time then one made sure they were invited at least two hours earlier than necessary, thereby allowing for the carefully late and casual arrivals.

Long before this however, at home in England, I gave

dinner parties in the normal way, and it was not often that my friends were late, unless of course something serious had happened to detain them. Still believing my school lesson about Punctuality and Princes, it naturally did not occur to me one evening when I actually invited a real prince to dinner, that he would be anything other than punctual. The prince in question was the new husband of actress Dawn Addams and he was acknowledged in London society as Prince Massimo. At a cocktail party one night, I met the two of them just recovering from their honeymoon, and in a happy moment invited them to my house for dinner. They accepted graciously, and on the evening concerned, with my cook preparing mouth-watering dishes in the kitchen, all timed to perfection, Dennis and I waited for them to arrive.

Time went on and they did not come, we had some other friends there too, who had arrived at the appointed time and were, after a few drinks I noticed, becoming restless and quite hungry. The cook was now making her presence felt, banging pots and pans louder than usual, just in case we had forgotten about her, but I was apprehensive about starting the meal as it was not often I had royalty to dine and, being much younger then, I cared what people might think.

Finally, after two hours had passed, and the other guests could drink no more, faint from lack of food, with conversation running a trifle thin as a result, I announced that with or without the prince we would eat and so, to the relief of all concerned, not to mention the cook, we began. It was a super dinner, despite the delay, and roughly an hour later whilst drinking coffee, we suddenly heard a ring at the front door.

'It's them,' said the cook, almost as though Frankenstein and Dracula had just arrived. Dennis's remarks were less than complimentary, he felt that as they were a good three hours late and had not even had the decency to telephone, they should be treated accordingly. He instructed the cook what to do, and so we all sat back and listened to the following conversation.

It was quite apparent that the couple were much the

worse for drink (or as the cook put it later, 'Cor, I could smell it so strong, it nearly knocked me back!'), and when they proceeded to enter announcing they had come for dinner, she stood her ground like Boadicea and stated, 'I'm very sorry, they all had their dinner at nine o'clock, it is now ten, and everybody's gone out.' 'But that's preposterous,' said the prince, 'we've only just been able to get away from a cocktail party.'

'Yes,' replied the triumphant cook. 'You were invited for seven, and it is now past ten, so you've had it!' With that, she closed the door firmly in His Highness's face, amidst great mirth from the occupants within.

I do not know what the reaction was after that, but for a few minutes there was considerable snorting and muttering outside the front door. I never met the prince again, but some twenty years later after they had been through a bitter divorce I again met Dawn, who never mentioned the incident, so I could only assume she did not remember it. Some things are better forgotten it seems, even the important lessons one learns at school.

Q is for QUEEN

Our gracious figurehead, and a lady who not only does her work well and thoroughly, but with never ending energy and enthusiasm. I have often thought that if I were the Queen of England, I would probably sit back and enjoy the privileges allotted to me as sovereign, but perform only half the duties, waving my subjects away rather like Queen Victoria did, as I was the Queen and there was nothing anyone could do about it.

I have met our Queen on two occasions, one was at the Royal Command Performance in 1955, when I merely curtsied and exchanged a few pleasantries with her, and the other was an auspicious occasion, when I was asked to go along to Windsor Castle and take part in the cabaret there at the annual Xmas party and ball, which is held for the staff, and members of the Royal Family who are staying there at the time.

There were two other acts doing the show with me, namely, the marvellous Tommy Cooper, and the unmatched comedy team of Morecambe and Wise. As usual I regarded the whole prospect with excitement, but not nerves, as unlike anyone else I know in show business, I do not and have never suffered from nervousness when performing. Many people call me 'over-confident', some perhaps even think me cocky, but it is a fact that due to my early enthusiastic ambitions about becoming an actress, I have never been able to suppress my longing to get on stage and do it, and if the critics are out front so much the better, then I really set all my motors running and give them something to look at. 'Showing off' is what it would no doubt be called in most circles!

Once when a student, I tried to make myself nervous before going in for an acting exam at the Dramatic Art Academy I was attending, merely because it seemed to me that it was the thing to do, as everyone else became racked with nerves before a performance, but all I succeeded in doing was making myself dry up and forget my lines in the middle of the play, and I vowed then that if *that* was what being nervous did for me, I would definitely stay in the driver's seat from then on.

So I set off to Windsor Castle feeling ice-cool in my normal fashion, when for all I knew Tommy Cooper and the rest were throwing up in their bathrooms at home. We were shown into a magnificent place which looked like a throne room in some Hollywood movie about Robin Hood, after weaving our way through fascinating corridors sporting suits of armour, which I longed to hang around and gaze at. The ball was already in progress in the next room, and I had no idea what it was all going to be like once I hit the stage, but undaunted I made myself ready, and awaited my cue. Tommy Cooper went on first, and from the sound of things, as always, he had them rolling on the floor with laughter. Then it was my turn. Confidently I strode out into the ballroom, quickly looking for the stage, and to my amazement found there was not one there. The sight that met me, was that of the Queen with the Queen Mother on one side of her and

Princess Anne on the other, with a few castle dignitaries filling up the front line. Behind this distinguished group were all the castle staff sitting in a sort of half horseshoe shape, and none of it was as I had imagined. At the very least I thought the Queen and members of the Royal Family would be right at the back on a platformed seating arrangement, and I would be safely a long way down from them on a stage.

As things were, it was all very informal, which, I was told afterwards, is how it always is but at the time I felt rather as though I was doing an audition for Lew and Leslie Grade, or some other theatrical producers, only in this case the adjudicator was Her Majesty. I started my act as usual with the opening number, received polite applause and went on to the next, which was a bit saucy as it was a parody on the Noel Coward song 'Let's do it'. I figured it must be going well, as I could see the Queen Mother laughing at some of the naughtier lines, and tapping her foot to the music.

It was then that it hit me as to what I was doing. I kept trying to play to the entire audience, but due to the fabulous diamonds in the Queen's tiara sparkling and twinkling in front of me, my eyes kept returning to her in a hypnotic fashion. Suddenly for the first time in my entire life, it happened, I became paralysed with nerves, for I became aware of myself as if looking through a mirror, and all I saw was Diana Fluck from Swindon standing in the middle of a large room in Windsor Castle, with the Queen sitting bolt upright in front of me, and also being forced through courtesy, to watch me for the next twenty minutes or so, whether she liked me or not. What did I think I was doing, I asked myself inwardly. How dare I stand up here in front of the Queen of England and try to entertain her?

How I got through the rest of it I will never know, but thankfully I did, and the reception I received was good, much to my surprise. After Morecambe and Wise had finished their act, we were then lined up in the throne room as I called it, and before we commenced supper, were told the Queen and her Family were coming in to meet us.

What followed next I will never forget! As this was not a formal occasion, the Queen could take her time and talk as long as she wished to everyone, particularly as she was in her own home, and not on a tight schedule, and this she took good advantage of.

When it came to my turn she congratulated me on the show, and stood there chatting away for what must have been a good five minutes, asking me about Hollywood, films I had made, especially *Yield to the Night*, and many other topics of conversation. For the first time in my life I was humble, and kept apologising for the rather risqué song I had sung at one point, but she would not hear a word against me, and added that she was sorry Princess Margaret had not been here to see it, as she was a great fan of mine.

As if this were all not enough, the Queen Mother, who is the most delightful person it is possible to meet, as she has a special way of making the person she is conversing with feel as if they are the only one in the world worth listening to, proceeded to expound on her daughter's already warm praise. When I told her that at Christmas-time I was appearing in pantomime, she clasped her hands with glee and asked excitedly, 'What are you playing?' 'The prince Your Majesty,' I replied, and then realised what a silly answer it was on my part to someone of her status. 'Oh the prince,' she cried, 'such a wonderful part isn't it?'

R is for TED RAY

I have been friends with the Ray family for many years. Father and comedian Ted was my first acquaintance when we worked together on a radio show entitled *Calling All Forces* way back in 1952. Ted was at his most popular peak due to the success of his own radio series, namely *Ray's a Laugh*. It was during this time that he introduced me to his two sons Robin and Andrew. I was eighteen years old, Robin a few years younger and studying music, Andrew barely twelve but already a child star, having been chosen to play the lead in a film called *The Mudlark*. I can remember my first meeting with his in his neat little great-coat and long socks as he politely shook hands, never dreaming one day we would become firm friends in our thirties, and that he and I would devise the wicked game of 'hotseat.' Robin has come a long way since those days too, for he is now an authority on classical music and a frequent host on television shows. However, for the time being I am dealing with 'Dad,' and though I emphatically denied the use of drugs or pills when writing about marijuana and the like, I am afraid at this juncture I must contradict myself, and confess finally, that one day all those years ago Ted Ray and I got 'high' on pills!

The place was Hamburg, Germany, one bitterly cold morning in 1952 where we had been performing a radio show for the troops stationed there with the occupational forces. Thankful to be leaving, Ted, the other stars and I arrived at the airport in readiness for the flight home. Whilst waiting in the lounge, drinking coffee, Ted asked me if I liked flying, and I replied that I was a fairly good passenger, but it depended naturally on the weather conditions. In those days there were no jets to fly above the storms, and one had to put up with the bumps and jolts of travelling in propellor-driven aircraft. Ted produced some travel pills which he assured me were marvellous when flying as they prevented any sickness one might encounter, especially on a morning such as this.

Thanking him I swallowed the prescribed two, as did he, and eventually our flight was called. We boarded the plane, but after a long wait we were all told to alight and return to the airport lounge, as the weather conditions had produced problems for the plane in some mechanical way. Wearily we did as requested and settled back to another session in the waiting-room, when suddenly Ted and I felt very strange. We began giggling and behaving in such a lighthearted way that it provoked some angry glances from our fellow passengers who were not feeling to pleased with life anyway thanks to the delay.

We could not imagine what was wrong, or why we were acting the way we were, and then it hit us . . . the air-travel pills which Ted had so liberally dosed us had started to work, and by rights we should have been up a few thousand feet instead of down on the ground. This resulted in our giddy behaviour, and there was nothing we could do to stop the wretched things from taking their course! Ted did his best to gag through the ensuing hours but by the time we *did* actually fly, the pills had stopped working, and we both felt extremely ill on the journey back.

I have never taken travel pills since, and whenever I see Ted he always reminds me of our horrifying flight from Hamburg, the day when I can say with all honesty that I was happily very briefly under the influence of drugs.

R is for SIR CAROL REED

The late and great film director who was probably the best England ever produced. Every actor and actress's ambition was to be cast in one of his films, and I was no exception. I remember one day Dennis and I were driving around Sloane Square in London and we saw Sir Carol alongside our car in his Rolls Royce. Dennis turned to me and said, 'Some day darling you will make a film with that man and it will be the beginning of real stardom for you.' His words proved to be right, for a year or so later I was given the leading role in Sir Carol's film *A Kid for Two Farthings*. This became the turning point of my career for until then I had been regarded as a publicity seeking sex symbol, but when the news broke about my being cast in this film, people's attitudes changed considerably and directors and producers, who before would have turned their backs on me, now eagerly came forward to shake my hand and get in while the going was good.

A Kid for Two Farthings was acclaimed as one of the top money spinners of 1954 and that, along with the marvellous notices, also counted a great deal with the distributors who really control the film world. The script had been written by the brilliant Wolf Mankowitz — it turned out that life had brought us together a long time before we began making the film, as during the war when children were being evacuated from London to safer areas away from Hitler's bombs, Wolf had been evacuated to the very road in Swindon where I was born and had lived. Little did I know as I looked through my mother's front window at the straggling line of children waiting to be billeted at different houses, that one of them some day was going to write a film in which I would star!

We had wonderful times working on the set because acting for Sir Carol was such a joy. He treated actors like superhuman beings and was always aware of their sensitivities and nerves. On one occasion when approached by a sound man and informed that the actors in question were not speaking loud enough for the sound system to pick up clearly, he replied, 'The mechanical

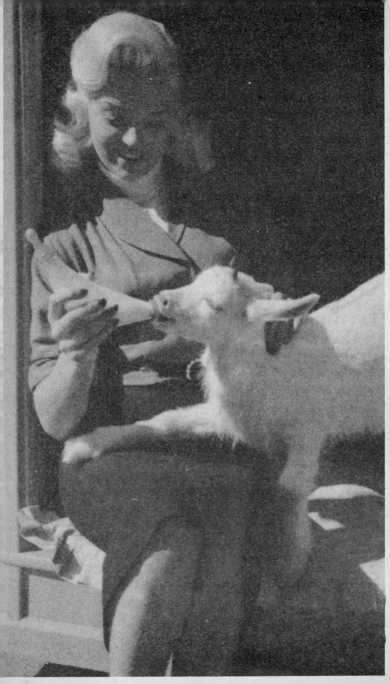

devices must follow the actors,' and that was the end of that. Primo Carnera, the gigantic ex-boxer and wrestler, was in the film and despite his enormous size was as sweet and gentle as a kitten.

Such is the fantasy and fun of making films that the strangest situations sometimes develop. On this occasion an old tramp was needed for quite a number of scenes, and somewhere one was found — a dirty looking old reprobate with a long beard. He lived on a disused bomb site in the East End of London and it was feared that although he obviously needed the money he might well go off and get drunk, or not turn up at the studios on time as he was hardly trained to know about things like studio protocol. So the production department sent a large chauffeur-driven limousine to his bomb site home every morning to bring him in on time. What his fellow tramps thought as he rose from the rubble and stepped into his car, heaven only knows, but I do know that, typical of human nature, he started getting rather 'flash' as time went on, and no doubt was brought down to earth with a bump when it all came to a dizzy halt, as everything in life must.

Sir Carol Reed died tragically — British films also died a little when he left us, their quality was never quite the same again.

R is for ROMANCE

There is nothing so wonderful, or so guaranteed to bring out the beauty in a woman as romance! It is the spice of life — and I should know for I have had my share. The trouble is it never lasts and that is why it is such a mysterious and exciting thing. One of my very first romances, if it can truly be called that, was as a thirteen-year-old girl at home in Swindon. He was a dark, tall schoolboy whose mother had a lovely house with a private lake at the back where we used to go boating on lazy summer afternoons. Little did we know in those far off days that eventually I would be Britain's top sex symbol and he would be the author of *The Naked Ape*, namely Dr Desmond Morris. I hope he did not base his scientific findings on me!

R is for ROSE

'A rose by any other name would smell as sweet,' Shakespeare once said and how right he was, the rose being my second favourite flower (the first being a daffodil). But this story is not about the floral kind, it concerns actress Jean Marsh who had such a fantastic success in the television series *Upstairs, Downstairs*, for not only did she act the demure Rose, parlour maid and loyal servant, but created the show together with another clever lady.

Jean and I have been friends for well over twenty years now and she always had a pretty kooky sense of humour. But the joke, if it can be called that, was on us one night when my first husband Dennis taped a conversation without our knowledge and broke up two marriages in one go!

Actor Jon Pertwee, late of *Dr Who* fame, and Jean had been married for some time when he and she came down to stay for a weekend with Dennis and I — a thing they had done many times over the years.

This particular Saturday Jon had to go to Croydon to do a late night cabaret show, so he left Jean with us. It was early evening, just before dinner, when Dennis, with a strange look in his eye which I should have detected, said to another of our guests, 'Let's go and have a quick game of tennis.' And away they went down to our tennis court at the far end of the grounds. Once we thought they were safely out of earshot, Jean and I embarked on a lot of 'girls' talk' which involved some revelations on her part about a man she was secretly infatuated with (plus her remarks about life and marriage with Jon) and me mooning over a muscleman I had met on the set of the film I was making, describing his green eyes in a stupid way I suppose, the way girls do when left together alone to chatter.

In due course Dennis and his friend returned and my cook announced dinner was ready.

'You go on in,' said Dennis, hanging back in the drawingroom.

Just as the first course was being served there was a crash, and a roar like a bull from Dennis. Suddenly he appeared at the diningroom door in a terrible rage, calling Jean all the names he could lay his tongue to and none of them very complimentary. It seems he had craftily set up a tape recorder to find out what we would talk about when he was not there, and also because he suspected that something untoward was going on in Jean's life. Of course my idiotic twittering about the muscleman had shocked him too, for he was an extremely jealous man, who always thought other men were trying to make it with me. I learned much later in life that he was doing all the things *he* accused other men of doing to me and judged them all by his own behaviour, but it did not help at the time.

All hell broke loose — he smashed furniture and nearly destroyed our drawingroom in his temper, until finally Jean and I left the house in my car and drove back to her flat in London. I took some overnight things but planned to return and collect my other belongings when he had calmed down. The marriage was obviously over.

Dennis sat there after we had left, brooding and drinking until Jon arrived back in the early hours of the morning, tired from his show and puzzled as to where his wife and I were. Dennis explained what he had heard and that our marriage was over as a result. He and Jon sat looking at each other across the huge fireplace, drinking more wine, with Jon trying to cheer him up and pour oil on troubled waters. Eventually Dennis, who had had enough of Jon's weary attempts to prove things were not as bad as they seemed, shouted in a fit of anger, 'You bloody idiot. You think your wife is so marvellous, well just listen to this!' and promptly played the offending tape to the horrified Jon.

It was a mean thing to do, but Dennis was like that. His philosophy was that if his marriage was going on the rocks then everyone else's should go too. Quite naturally Jon was very hard hit, and not only did his marriage to Jean break up as a result, but he had to spend a long time in hospital getting over it — unlike Dennis, who decided that he was going to break up every marriage he could from then on, and *did!*

S is for SCORPIO

They do say this is the worst sign of the Zodiac and they are probably right! I am a Scorpio, I hasten to say — and, oddly enough, so were my two ex-husbands. Even my third husband Alan narrowly missed it by two days, but only because he was lazy about being born! I am not particularly attracted to Scorpios so I do not know how I married two. My downfall sign is Capricorn in love but I have already covered that under the letter C. My agent is Scorpio and so is my dentist, and the doctor who saved my life when I had meningitis. I know a few Scorpio women whom I admire tremendously because they have fantastic drive and guts, like Stella Richman, who is one of the heads of London Weekend Television and at a point in her career bossed twenty-four men on television business projects. 'Scorps' are bossy people, I'm afraid. In fact actress Jill Bennett with whom I appeared in the West End play *Three Months Gone* nicknamed me 'Bossyboots'.

We are passionate, jealous, efficient and very determined. When we love, we love, but God help you when we hate! Nothing and no-one will stand in our way if we want something; and we would, like the scorpion who stings itself to death, rather die than admit we are wrong. There is also a saying which all should heed — 'The devil has a field day when he finds a Scorpio with nothing to do.'

S is for STARLETS

A ridiculous title, dreamed up by film studio publicity departments for young actresses who had not yet made the

S is for SONS

Top left: Mark
Top right: Gary
Left: Jason

213

grade. Starlets were to be found posing at premieres and on the beach at Cannes in film festival time but hardly ever were they seen acting in films.

I was given this title by the Rank Organisation at the beginning of my association with them, but thankfully shed it quite quickly, as I was fortunate enough to do a great number of films, and finally achieved the accolade of having my name up in lights in Piccadilly when I starred in the film *Diamond City*. A thrill I will never forget, particularly as I was just seventeen years old at the time.

It was always sad in the heyday of the film world to see the unending procession of young girls strutting and preening for the press, with their eyes on stardom, and in many ways they reminded me of shoals of seals, lying on a beach posing for a while in the sunshine, then being washed away by the merciless tide never to be seen again.

One unfortunate starlet, Simone Sylva, decided to go the whole way by stripping off the top half of her bikini while posing with Robert Mitchum at the Cannes Film Festival of 1954, thus ruining her career before it had begun, so disgusted was everyone by her behaviour. In these days no-one would bat an eyelid.

One starlet more famous for her off-screen activities than her acting was the now late Carole Lesley who sadly committed suicide.

I knew Carole well during her modelling days, and she was very pretty but she was very insecure and needed constant flattery and reassurance. Eventually she landed a film contract with Associated British Pictures with whom I had just made *Yield to the Night*.

The same director, J. Lee Thompson, was directing his follow-up entitled *Woman in a Dressing-gown* starring Yvonne Mitchell. Carole's role was that of a rather slovenly girl without make-up and in drab clothes.

The first morning on the set everyone was waiting for her to appear and the director was irritated by her late arrival. To add to his annoyance, she was not looking the way he wanted her to at all. Her hair was perfectly coiffeured, make-up flawless, and she was dressed beautifully.

There was an altercation and Lee insisted she return to the make-up department and get herself roughed up and de-glamourised. Carole openly refused, as with her insecurity she felt she could not be seen without the beauty aids.

An argument ensued, Carole burst into tears, and Lee stamped his foot and shouted, finally screeching at the poor girl, 'You call yourself an actress? Do you know Diana Dors went all through *Yield to the Night* for me without a vestige of make-up and her hair dyed black? What the hell kind of an actress are you?'

The hysterical girl stared at him and retaliated as only she knew best. 'I'm not an actress . . . I'm a star!' she cried.

S is for STARS

The word 'star' is a very misused one and is thrown around with the same abandon as the word 'love', in essence, when a person uses either, it does not always strictly mean what it implies!

There are very few 'stars' left in the world today particularly in films. 'Stars' are connected with pop music or football, whereas once the silver screen boasted the complete monopoly. When the British film business was at its height, the name 'starlet' as described earlier, was invented and actually meant that the actress had not yet achieved world stardom, but had every hope and possibility of doing so. Nowadays only a handful of 'superstars', as they are now referred to, exist, and with the exception of Elizabeth Taylor and Sophia Loren, most of them are men. To be a 'superstar' means one can carry a film and make the money pour in the box offices merely on the strength of a name. This can be a continual headache to agents, producers and artistes themselves, for many an actor has been left very depressed when he sees his name down among the 'wine and spirits' as the old pro saying goes (meaning the bottom of the theatre programme where courtesy credits are bestowed on tradesmen who provide various props etc, for the play); so it is very important for a star to have a clever agent who will fight for the correct billing.

Such was the case once when a big West End producer had brought the stage production of *Call me Madam* to London from Broadway and proceeded to bring over the female American star Billie Worth who had scored such a great success with it. He had teamed her up with an actor of great star distinction here, the now late Anton Walbrook. Somewhere along the line however, Miss Worth's agent had cleverly ensured that she received top billing in the show! But Mr Walbrook's agents were not about to allow their client to appear second to her or anyone, and so the long battle commenced between the producer and the opposing agents, as to who should have 'top' billing, and merit the real title of 'star'. Arguments were raised on both sides about the success of Billie Worth's performance on Broadway, and Anton Walbrook's stardom over here, together with the fact that she was virtually unknown in this country, yet the tricky part was that her contract and claim for star billing had already been signed! After long and tedious hours of deliberation with the situation having reached deadlock, Billie Worth's agent suddenly came up with the final idea which entirely eclipsed the steadfast agents of Anton Walbrook. 'Just a minute here,' he announced carefully keeping the excitement in his voice under control, 'There is *no* way you can allow your client's name to appear in lights over the title stating "Anton Walbrook in *Call Me Madam*" . . . imagine what it will do to his reputation!'

That was the end of the matter, and Billie Worth starred in *Call Me Madam*, which ran very successfully, with Anton Walbrook graciously giving way to second billing underneath.

T is for TAURUS

Through the book I have made odd references to certain signs of the Zodiac, and at this juncture I would like to say that I now have a message for all those people born under the sign of Taurus the bull . . . you may come out now!!

216

T is for TELEPHONE

One of my weaknesses in life is the telephone, and my favourite pastime in the morning after I have had coffee and read the papers is to call friends for a gossip. Now that the price of calls have risen to astronomical proportions, much to my husband's relief, I have had to curtail my activities in this field, but his best description of me and the telephone are still summed up by the words, 'She's wearing that Jewish ear-ring again.'

In the past I have played many a good joke from the safety of my telephone, and some have been nothing less than hysterical. There are always people in show-business, despite their apparent shrewdness, who can be hoodwinked and hoaxed, whereas others catch on immediately no matter what strange voice I am using. Actor Gordon Jackson, of *Upstairs Downstairs* fame, was a classic example of Scots shrewdness, for on one occasion when I rang him with some ruse or other, hardly had I opened my mouth, than he exclaimed, 'Hello, Diana. How are you?' which caused total amazement on my part as I thought I had been giving a sterling performance complete with accent to disguise myself.

Singer Dorothy Squires is a person who does not like to be hoaxed. I once conducted a whole conversation with her, pretending to be a newspaper reporter and wound up asking a very impertinent question as to what she was going to do for sex when her husband Roger Moore was away on location. Dot was not amused, hung up, and did not speak to me again for a long time. When she did, it was to ask in quite a hurt tone, 'Why do you always make fun of me, Di?'

One of my best telephone jokes was carried out on actor William Franklyn. Now Bill is a darling and also very intelligent, but he is a perfect target for a hoax as it never occurs to him that that is what it might be, regardless of the situation.

We have worked together many times on television, and

217

on the last occasion Bill would come to rehearsals wearing a very smart, rough woollen jacket. He seemed so fond of it, he also wore it on the show, and later when I happened to see him doing an interview on another programme, he was wearing the jacket again! It was at this point I decided to play a trick on him, not the first I have done over the years I might add. I rang his number pretending to be a wardrobe mistress from a television studio where they were filming the series *Black Beauty*. After announcing myself by an anonymous name, I launched into a whole thing about having just seen him on the box wearing a beautiful jacket, and asked him where he had had it made, as I was anxious to get one like it for an actor who was working in the show. Bill carried on a lengthy discussion about the garment, its texture, the price, where he had had it tailored and so forth, obviously highly flattered that his taste in clothes had prompted someone to telephone. I then ventured that he might consider renting the thing, and he mulled this point over quite happily, silently totting up how much he could charge. As he was doing this I said, 'This jacket is just the sort of thing we need for a particular scene in a barn, where the doctor rapes the girl,' thinking it would give him a small hint that things were not quite as they seemed, for by this time I was convulsed with laughter and could not keep things going much longer. So carried away was Bill by now that he did not see anything odd about a girl being raped on a children's television show, and continued rattling on delightedly. In the end I could stand it no more, and said in a loud voice, 'Well, Mr Franklyn, there is just one more thing I would like to ask you. Have you yourself ever had sex whilst wearing this jacket?' I sat back waiting for the reaction, which was just as I had imagined, utter astonishment and then totally helpless laughter! Such is Bill's sense of humour, that far from being angry like Dot Squires, he went around telling the story to everyone for months afterwards, and even related it to the dignified magazine *Queen*, setting out the whole story with much more salty language for the tag line! This appeared alongside tricks which other 'witty' women such as Princess Margaret and the Duchess of

Devonshire had played, but thanks to Bill's description mine was of course the DIRTIEST!

T is for TEXAS

I had always thought that the Lone Star State was a hotbed of dust, oil and horse manure. My excursion to Houston, Texas, was to appear in a nightclub there owned, I was informed, by an incredible character named Glen McCarthy, who was the original oil-strike millionaire, portrayed by the late James Dean in the film *Giant*.

I went to the club where I was to perform and met Glen McCarthy, who did not look at all like James Dean, but whose behaviour did rather match up with Texans I had known before. He was charm itself though, and spent most of his time drinking a terrible concoction called Cold Turkey. I never dared ask what the ingredients were, but judging from the amount he consumed, and his subsequent behaviour, I could only assume the thing was lethal.

Opening night arrived, and it was as if all Houston had turned out for the occasion. The Maitre d', who also spoke with a thick Southern accent, proudly told me there were so many millionaires in the audience they made 'Glen McCarthy look like a pauper. But then Mr McCarthy *is* down to his last four million,' he said sadly, shaking his head. I found out later he was right. Four million dollars in that town was chicken-feed.

My stay in Texas was fascinating, their social life is lived on a much higher scale than ours, and the hospitality was superb. No dust, horse manure, and gushers there in Houston, but beautiful homes, elegant parties and cultured, courteous people. The old Texan toughness was still there however, for under the surface, men like Glen McCarthy and his contemporaries still lived and behaved as they had done years before they struck oil. Nightly Glen would sit morosely hunched over his beloved Cold Turkey, and none of his staff dared displease him, 'My name is Glen McCarthy, and I bow to no man,' he would shout occasionally, just in case anyone was in any doubt.

His attitude to me was always polite and respectful though. 'Why that Miss Dors is just as sweet as a honey bee,' he would drawl with his Texan accent, which was quite a different statement from the usual curses which came out of his mouth, depending on the amount of Cold Turkeys he had swallowed.

One night there was a scene in the club, which really summed up the whole place to me. Glen had been at the bar all day as usual and, feeling like a bit of good old Texas fun, he deliberately picked a quarrel with one of his best buddies, who was of course a multi-millionaire! The argument grew worse and worse, as both men, fortified by drink, let forth a verbal barrage which infiltrated from the bar into the cabaret room where I was trying to perform my act.

Eventually and not surprisingly the whole thing led to, not just blows, but a punch-up such as I had never seen on the screen in any cowboy film, and it raged on for about half an hour, with the two men knocking each other over tables, chairs and bar-stools, and no one daring to interfere. As Glen was the boss, they could hardly eject him. Finally amidst much blood and gore, and a wrecked club, Glen proudly announced himself the victor, whilst his opponent was carried off to the hospital with heavy wounds.

I suppose only in Texas would the champion arrive at the hospital the very next day, armed with fruit and flowers for the unfortunate patient, thanking him for one hell of a good evening!

T is for TERRY THOMAS

Thomas Terence Hoare Stevens, better known as frightfully English comedian Terry Thomas, has been a friend of mine for nearly thirty years. I first worked with him on an early television series of his entitled *How Do You View* which was then his 'catch' phrase. He is also godfather to my second son Gary, and whenever he was making films in Hollywood he would stay at my home in Beverly Hills, and allowed me the same hospitality at his home when I came over to film in England.

Terry would always amuse the members of my staff when they went in with his morning tea. There he would be, sitting up in bed despite the warm California climate, wearing a red flannel nightshirt and little red nightcap with the usual tassel dangling on the end of it. At his home in London he had a shield above the bed, sporting his coat of arms and family motto — the head of a benign looking cow, and the words *I will not be cowed* written above it.

Terry liked a drink when he returned tired from the studio, for he found Hollywood really too fast compared with his somewhat slow genteel British way of life. This, and the pressures of work perhaps made him drink more than he should have done sometimes. One night whilst I was staying at his house in London where I was working, a rather frightening thing happened, due to his consumption of too much champagne!

He had been out to dinner with his agent discussing important business matters, and as the evening went on had obviously drunk more than was good for him. Luckily the agent was still reasonably sober at the end of the meal, and was able to drive him back to my home, safely depositing him in the drawing-room, before going back to his own house, exhausted by the night's activities. Suddenly he was woken by the urgent ringing of his telephone. It was a terrified Terry crying down the other end for help, and all he could decipher from the garbled chatter were the words, 'Help! I've killed her! Her head's come off.' The agent leapt out of bed in a panic, assuring Terry he would rush over immediately.

With a screech of brakes he pulled up in the driveway, and bursting open the front door found Terry still sobbing about the severed head and muttering 'I've killed her.'

'Who? Who?' implored the agent desperately. Then to his amazement and relief he saw the 'victim'. It was not, thankfully, a human being but a gold cherub which had been standing in the middle of a round velvet seat holding a bowl of flowers in its hand. Terry had drunkenly fallen over the thing, and amidst the confusion in the darkened room, thought he had really beheaded someone. I was not informed of all this until, upon returning, I noticed a new cherub had been quietly and subtly replaced by my embarrassed house guest.

T is for TWO-WAY MIRRORS

I want to begin this subject by stating that I am not a voyeur. My first husband Dennis revelled in this occupation, along with a close male friend of ours, and when they used to persuade me to hide in the cupboard with them to spy on some sexual sport, I never found it particularly interesting. Funny yes, but certainly not exciting in a sexual way. More often than not I would let them get on with their 'wardrobe games' as I called them, and find myself something better to do.

One day to Dennis's utter delight he found a shop which sold mirrors, and whilst browsing around, came across an invention which was a two-sided mirror. Excitedly enquiring as to why this had been devised, he was told it was used by shop-keepers mostly, who wanted to keep an eye on their staff, and discover whether they were fiddling the cash.

Dennis was almost as thrilled with his purchase (it only cost him three pounds, fifty pence) as if someone had given him a priceless antique. It was a round mirror, so he installed it into the middle of a circular bedhead we had, and cut a hole in the ceiling above, so that people could lie on the floor of the bedroom above, and gaze down through the magic mirror, without being seen by the occupants of the bed below.

It was, of course, essential that the man in the love-making duo knew what was going on, as otherwise one or the other would possibly have turned out the light, and plunged themselves, along with the spectators, into total darkness, thus spoiling the fun!

There were two men we knew who were willing to

'perform', if that is the best word for it. One was a business man, and the other a well known newspaper show-business columnist, today married to one of the top comedy actresses in television. In those days he was a mere trombone player at the Victoria Palace Theatre, and bore an uncanny likeness to the actor John Mills. I mention this, because it played an important part in the wooing of young actresses and such like. Whilst the business man merely pretended to be a film producer who might cast them in his latest film, the trombone player convinced them they were actually making love to John Mills himself.

It really rather amazed and disgusted me as to what women would do, and how they would let down their sex, in their efforts to be able to say they had had an affair with a film star.

I have not room under the letter T to go into descriptions of the nights of frolics and fun which went on under that mirror, but if I named all the well known people who have laid flat on the top bedroom floor, on an old mattress placed there by Dennis to make viewing more comfortable, it would read like a *Who's Who*. Besides which it is not my desire to hurt anyone by writing this book. Anyway it was all just a bit of nonsense in days gone by — far better than taking drugs.

One rather sad event happened as a result of this however, it started as a practical joke and nearly finished very seriously. The man who posed as the producer, upon seeing some of the mirror broken and thrown in our dustbin (after what must have been an almost too exciting session one night!) stole a piece and installed it in his flat between the bathroom and bedroom wall. He must have been peeping at girls for quite some time, before one of his 'dates', whom we knew well, suddenly heard a noise and discovered the naughty piece of mirror, realising full well what it was. On reporting this to Dennis he went mad with rage, suddenly becoming very Victorian (which was right out of character), by saying, 'The crafty sod has probably been looking at my wife as well when we have been round there.' His defence of me was chivalrous, but I did not

223

really regard it as too much of a compliment, for I knew he was simply furious that the fellow had pinched his mirror. Not only that, but the man had obviously been having secret sessions all to himself, without letting his friends in on it. Dennis could not rest until he had paid him back for his treachery, so he hit upon the plan of really tricking him into thinking the police had found out about him, and were going to prosecute him under the 'Peeping Tom' act.

His first move was to contact a stunt-man we knew, and get him to dress up like a detective. He gave him the address and details of the offence, and arranged for him to go along at a certain time one afternoon when we would all be there to see the fun. He also got a solicitor friend to type out a proper warrant, so that the 'detective' would look even more authentic!

The afternoon arrived and we had all assembled at the flat for tea. The culprit and his steady girlfriend were blissfully unaware of what was to take place, when the doorbell rang. The girlfriend answered and walked into the drawing-room looking pale, saying the police wanted to see him. Looking curious he went to see and we heard our stunt man playing his role to perfection, reading out the full charge, and stating that a complaint had been made by a young girl who had been entertained there, because a two-way mirror was in the bathroom wall. Our stunt man had brought another one with him dressed up as a uniformed policeman. We heard them march into the bathroom, having been told where the offending thing was. More detective-style conversation followed and he was informed that he would be hearing from them in due course, since a charge would be made and he would have to go to court.

When they finally left, his girlfriend went beserk, for naturally she had heard and seen all. It had also showed her that he was having girls up to his flat whenever she was not around. At that moment, however, he was so terrified about the police case and his family and business, that the least of his worries was her finding out that he had been unfaithful. Dennis, mischievously played his part well, and not only expressed horror at the police matter, but

224

berated him for having a piece of his mirror and not telling him about it, which was what he had been bursting to do all along.

It was a cruel joke, but we did not expect it to go as badly as it did. As the days went by, we couldn't bring ourselves to tell him it was only a hoax. He had resigned from his club, and made a clean breast of it to his family so they would be forewarned when the case hit the papers, all before we could stop him.

'Something must be done,' said the solicitor who had typed out the phony search warrant. 'I'm afraid he might commit suicide.' So we decided he should ring him up saying he had telephoned the police station to enquire about the matter, that they knew nothing of the affair, and he had obviously been hoaxed. This he did, and thankfully the poor man breathed a sigh of relief. He had lost his mirror and his girlfriend, but by then he did not care! Naturally Dennis was the top suspect, and when challenged admitted it. As usual, with his charm he got away with it, like everything else in his life.

U is for UNDERWORLD

It is an odd fact that villains, actors, and lawyers, are all relatively speaking in the same mould.

Lawyers conducting their cases in court, either prosecuting or defending villains, are the nearest people to actors one will find, as they stand there in the centre of the stage, ennunciating in rich clear theatrical voices, and waiting with dramatic pauses to let their words sink in, whilst probably using their spectacles or papers as props to fiddle with, à la Method School of acting.

Actors by and large, being essentially gypsies at heart, feel a strong bond, and indeed display a fascinated interest with villains, especially as many of them have to portray these characters in films and plays. We were all described as rogues and vagabonds in the old days, when actors were not allowed to enter a town, so frowned upon was their profession, and that is how it should have remained, for all this bestowing of titles on our kind is a farce. As one actor bemoaned years ago after the great Henry Irving had been made a 'Sir', 'The trouble was, Henry should never have accepted the Knighthood'.

Villains do not necessarily wish to become lawyers, but I know many who would love to be actors, and who are as intoxicated with show business folk, as we are with them at times.

The notorious Kray twins who incidentally have the same birthday as myself were always around the fringes of show business and indeed did a great deal of good work for charities before they were imprisoned for life.

I once made the acquaintance of the reputed leader of London's underworld at that time, Billy Hill. He was on the face of it a very charming and polite gentleman, to such a degree that I could never understand how he had become the alleged King of Crime. A funny incident happened with the pair of us on one occasion due to a car-dealer friend of mine who continually boasted that he and Billy were on the greatest of terms, business-wise and socially.

One evening purely by chance Billy Hill arrived at my house with another rather dubious friend, whose activities I had known for some time were not actually tied up with the Red Cross. Whilst they were there the telephone rang, it was my car-dealer chum.

'Get him over here,' ordered Billy, who knew him only slightly and was irritated by his continual insistence of friendship. Without mentioning the presence of the two top gentlemen of crime, I casually invited the car-dealer and his girlfriend to my home and we sat down to a game of poker. Eventually the doorbell rang, and in walked the couple breezily.

'Oh, I believe you know Billy very well,' I began still holding the cards in my hand and trying to appear nonchalant! Billy looked up from what was obviously a good hand, as he was smiling, a thing he did not do too often! 'Sit down and join the game', he said. This was an *order*, not an invitation, and the car-dealer, who had gone white at the sight of the man he had professed so often was his best mate, went an even seedier shade of green, nearly falling over a chair in his efforts to get to the table on command. Suffice to say the evening did not go too well for him. The cards, even if they had been running his way, would not have made him feel any happier at being in the presence of the 'King', and sadly before many hours had passed he lost several hundred pounds. The next day he telephoned me and with a false laugh, said, 'Fancy old Billy being there last night . . . I did lose a lot of money, but I tell you what pet, I didn't mind, I regard that cash as an investment.' I noted that in the future he never bragged about knowing Billy or any other villain again!

In America the underworld is a vastly different matter. The crime syndicate, I read one year, made something like six billion dollars profit, and it is a well known fact how the Mafia and all the gangsters began in Chicago in the old days. I once played at a very dubious nightclub there, which was controlled by big racketeers, and to give my reader some idea of the atmosphere of the place, the week before I appeared, three people, two men and one woman, were found with their throats cut in the alley at the back, for disobeying the rules. One night I remember, the boss who fancied his chances with me, suddenly paled as a large car of the Al Capone style drew up and five men got out, 'Hey, here come some of the big guys,' he muttered, and hurriedly pushed ordinary customers' tables to one side, as he prepared the best seating arrangements possible for them to view my show.

Once in a nightclub in Hollywood I was introduced to a very good looking man who was immediately flattered and bought me champagne, when I expressed my opinion that he was the living double of the late film actor John Garfield, an idol of mine! After he had left I was then told that the man who had paid me such charming courtesy, was a well known member of the Mafia and was actually known as 'The Executioner'.

But only in America could such an incident happen as it did when a very well known and highly respected Hollywood lawyer was making his way up the ladder as a youth of nineteen in Chicago. He was in with the Mob, working as their legal adviser even then, and had apparently made a deal with the judge in one particular case, to get his client off. Suddenly the judge did an about turn and sentenced the unfortunate defendant to a jail term, 'You dirty rat fink,' cried the lawyer, so saying he leapt out of his seat, and punched the crooked judge right in the nose! No matter what our justice is like in this country, and it does leave a great deal to be desired, I cannot imagine any of our renowned Q.C.s jumping up in wig and gown, and letting a dignified Old Bailey judge have one smack in the hooter! Thank goodness for staid old England.

U is for URBAN

This word will convey nothing to anyone, but as we are on the letter 'U' it triggers off a whole scene which happened to me in Sweden when I went there a few years ago to make a rather sexy film.

I was portraying a Madame in a brothel, and Urban was just about the most handsome young man I had ever seen. He was playing my Greek boyfriend in the film, and it was probably just as well my husband Alan was there too, for if I had been single I would most certainly have fallen for Urban!

The producer of the film was an incredible character named Vernon Becker. I say incredible, for as he had been born far too late to be a Hollywood producer, the kind of film business he would have revelled in was long past, and so he had to be content with playing a Cecil B. de Mille type role in Sweden, where he had already made several sexy films and had had a ball, casting and producing them.

The film commenced and while we shot most of the brothel sequences in what had once been a Swedish palace, Vernon spent most of his time either on the telephone to New York, or casting young Swedish starlets. He was an ebullient, comical man, with a heart of gold, and I came to grow quite fond of him. The Swedes, as everyone knows, are completely honest and open about sex, there are no bans on it, they discuss, practise, and show it on television at children's peak viewing time into the bargain! Urban kept on trying to explain to me that 'it is normal', in his clipped Swedish accent. One day he took Alan and I to a typical Swedish sex shop, and amongst all the pornographic paraphernalia, we were horrified to see sex books containing pictures of young children taking part in sex acts. This appalled us, but once again Urban assured us that in Sweden it was all perfectly *normal*! While I did not approve of this last piece of Swedish behaviour, I had to admit that if nothing else their normal sexual attitudes to life were a lot healthier than all the violence we are forced to witness here and if one thinks about it, the Swedes who abhor violence and refuse to show it on their screens, have never been involved in a war such as the rest of the world has.

Vernon was getting very excited as he wanted to find some beautiful girls for a certain part of the film which involved seeing various performances of sex given on a stage. 'I am going to cast my film by going to some of the sex clubs here in Stockholm, and finding the best acts they have,' he announced one day. 'Why don't you and Alan come with me? It's really something.' He was behaving like a small boy about to enter an unlimited candy shop, so coupled with our natural curiosity as to what went on in these establishments, we accepted his invitation.

Our car drew up outside an intimate looking place called *Le Sans Moral*, which roughly translated means 'Without Morals'. We were ushered in by a dignified-looking manager, who bowed his way in front of us to a large room fitted out with armchairs, sofas, and a small stage. Drinks were provided, and Vernon, unable to control himself, began asking 'When does the show start?' as if he were present at a Broadway first night.

'Any moment, sir,' said the manager, very much in awe of us all.

Eventually, to Vernon's delight, the room was darkened and the curtains drew back on the stage to reveal a large

German lady who slowly stripped, waving an enormous peacock blue ostrich feather fan in front of her oversized frame. It was all rather boring, as she was not even pretty to look at, but quite obviously considered herself to be extremely alluring, and Vernon did not help the proceedings by shouting out loud criticisms of her act (if that is the right word for what she was doing), with statements such as: 'Well at least *she* is enjoying herself if no-one else is.'

I could tell that the treatment he received from the grovelling manager had obviously gone to his head, and he was playing the big Hollywood tycoon with even more fervour than normal. I did not like the German lady either, but wished he would keep quiet as by now she was glaring at us from behind her fan, and I knew something was going to happen if he kept on heckling. I was right. After about the tenth shout from Vernon as to what a bore she was, she strode down from the stage, and hovered over him like Attila the Hun, tearing him off a terrible strip in her gutteral German accent. 'Now shut up,' she finally ordered and stamped back on to the stage to continue her contortions.

Happily her performance ended soon after this incident, so Vernon did not have to hide his feelings any longer, and the next artiste appeared. This time it was a beautiful redhead, who had taken the trouble to dress her whole act as if she were playing in a sophisticated musical comedy. She went through the motions of stripping, with the aid of a proper story which she mimed for us. The whole thing was actually quite charming, and continued with grace and artistry, until she came to the grand climax. Suddenly having taken off all her glamorous clothing, she seized a candle, lit it, and standing on her head in an upside down pose, placed the thing in a very intimate part of her anatomy, making it twirl around in a circular movement. Vernon was beside himself with excitement. Until then his loud remarks had been fairly funny, but this last piece of action really infused him with genius, and hysterically he yelled out 'Guess what she does for her *second* birthday?'

Mercifully there was an interval after this, and we made our way to the bar, where the redhead eagerly awaited us to see if there was a chance of her being cast in Vernon's epic. I was so embarrassed by his 'birthday' statement that I found myself actually congratulating her on her act, as if it were a straight first night at the London Palladium!

Undaunted, Vernon sat back in his armchair and announced that coming up after the interval, were a man and woman he really wanted to see, for their sexual gyrations would, he was sure, be advantageous to a particular scene in his film. The curtains drew back, and there were the couple waiting to act out a sex scene for real! I took a deep breath and nudged Urban saying surely they were not actually going to 'do it' on stage, only to receive his usual and by now stock phrase, 'It is normal.'

Whether it was the presence of Vernon and myself, or whether the man in the duo, was nervous, and just plain tired, (I learned afterwards that this pair went around doing *seven* clubs a night), I do not know, but whatever the reason, this was certainly not going to be his star moment. Try how he may, he could not perform at all, and no amount of coaxing by the lady could get him going! Vernon's loud heckling did not help matters either, and finally in desperation, after ten minutes frantic effort to put on a good show, he strode off the stage in disgust, leaving his poor partner in a most unflattering position, looking utterly dismayed at the events.

'Ho, ho, ho,' roared Vernon, holding his sides with laughter. 'He blew it. This was his big chance to get into movies, and he blew it. I can see him now back in the dressing-room throwing up in the sink.' And he continued to shake with mirth at what was the most incongruous show-business situation I have ever witnessed.

V is for LAS VEGAS

Another playground for the wealthy, although it is nowhere near as romantic as Venice. Still it is one of my favourite places in the world and somewhere that is

impossible to describe to anyone who has never been there. When I first saw it looming up in the desert from the windscreen of my car I thought it was a mirage, and really it is, for being in this unbelievable town with its fantastic lights, which make Broadway look like a coal-hole, and its gambling facilities situated everywhere from the hotel lobbies to the hospitals, is like living in a dream.

I have appeared there three times in cabaret, and the first time at the fabulous Dunes Hotel I led an existence which nearly drove me crazy! I did three shows a night — the opening one which they called the 'dinner show' commenced at 8 p.m., the next at midnight, and the last at 2 a.m., which meant that I did not come off stage until nearly four in the morning. One can hardly go straight to bed for the adrenalin is still working overtime, so I would play around, see some lounge shows, eat breakfast at seven and watch the sun rise over the desert. As the temperature outside was one hundred and nineteen degrees in the shade at that time, it was best to sleep all day in one's air-conditioned room, waken at six in the evening, have coffee and toast and within two hours be standing in the wings waiting to go on again, fully made-up and gowned. This went on for seven relentless nights a week, with not one night off for two months, and by the time it came to an end I had gone nuts. No wonder the town has been named 'Lost Wages' by entertainers who have played there, for between shows there is nothing else to do but gamble, and many artistes lost their salaries — sometimes weeks in advance. Such was the case of one young Italian boy who was singing with a group in my show and had not only lost all his wages, but his fare back home to Italy.

One heard so many terrible tales of people being in such debt to casinos that they could never leave the town. Comedian Red Skelton, with whom I once had the pleasure of working on television, cracked the greatest gag about the air-conditioning which was kept at ice-cold level in all the hotels, necessarily so with the sort of heat out there. 'The best way to commit suicide in Las Vegas,' he quipped, 'is to go up to your hotel suite and just sit there nude with the air-conditioning on.'

I met so many stars, gangsters and strange characters. It would be impossible to name them all, but the oddest man I met was the editor of a weekly magazine all about Las Vegas. Some time after our first introduction he came into The Dunes gambling casino one night, and saw me idly playing Blackjack — giving myself a twenty dollar maximum win or lose. (I have never been a real gambler thank goodness.) He sat down at the table and offered in a rather flash way to play for me. I allowed him to take my seat and stood beside him watching the cards being dealt. What happened in the next ten minutes was too horrifying for words. He began by not betting too highly, and when the cards started going against him proceeded to *up* the stakes, trying in vain to win some of his money back. This of course, as all gamblers know, never works. In fact they call it 'desperation stakes'. In short, from sitting down with about forty dollars in hand, he lost, in that small space of time, one thousand dollars, and left the table looking extremely green around the gills, not at all like the slick fellow who had arrived ten minutes earlier. I did not see him again during my stay in Vegas, but I heard an incredible sequel to his life story which occurred some years later. It seems that, with his hectic schedule he never got around to eating. So he kept a drawer full of candy bars in his office desk for each occasion when hunger overtook him. He had a craving for candy anyway! One day he was rushed to hospital complaining that he felt very ill, and when the doctors examined him they found he was suffering from a severe case of 'beri beri' . . . it could only happen in a town like Las Vegas.

V is for VENICE

That most romantic of all places for lovers and ordinary people alike. My first encounter with Venice was at the film festival held there in 1955. All the Rank stars going over were under contract to that organisation to give it a big boost for Britain. The press had been pestering me for weeks as to what publicity I was going to pull to make

some headlines, and also what fabulous clothes I would be wearing. Their last question gave me an idea and that is how my famous mink bikini came about.

I was smuggled out of the Excelsior Hotel by a publicity man and a photographer, and the pictures they took of me propelling a gondola wearing my mink bikini not only caused world-wide publicity, but later inspired a show which ran very successfully in the West End, which lampooned me and the whole festival, entitled *Grab Me A Gondola*.

So many things happened during that week in Venice. It is a pity the show could not have dealt with what went on *behind* the scenes — it would probably have been even more successful. I returned to my hotel suite one day after sunbathing on the expensive beach with its colourful awnings and cabanas making the whole scene look like a film set, to find an enthusiastic Italian photographer hiding in the wardrobe anxiously waiting for me to disrobe entirely so that he could leap out and get a few nude exclusives! Needless to say he was forcibly ejected by the management and was not seen again.

There was also a rather embarrassing moment on board a grand ship of Her Majesty's Fleet, moored there for the festival to wave the British flag. All the stars had been invited to a cocktail party and high ranking officers in their elegant white uniforms mingled with the stars against the beautiful Venetian background. I was having a conversation with the Admiral and his wife, a formidable lady, who asked the question we had all been asked a hundred times that evening, 'Do you like Venice?' and, 'Do you think the canals smell?'

I answered for the umpteenth time that I did not think the canals were half as bad as they were made out to be. Hardly had I said it when we perceived a large birth control sheath floating by. The Admiral coughed and his wife blushed heavily, quickly changing the subject to the last film she had seen me in.

My other two recollections of the event were the night of the big premiere of Britain's film contribution and the reception that followed. I made my entrance into the large room at The Excelsior, looking, although I say so myself, quite stunning in an all white evening gown covered in rhinestone embroidery, a white fox stole around my shoulders and feeling extremely dignified. I was alone, as Dennis my husband had gone somewhere and arranged to meet me later downstairs.

What I did not know, as I stood there being photographed in all my glory, was that the press were having a quiet laugh up their sleeves about the fact that my dear husband had arrived earlier and regaled them with the account of his sexual activities with actress Mary Ure.

Absolutely the last and final nail in the coffin of the festival was the head of Associated British Pictures, who was not short of a few thousand, borrowing the money for his excess baggage from me at the airport, and never having the decency to pay it back.

V is for VINCENT

I only know one Vincent and of course I mean Vincent Price, who I can honestly say is one of the greatest and dearest men in show business. I first met him in Hollywood years ago when we worked on a television show together, and since then we have worked on many others, among them *Movie Quiz* in which we both triumphed as we consider ourselves great movie buffs. He also did something pretty nasty to me in a film entitled *Theatre of Blood*. But I can forgive him that just as I could forgive him anything, because I adore him.

Long before we met, when I first went to Hollywood in 1956, the head wardrobe designer from Warner Brothers, Howard Shoup, told me: 'If you two ever get together, you will just leave the ground,' and he was right. His sense of humour is superb, and one thing I adore about Vincent is that he does not mind in the least that his fame has been built up through his success in horror films. In fact he revels in it! Unlike Christopher Lee, who practically has a seizure if one hints at his playing Dracula. I was making a

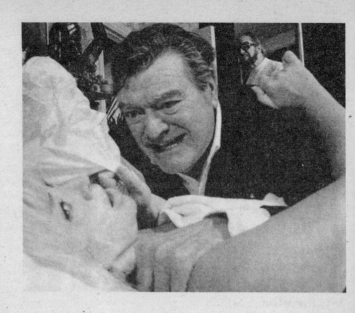

film on location in Devon with Christopher and that other master of horror, Peter Cushing. One evening Alan, Georgia Brown (who was also in the film), and several others, were dining at a restaurant down by Dartmouth harbour which was steeped in atmosphere with its old wine bottles and cobwebs all around the walls. Suddenly the doors opened and in walked Christopher and Peter, both looking grave. Alan's exuberance got the better of him and in a loud voice he cried, 'Look out, the sun's just gone down!' Had it been Vincent Price he would have roared with laughter, as did all the people at our table, but Christopher and Peter continued to glower, and passed on by.

Vincent fell in love with actress Coral Browne when we were making *Theatre of Blood* and it was a romance we all approved of. Coral is a great character herself and has been known to make some pretty salty, witty statements regardless of the consequences. But when she and Vincent were together they were both quiet and coy. As he put it, 'We are so happy, we look like a couple of contented cats.'

238

The best story about their courtship involves Coral. Before they married Vincent agreed to completely redecorate and fit out her flat in London. She went around ordering carpets, curtains and antique furnishings. At Harrods she found a very expensive, beautiful antique bed and arranged to purchase it on the understanding that immediate delivery was guaranteed. The salesman was slightly crestfallen and explained as delicately as he could that although she had paid for it, the delivery would be a problem, and it might take weeks, perhaps even a month or so.

'My good man,' announced Coral, 'I am fifty-nine years old, I have just taken a lover of sixty and I want that bed delivered TOMORROW!' She got the bed!

W is for WALK-ONS

I am often asked what advice I would give to budding young actors or actresses at the start of their career, and apart from the first answer of, 'Don't do it,' my second would be, 'Watch out for "walk-ons"!'

There is also another bit of advice given to me at the beginning of my career. 'Always be nice to the people on the way up, you meet the same ones on the way down.' This need not necessarily apply only to walk-on people, but I have lost count of all those who have appeared in small parts in my films, and who are now big stars. Therefore, whether it be producer, agent or walk-on, always be nice when you are at the top, for they will surely be there as your star begins to wane.

Marilyn Monroe was perhaps the classic example of someone who walked, or rather wiggled across the screen in her first film, and then became a super-star. Happily I was not starring in that movie, but whoever was has probably rued the day they did not bother to even say, 'Good morning,' or perhaps buy her the odd cup of coffee.

When I starred in my first Hollywood film, John Wayne was asked to play a surprise 'guest role' at the end. This involved his appearing in a scene with a pretty girl on his arm, supposedly his wife, who did not speak a word, but merely smiled and let him do the few lines necessary. I think I might have nodded in her direction, but how was I to know that one day she would become Angie Dickinson?

By the same token when watching old movies of mine on television I have developed a game of 'star spotting' with walk-on's and small parts, thereby detecting such names as Stephen Boyd, Alfred Burke, Oliver Reed, Patrick Cargill, Michael Caine and on and on. The list is endless and it is quite a fascinating game to play.

So to those of you who yearn for stardom, remember my advice and experience: be on the look-out for walk-ons or understudies. They are always there waiting in the wings, in case you ever let stardom go to your head, or worse still, begin to believe your own publicity!

W is for WELSHMEN

I hope I do not lose too many Welsh male fans when I say that in my opinion, Welshmen, by and large, make rotten husbands! Rather like the Italians who marry early and then proceed to have a good time on the side, leaving their wives permanently at home, the average Welsh male behaves in roughly the same way. They do not all take mistresses, like their Italian counterparts, but the opposition is darts and beer, for there is nothing a Welshman enjoys more than a good night down at the local with the boys. To be shacked up in a lady's boudoir would definitely take second place!

I have been married to a Welshman, Dennis Hamilton, but he did not fit into this mould, probably because the worst thing one could accuse him of was being born there — he detested Wales for some reason. I have had a love affair with a Welshman, and that was all right, but if I had been foolish enough to marry him then he would surely have taken the same route as all the rest. I also have quite a few Welsh cousins, thanks to my grandmother's retreat to Wales with her lover, and amongst the male members of the family I have noted, with dismay, the attitude towards their long-suffering wives. It seems once a wedding ring is on the finger, all romance flies out of the window, and the girls are lucky if they see their husbands for longer than it takes to wash and shave on arriving home from work before rushing off to the pub or a rugby match, as the case may be.

One should not generalise I suppose but it is odd how certain countries have their own behaviour patterns, and in my experience the Welsh do carry on the way men did in the Victorian age, thinking, 'the wife's place is in the home, preferably the kitchen, and that is where they should stay with no thoughts or interests other than their families.'

Richard Burton, despite his sexy screen appearance, is a typical Welshman and very proud of it. His principles and beliefs were shaped in the rugged countryside of Wales where he was born, and though I am sure he never left Elizabeth Taylor sitting at home whilst he played darts and swilled beer at the local, his background and slightly narrow Welsh outlook was quite apparent when he rang his ex-wife Sybil in New York one day to see how she was getting on. He had run away with Liz and left Sybil to cope with life and their children after many years of marriage to him, and she was still reeling from the shock of it all. But politely she told him that things were all right and she had been trying to rebuild her life by going 'out on the town' a bit and having a little fun, which heaven knows she deserved! 'Sybil,' said Richard sternly, as only a Welsh husband could, divorced or otherwise. 'I do hope you are behaving yourself.'

When I was first told this story by a great friend of his, I laughed at the preposterousness of it after his outrageous public behaviour with Liz Taylor. It also made me think of the time many years before, when, still married to the long-suffering Sybil, Richard had been a frequent visitor to actress Claire Bloom's tiny Chelsea home. Alas the house I lived in with *my* Welsh husband was literally next door, and Dennis had no scruples! He spent many an exhilarating hour peeping at them through Claire's window at the back. As I said at the beginning Welshmen make rotten husbands!

W is for WORKING MEN'S CLUBS

It was my unhappy lot for nearly ten years to appear in cabaret in these working men's playpens. In the early Sixties these clubs were popping up everywhere.

I have appeared under the most appalling conditions. No musicians except perhaps an organist, a sleepy drummer, neon lighting and rows of rowdy men swilling beer.

I once wondered how Frank Sinatra's act would have gone at Doncaster say, with one dodgy organist and two neon lights.

A story which typifies the atmosphere of a working men's club concerns that beautiful singer Matt Munro who had just paused dramatically in the middle of a sentimental ballad, when someone shouted roughly, 'Pies up.' At this news the audience rose in a frenzy of excitement and rushed to the back of the club. It was apparently their custom to serve hot pies and sausage rolls during the evening, and they had chosen, with typical insensitivity, to do it whilst poor Matt was trying to give them his dramatic rendering.

One rather disconcerting thing happened to me when I was engaged to appear at a club called excitingly, *The Dolce Vita* in Newcastle-upon-Tyne. It was the middle of winter, very cold, and I contracted laryngitis on the opening night. This was 1964, cabaret was new to people then, and a great attraction, so, crowds were lining the streets to get in, much to the delight of one of the club owners, a Jewish gentleman who had quite a sense of humour in his own way, providing the money kept rolling in!

I called a doctor and he ordered me not to try to speak above a whisper for several days.

'But what can I do? I am opening at *The Dolce Vita* tonight.' He recommended that the club owner should sort that one out, so unhappily, I made my way to the club and having found him, proceeded to squeak out the awful facts.

'Never mind, never mind,' he said thoughtfully. 'I tell

you what I'm going to do. I will go out there on stage and tell them you've got this laryngitis, and that the doctor has forbidden you to perform tonight, but in true professional tradition you are defying his orders and *insisting* on appearing.' He stood back with a big smile of satisfaction, as if inspired with the genius of his excuse. I stared at him incredulously, his proposed speech sounded all very well, but what was to happen after I walked on to the floor and the tumultuous applause had died down? for I would not be able to even croak!

'Yes, yes. But what shall I *do* when I get out there?' I pleaded.

'Fuck 'em! I've got their gelt,' he replied.

X is for CERTIFICATE X

I suppose my name is synonymous with this dreaded stamp by the censors of films. But looking back, I have not appeared in many which have been awarded (if that is the proper word) Certificate X.

X conjures up sex, violence, and all things shocking when it comes to censorship, but in the heyday of my film career, the things which were frowned on, and indeed completely barred were, by today's standards, very mild. My first brush with film censorship, and what I still feel today was the ultimate in hypocrisy, was when I was making a frivolous little film entitled *Lady Godiva Rides Again*. I was not playing the lady in question, in fact nobody was, as the plot was all about beauty contests, and crooked managers etc. There were so many girls in the film, all parading around in bathing suits, that the male members of the cast and production crew had a field day, especially on location. The film itself was a harmless bit of comedy, and certainly did not receive an X seal. Naturally *I* was the only one who was in any kind of trouble and all because I was wearing a bikini!

One has to bear in mind that this was 1951, and whilst bikinis were very definitely *in*, the Americans for some reason, still smarting after the effects of the wickedest movie they had ever produced, namely *The Outlaw* starring a sexy, large-bosomed lady named Jane Russell, were playing it extremely cautiously about sex and the female form. I was told by the wardrobe department that I was to have two lower halves made for my bikini, one was the normal type girls are still wearing today, and the other cut slightly higher, so that it covered my navel! apparently one was not supposed to have a navel in America. It had been all right for Jane Russell to show her ample bust, but if England tried to match up with a bit of competition, even by displaying a harmless navel, then the American board of censors would not allow the film to be shown in their virgin country, so our producers had to play along with them, or lose money.

Every scene I did when wearing the outrageous article, had to be filmed twice, once for England, and then a quick change over to the more conservative half of the thing, for America. How hypocritical can anyone become?

In those days no one was *ever* filmed in a bedroom scene together with anyone else, unless one person was in bed, and the other, whether it was man or woman, kept one foot squarely on the floor! As for filming a couple of married people in bed together? Well, it was all unthinkable, and thank goodness we have progressed far beyond it all, although I do not approve of the permissive society altogether. When I think of the films made today, and what actress Vanessa Redgrave was doing to herself in *The Devils*, I wonder about the necessity of censorship in the first place, and must admit I feel slightly angry after the things I have had to put up with in the past. If I had appeared as she did in that film, it would most certainly not have been classed as art, but dismissed as pornographic, and I would never have worked again!

The Americans carried their panic about women's bosoms to crazy lengths. It has all stopped now of course, and they are the leaders in everything in films today. But not that long ago, when I used to appear on American television, pieces of coy-looking gauze were meticulously stitched on to the top of my low-cut dresses, for fear I showed too much cleavage!

My last word on the subject of *X*, sadly affects this book, for although I have told the truth as honestly and fairly as I can, whether it be humorous or not, I have to admit that I have had to stop myself from writing certain perfectly true stories, due to the fact that although they may sound amusing when told in the right company, many readers would and could be upset by them. Perhaps one day I may write a sequel which will incorporate all those things I have not dared to write even now, and so for the time being they must all remain under the shadow of the dreaded Certificate *X*.

X is for FATHER XMAS

This was an occasion when Father Xmas did *not* come down the chimney — but then it took place in Hollywood and was not even Christmas either! A very popular goodlooking pair of stars, way back in the early sixties, were tied together in Holy Deadlock — sorry, I mean wedlock, and had been in that state for some years after a highly publicised wedding which delighted all their fans and made them look like young Mr and Mrs America. But they had reached that time in their association when they found out — like most of us do — that marriage has nothing to do with sex! So life for them hit a low ebb. The husband also got to the point where he needed heavy doses of sleeping pills to get him off at night in order to arrive fresh and rested at the studio next morning to star in whatever film he was making. And as he was a very popular star he worked all the time. Meanwhile his wife, who also made many films, was not engaged in a production at the time of this story, and with her husband out at the studios all day and the resulting decline of her love life, she began casting her beautiful eyes around Hollywood for a suitable lover.

In that town there is never great difficulty in acquiring this particular item and she soon found what she was looking for — a handsome young actor who was currently out of work. Everything would probably have gone along swimmingly if they had had an affair in the normal way with him creeping out before the husband came home at night, and her waiting to greet him with the martinis mixed and a welcome kiss! But our heroine wanted a few more extra thrills than that and she and her lover agreed to embark on a much more exciting type of intrigue.

The lover, I might add, was a good friend of the husband and this is important to remember as it saved his bacon when the 'shit hit the fan', as the saying goes.

Their plan involved waiting until the husband retired to the king-size matrimonial bed having liberally swallowed his sleeping tablets, guaranteed to knock him out cold. His wife would lie there beside him and when he was snoring peacefully, the lover would climb on to the roof and gently slide down the bedroom chimney. (Hollywood chimneys are not dirty old things but merely ornate affairs which look impressive but never have fires.) Then he would crawl into bed with his sweetheart and there, with the sleeping husband oblivious as to what was going on, make passionate love until dawn, when he would climb up the chimney and leave. This method of entrance and exit had to be used for fear of being seen by the servants.

It appears that this state of affairs, if you will pardon the pun, had been going along fine for quite some time until one night the worst happened. The husband either forgot to take his pills or they did not work, for as he and his wife lay there in bed, he heard someone scrambling around on the roof, and thinking it was a burglar telephoned the police immediately. The wife of course was unable to stop him as she had to pretend to be frightened at the prospect of an intruder too.

When the police arrived they found a shame-faced young actor on the roof, and the husband on seeing that it was his friend, apologised to the police saying everything was all right as he knew him well. When asked what the hell he was doing up there the lover quickly replied that he was about to play a prank on the couple, so the story ended happily.

I do not think he tried playing Father Christmas again,

and anyway the husband and wife were divorced not long after. How do I know all this is true? Because the Capricorn boyfriend I discussed back in this book under the letter 'C' was a young actor in Hollywood and had a cousin in the Los Angeles police force. He had been one of the patrolmen called to the house that memorable night; also my Capricorn boyfriend knew the 'Father Xmas' actor extremely well, and received a first hand account of how it felt to be caught up on the roof when it was not even the Yuletide season.

X is for X-HUSBANDS

Strictly speaking this item should be written under the letter E, as in ex-husbands, but by and large the ones who have been married to famous women are probably much better off hiding under the title of X, meaning they are censored, and more or less banned completely!

Ex or X, a husband you have finished with is not much use, unless of course he is very rich and still providing you with plenty of alimony, a situation I have never experienced, I am sorry to say. Ex means in the past, and X is usually more prevalent when it comes to husbands of famous wives, particularly actors, whose careers have not gone the way they had hoped, and who would prefer if possible to remain anonymous.

To be married to a sex symbol or love goddess whichever way it is described, is not an enviable position to be in. Consider the subject of Brigitte Bardot and her Ex-husband Jacques Charrier dealt with far back in this alphabet encyclopaedia, and his subsequent nervous breakdown as a result of being 'Mr Bardot'. Aside from myself, and I am just as well-equipped to speak as anybody, one has only to look around at all the famous sex-goddesses there have been, and count the number of husbands left littered along the wayside, some revealing their intimate stories to the Sunday newspapers, claiming to have masqueraded as their wives' 'managers' under pressure, which according to them was the reason they did not make the grade on their own.

Whilst it is not easy being married to a famous female star, sex-symbol or otherwise, and I am not holding a flag for all of them, for I know that in many cases the wives are just as much to blame for the break-up of the marriage as their husbands, anyone must be able to calculate that it cannot be the fault of the ladies *all* the time, as more often than not the sex-symbol who has a long list of husbands and lovers behind her is not merely fickle or unfaithful, but genuinely desirous of a normal, happy married life with one man. The fact that she is sexy is an even larger indication she is probably made this way, for I have always maintained it is the quiet, retiring little wallflowers who are the worst. These are females who have to prove they are desirable, whereas the obviously sexy women do not. In Hollywood years ago it was a well-known fact that one top movie star famous for her 'little girl' looks and film roles, all innocently cute, was the biggest nymphomaniac in town!

Marilyn Monroe did not have to prove that she was sexy, indeed like many of us, she spent a great deal of the time fobbing the wolves off! A sad part of a love goddess's life too is the loneliness, no-one can possibly imagine that the very dream girl they have ogled up there on the screen is perhaps sitting at home alone after the break-up of a marriage, wishing the telephone would ring and someone would take her to dinner. Men think, quite naturally, she has an army of admirers fighting for her favours, and even worse that she might refuse their offer to go out, thus wounding the male ego!

This so many times is just not true! The tragic remark by Rita Hayworth when she said that 'men go to bed with Gilda' (her most famous portrayal) 'and wake up with only me in the morning' is the saddest statement I have ever heard.

The late Jean Harlow, platinum blonde and fore-runner of the sex-goddesses, lived life in such a turmoil regarding her sexy image, she would disguise herself and go to some other town away from Hollywood, trying to 'make it' with taxi drivers and the like, merely to prove that she could attract a man without being 'Jean Harlow'.

Whenever I see a famous female star with a husband in tow, described as her 'manager', I have to smile, for it is in most cases, the only description which can be politely given for the presence of a man who has failed in whatever career he chose, and is at the time clinging on to his meal ticket. Harsh words these, but so often right.

Sex-bomb Raquel Welch, with whom I once made a movie in Spain, and her Ex, Patrick Curtis, were a classic example of the manager/star team, but for a change the title of 'manager' was correct. Patrick had moulded and made her, but Raquel was in private a frightened, insecure woman, governed by her husband, but desperate to carve out a good acting career for herself. She asked my advice as to what to do and I told her to get into the theatre, although I knew it was a hopeless task for her.

Beautiful blonde Lana Turner, also no slouch when it came to being a screen goddess, has a list of seven X husbands behind her, and try how I might I cannot make myself believe that it was always Lana's fault that the marriages failed. Not one of her Xs has contributed anything to her life, during or since the times they were together, and the same can be said for so many more who spring to mind, Betty Hutton, Veronica Lake, Hedy Lamarr, Dorothy Lamour, Ann Sheridan, Jayne Mansfield, Linda Darnell, the names are endless, alive or dead.

'Hell hath no fury like a woman scorned' the saying goes, but show me an X husband who is not right there squealing about the sacrifices he has made, and the terrible way he has been treated, whether his ex-wife is a screen star or a shopgirl!

Y is for YACHT

Only very wealthy people own them and I have spent the odd weekend on a friend's yacht in Monte Carlo. But the oddest weekend I ever experienced on a yacht was back in Hollywood in the summer of 1956, soon after I had arrived there in a blaze of publicity to make a film for RKO. After my great success in *Yield to the Night*, I sat around in England for eight months waiting for an offer of something really worthwhile as a follow up, but nothing happened. Finally I went to Hollywood to make a not very good film, mainly because I had always wanted to go there, and also because the money was extremely tempting. I did not in those days have a clue about the 'wheeling and dealing' that went on. Besides I have never been very business-minded. It came therefore as a pleasant surprise when Dennis and I were invited by William Dozier, head of RKO, to spend the weekend on a luxury yacht with his wife, ex-actress Ann Rutherford (once Mickey Rooney's girlfriend in all the Andy Hardy films). We accepted and were driven to the harbour at Balboa, in order to board and proceed to an island named Catalina. The yacht belonged to a rich businessman who was waiting for us with his girlfriend, Bill and Ann, and two other passenger guests, an agent and a film starlet client.

We set off and it was a wonderful experience. I had never seen flying fish before, and when we were not sunbathing and gazing at the sights on voyage, we played cards and talked. All in all a very friendly and convivial gathering. What I did not know was that although it seemed like harmless fun, everyone on the yacht was there for a purpose. The man who owned the yacht owed the head of the studios a favour, and was working it off by letting us all relax on his boat; the agent wanted to do a deal with the studio boss for the starlet, and get me to sign a contract making him my sole representative; and the studio head wanted the agent to chat me into signing a long-term contract, for not too much money, with his studio. So, amidst the cheerful banter there was an awful lot of high powered business going on all unbeknown to me.

At the end of it all I did not sign with the agent, nor did his girlfriend sign with the studio. I made only one more film for RKO for a *lot* of money, so maybe the weekend was not quite as successful as everyone had planned, except for the owner of the yacht who had at least paid off his debt!

My only sad recollection of the cruise however was

when we got to Catalina and I looked across the harbour and saw a beautiful yacht called the Santana moored there. It belonged to the late Humphrey Bogart, and he was sitting on deck talking to the late Jeffrey Hunter. Bogie was in the last stages of his terrible fight with cancer, weighed seven stone or so, and looked pale and grey. He waved a frail hand, and that was the last time I ever saw him.

Y is for YIELD TO THE NIGHT

If an actress has any sort of successful career, then it is an odds-on bet she will have made many films. In my case I have made somewhere in the region of sixty-five films, but I can count on one hand those which pleased me and were also good! I remember one of my films being criticised in the press as British film-making 'at its worst', but after a while you learn to harden yourself against this sort of thing, and anyway if you know in your heart it is bad, they why blame the critics for knocking it!

A Kid for Two Farthings was my first and best film up until 1956 when I was offered the role of the condemned murderess in *Yield to the Night.* At the time, everyone thought the film moguls were cashing in on the unfortunate story of the tragic murderess Ruth Ellis, the last woman to be hanged in England, but strangely enough the story had been written two years before, by authoress Joan Henry, with *me* in mind for the leading role. I was so excited at the chance of being able at last to prove that I was not merely a glamorous sex symbol but an actress, and I tackled the part with alacrity.

The Rank Organisation had been offered the script first but they had turned it down, so Associated British Pictures bought it, and it was probably just as well, for although I had a 'one picture a year' deal with Rank, they would *never* have cast me. Their refusal of the film was a bad mistake, for it was the *only* British film to be chosen for the Cannes festival that year, and John Davis, head of the Rank Organisation, had then decided to set a whole new publicity ball rolling by taking his stars to film festivals, in order to give them glamour and atmosphere, and of course

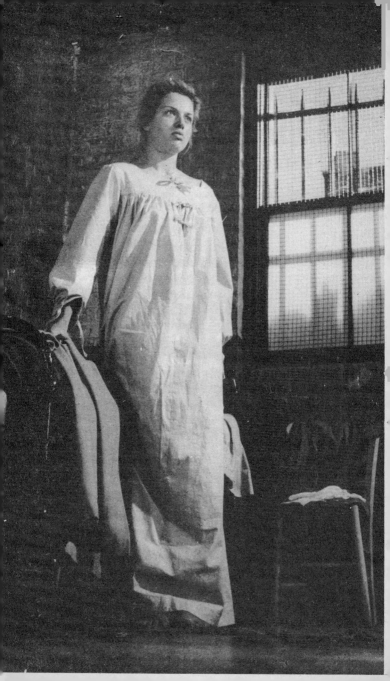

help sell British films to foreign markets.

To put it politely, he was considerably annoyed that his 'refused film' had been chosen, with me in the lead, and not one of the Rank films had made the grade. However he was committed to go with his 'stable of stars', and I went under the ABC banner. The *big* night came for the premiere, and I remember standing on the balcony of my bedroom at the Carlton Hotel, looking down at all the lights twinkling along the Croisette, the Mediterranean sparkling in the background, and thinking, 'This is *my* night, and whatever else I do in the world, or with my career, there will never be another night like it.' I was right, the crowds thronged outside the cinema as I drew up in my powder-blue Cadillac, which matched my evening gown. Inside the atmosphere was electric! The director J Lee Thompson was sitting beside me, and tears were unashamedly rolling down his face, for he had lived and breathed this film for so long, and we all knew it was *good*. At the end the audience rose, applauding and cheering, but in the midst of it, a tight-lipped John Davis strode past me with not a word of praise or congratulations.

Later at the reception arranged by the Rank Organisation everyone had a place at dinner, except me. I was forced to wander down to the end of the room to sit with the press, who were disgusted at the treatment I was receiving, but warm in their praise of the film. It is odd how petty certain people can be, and I have never understood John Davis' behaviour, but it did not spoil my night. How could it? When you have a successful film like that, nothing matters. And whatever happens to me for the rest of my career, at least I can always point with pride at *Yield to the Night* and say, 'I did *that*.'

Y is for YORKSHIRE

If you are determined to lose your virginity — then what better place to do it than the beautiful dales of Yorkshire.

Z is for ZSA ZSA

There is no way one could complete this book when it came to the letter Z without mentioning Zsa Zsa Gabor. I have known this lady for twenty odd years, ever since the time I nearly bought the beautiful house in Bel Air, which had been given to her by one of her many husbands, Conrad Hilton.

To this day she still has a devastatingly beautiful face, and although the figure is heavier, the entire effect when she is standing in front of you is quite breathtaking and very, very feminine. Once when we were dining at the Luau restaurant in Beverly Hills she bought me a lovely diamond hair slide. Her millionaire husband Herbert Hunter probably the shrewdest of all her spouses was with us that night also, I say the shrewdest because he made sure that the extravagant items and jewels were bought in his name, and went with him when the marriage ended, including the fabulous heart-shaped diamond ring second only to the one Richard Burton gave Elizabeth Taylor.

Contrary to popular belief, Zsa Zsa has never done all that well out of her husbands.

The late George Sanders, who I think she truly loved did not do a stroke of work whilst they were married, according to Zsa Zsa, preferring to sit at home with pipe and slippers, leaving her to earn the money!

Another of her husbands who claimed to be an oilman from Texas, worth millions, really drew a blank. For that matter so did she, for as they stood side by side swearing to love, honour and obey, neither knew that the other was penniless, or practically so. Zsa Zsa believed he had oil wells gushing up millions of dollars a minute, and he thought that she received thousands of dollars for merely opening a supermarket! The net result was total disaster, after they settled back in his apartment in Dallas and the confetti had blown away. For the horrible discovery was made that none of these fantasies were true and Zsa Zsa would have to reconcile herself to being a suburban housewife each day, whilst hubby went to work.

I once did a pilot for a talk show here in London, and to

make the thing go with a zing, I sent for her. On every American chat show she has ever done, she just *will* not stop talking, even when told to 'shut up' as I had once seen happen there. I knew there would be no embarrassing silences with my guests due to flagging conversation if Zsa Zsa was on it.

After a big build up by the show's compere, Zsa Zsa finally made her entrance looking breathtaking in a flowing white ensemble, trimmed with white ostrich feathers, her golden hair piled high in cascading curls, and diamonds twinkling everywhere. All went well until she tried to take over the proceedings by getting up in front of the audience and doing a sort of rehearsed act with her daughter who was sitting anonymously in the audience. I let her have her head for a while, but was then given the signal by the producer to cut her short, which I proceeded to do, much to her dismay. 'It is very rude of you to treat a guest in this way,' she exclaimed in her Hungarian accent, and afterwards became rather pouty and badly behaved by answering my every question with a bitchy remark. In the end I had had enough of it all, for it *was* my chat show, so after admiring the large diamond rings she was wearing, and seeing her temper obviously cooling at my flattery, I leaned back and wickedly said 'Hmm . . . They are almost as big as mine!'

Z is for ZOOT SUIT

This may seem a strange subject for me to deal with and indeed most people, especially the younger ones will not know what it is. Simply, a 'zoot suit' as it was called back in the Fifties was a strange ensemble which represented the fashion of the late '40s, made famous by American jazz musician, Cab Calloway.

It did not impinge upon my life until one day in late 1958 I received a letter from America, stating that my three year picture deal with RKO worth somewhere around half a million dollars, had been cancelled by them, on the grounds of immoral behaviour which caused the studios to be embarrassed by the publicity.

Naturally I instructed lawyers to deal with the matter immediately. First of all to find out what dreadful crime I had committed which warranted this attack, though I knew in my heart that it was of course a high powered business trick on the studios' part to cancel the contract to their advantage. But I had to fight, and fight I did!

What was finally revealed was an article written in a terrible New York paper named *The National Enquirier*, notorious for its slanderous and libellious statements about well known people. The article amongst all the other clap-trap about such stars as Alec Guinness, who was reported as having got drunk and smashed all his wife's perfume bottles on her dressing table and so on, referred to my supposedly having attended a party at a house in Rotten Row (which of course was impossible as there are no houses there, just dirt tracks for horses). At this party, it went on to say, I am supposed to have jumped on to a table, taken off my bra, and done a sexy dance on the top of it, with my 'zoot-suited' boyfriend underneath doing who knows what to me whilst the dance was going on! Apart from the absurdity and impossibility of the story, in 1958 girls did not reveal their busts — so this particular part of it was frowned upon darkly.

The battle raged on between expensive American and English lawyers for something like three years at unbelievable costs. Finally I was only just able to win by producing my passport which showed that at the alleged time and date of the party, I was *not* in London but in South Africa appearing in cabaret. This was the winning stroke in legal terms, I was granted the case, and received an apology from *The Enquirer*. But, as always, the damage had been done.

RKO studios agreed to pay the money which was owing, but by the time the lawyers had received their shares and expenses there was not much left for me. It should have been a large amount of money which would have paid off my income tax and helped to keep me in my old age, instead of having to write this book to try and make an honest crust. Oh well, that's the name of the game I suppose!